Brenda McGraw
2/12/13

D1263681

BUSTED

BU$TED

THE RISE & FALL
OF ART SCHLICHTER

ART SCHLICHTER

with JEFF SNOOK

ORANGE*frazer*PRESS

Wilmington, Ohio

ISBN 978-1933197-678
Copyright © 2009 Arthur E. Schlichter and Jeffrey A. Snook

No part of this publication may be reproduced in any material form (including photocopying or storing in any medium by electronic means and whether or not transiently or incidentally to some other use of this publication) without the written permission of the copyright holder except in accordance with the provisions of the Copyright, Designs and Patents Act 1988.

Copies of *Busted: The Rise and Fall of Art Schlichter*
may be ordered directly from:

Orange Frazer Press
P.O. Box 214
Wilmington, OH 45177

1.800.852.9332
www.orangefrazer.com

Cover design by Jeff Fulwiler
Book design by Chad DeBoard
Photo credit page 43: *The Columbus Dispatch* Printing Company

Library of Congress Cataloging-in-Publication Data

Schlichter, Art.
  Busted : the rise and fall of Art Schlichter / by Art Schlichter & Jeff
Snook.
    p. cm.
  ISBN 978-1-933197-67-8
  1. Football players--United States--Biography. 2. Quarterbacks
(Football)--United States--Biography. 3. Compulsive gamblers--United
States--Biography. 4. Ohio State University--Football--History. 5. Ohio
State Buckeyes (Football team)--History. I. Snook, Jeff, 1960- II. Title.
  GV939.S336A3 2009
  796.332092--dc22
  [B]
                          2009020376

To Tay and Maddy, as I have told you countless times over the years, I never was a bad person, I just did some bad things in my life. I hope by reading this book, you will understand me better and realize how much I truly love you both. Mom, you're simply the best mother a guy could wish for.

—A.E.S.

To Savannah and Dillon, may you learn that the long and winding path through life is best traveled with a clear conscience, big heart and loving soul. Speak the truth, listen to your elders, taste success but don't swallow it, smell the roses and reach for the stars.

—J.A.S.

Table OF CONTENTS

Prologue

The first time I saw Art Schlichter, it was September 15, 1978—the night before Ohio State's season-opener against Penn State at Ohio Stadium.

Woody Hayes stood on the balcony of the OSU Student Union, introducing his players one-by-one to a huge crowd of Buckeye fans and students who had gathered below.

When Woody held a mic, it was usually entertaining, of course. His well-worn phrases and genuine enthusiasm, communicated through that familiar lisp, were music to the ears for Buckeye fans.

Every player had received a nice round of applause before the legendary coach introduced the freshman quarterback, the high school legend Buckeye fans had heard and read about.

Woody called his name, "Art Schlee...."

The rest of the young man's name had been drowned out by a deafening roar from the crowd.

Most of those fans, if not all of them, had never seen Schlichter play a football game. Never seen him throw a pass or run the option. Before Woody's introduction, most of them wouldn't have known the country's most highly recruited football player from a bagboy at their local grocery store. There was no YouTube, Internet or SportsCenter back then. There were no recruiting services to follow.

That moment was the first time Ohio State fans collectively had laid eyes on him.

It didn't matter, though, because they realized he was supposed to be a savior of sorts. He symbolized a new era of Buckeye football. And that in itself was worth cheering for.

With Schlichter, no longer would Woody's offense rely solely on a punishing running game.

"Three yards and a cloud of dust," which had produced three consensus national championships but none in the previous 10 seasons, was about to become obsolete just like disco and bell-bottoms.

With Schlichter, Woody's beloved Buckeyes were expected to finally move into the 20th century and join the remainder of the college football world.

With Schlichter, the offense would be balanced for the first time, and Woody's team would be able to come from behind if needed. God forbid,

Woody's team would *throw* the football on first or second down.

That was not only something the fans hoped for, it was something they wanted to see, something they *needed* to see after two straight losses to Michigan and three losses in the previous four bowl games.

Obviously, fans never realized there would be severe growing pains during this transformation from one era to the next.

They had no idea that Schlichter would throw a school-record five interceptions the next day in a 19-0 loss to the Nittany Lions.

And they certainly had no clue that season would end four months later in shocking fashion, with Schlichter's final freshman pass resulting in Woody momentarily losing his senses and punching the interceptor.

While the legendary coach would be ushered unwillingly into a premature retirement, Schlichter's fate would improve, before growing devastatingly worse.

He would become an All-American as a sophomore, leading the Buckeyes and new coach Earle Bruce to an 11-0 regular-season record and a Big Ten championship. He would then shatter all of Ohio State's single-season and career passing and total offense records before his four years concluded.

Although he wouldn't win a Heisman Trophy, he would become a bona fide legend among Buckeye fans by starting more games (48) and winning more games (36) than any quarterback in school history.

He played through the pain of several injuries. He offered his free time to charitable causes and he said and did all the right things off the field. He never appeared selfish or spoiled. He smiled for the cameras and said "Yes sir" and "No ma'am" when interviewed. He didn't smoke. He didn't drink.

All in all, he was too good to be true.

At least that's the way it seemed.

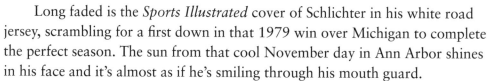

Long faded is the *Sports Illustrated* cover of Schlichter in his white road jersey, scrambling for a first down in that 1979 win over Michigan to complete the perfect season. The sun from that cool November day in Ann Arbor shines in his face and it's almost as if he's smiling through his mouth guard.

That picture depicts a snapshot in time, the previous life of Art Schlichter.

A few days before his final game at Ohio Stadium in 1981, Schlichter and I sat in the hallway of the Biggs Athletic Facility (now the Woody Hayes Athletic Center), as he reflected on his career. I was a sports writer then for the Ohio State student newspaper, *The Lantern*.

His body language made it obvious to me that his career had been somewhat of a disappointment. He would never say it, because he truly was a team player.

He knew that he had never beaten Michigan at home. He would never win a national championship or the Heisman Trophy. He would play in only one Rose Bowl during his sophomore season, and had grown increasingly frustrated with an offense labeled simple and predictable. The wide-open, four-receiver, take-no-prisoners passing attack he had been promised had never materialized, first under Woody and then under Earle Bruce.

"I was very positive about coming to Ohio State," he said. "I thought we could change tradition a little. I am still proud of the fact I was a passing quarterback at a running school.

"Having the opportunity to play college football would have to be the highlight of my life."

It just wasn't supposed to remain the highlight of his life as he progressed into his professional days and then into middle age.

When scouts projected sure-fire NFL stars of the future, Schlichter was included with Stanford's John Elway (whom Schlichter had out-dueled in a Buckeyes' 24-19 win earlier that season), Miami's Jim Kelly and Pittsburgh's Dan Marino, each a year younger.

Everyone, especially his father Max Schlichter, figured Art's future would include million-dollar contracts, national endorsement deals, NFL passing records and Super Bowl MVP awards.

By the time his rookie season with the Baltimore Colts ended, however, the sports world had learned that Schlichter's story indeed was too good to be true.

Details had trickled to the surface, revealing that he had hidden a severe addiction to gambling. On the field, he appeared to be an instant bust. Off it, he was a mental wreck. After he had gone to the FBI to report some Baltimore bookies had threatened him, NFL Commissioner Pete Rozelle suspended him for one year.

The sports world was shocked by the story, especially Buckeye fans.

It became clear that his challenges wouldn't be dodging linebackers, reading NFL defenses, or handling the two-minute drill to win a football game.

Art Schlichter's challenge was standing up to an invisible monster that had him by the throat.

It soon became evident that he would never break NFL passing records as Marino would or win Super Bowls like Elway.

Instead, he would fall hundreds of thousands of dollars in debt, become one of the biggest NFL flops of all-time as well as a full-fledged gambler and con man, committing dozens of crimes that would send him to prison for more than 10 years.

His reputation and image were tainted by the time Elway and Marino were NFL rookies, beginning their long road to fame and fortune that ultimately would lead to Canton, Ohio.

Schlichter, the high school legend, the Ohio State icon, the first NFL player suspended for gambling in 20 years, would become *infamous*.

The saddest part of this entire story is that he had the God-given talent to order his bronze bust placed in Canton as well. He could have played 10 or 12 years in the league, become a multi-millionaire, wore a Super Bowl ring on his finger and enjoyed a loving family by his side as he grew older.

Tragically, he experienced none of that.

"Do I think about those things today?" he asked, repeating my question as he drove down Interstate 71 one day.

"Nope. I never do. I let that go a long, long time ago. I never spend one minute thinking about what other guys did or how much money they made in their careers. If I did ... if I thought about those type of things, I would drive off this road right now and end it all.

"I won't let myself go there. It was what it was. Now, it is what it is. And I have to face the life I made for myself."

He has struggled for decades to find answers to what drove him to commit crimes, to break the law repeatedly, to lie, cheat and steal. Could it all fall under the ugly umbrella of an addiction? Did his father's master strategy to raise a sports superstar contribute to it? Was the pressure to change the way Ohio State played football just too much to bear for an 18-year-old kid?

Now free from prison for three years and counting, he has some answers. Art candidly reveals every ecstatic moment of his spectacular rise and every painful detail of his dramatic fall in the ensuing pages.

I spent plenty of time with him while compiling information for this book. In talking with doctors, therapists, his past coaches, a few of his gambling friends and mostly, with Art himself, I concluded that he is far from a terrible person. He is a good-hearted, intelligent guy, someone who loves his kids as a father should, but someone who was driven by the demons of a gripping addiction to do terrible things.

Therein lies the difference.

He had a sickness out of his control, as doctors told him repeatedly over the years.

It tore apart his life, his relationships and his family. It led to divorce, debt and prison.

Today, he lives with his mother in a small house in Washington Court House, the tiny town in Southwestern Ohio where the story began.

Schlichter faces ordinary problems just like any other average Joe in this sluggish economy, struggling to pay bills and child support. His credit probably is ruined forever.

Still, he must be given a pat on the back for not giving up, for not taking the easy way out of this life and for not saying, "Ah, the hell with it ... I am outta here."

He admits in this book that he came close several times. Now he believes he will never drop back and chuck that one final, fatal interception, at least not on purpose. After all, he has been called just about every name in the book over the years, but I am sure even his harshest critics never labeled him a quitter.

The fact is, there is too much left to do.

He has started a gambling intervention organization. He is quite skilled giving analysis on the radio before and after Ohio State football games, another talent he was blessed with. He provides financially for his two daughters, who live a three-hour drive away with their mother, who divorced Art in 1998.

"It isn't what I planned," he told me. "I can't take back all the wrong things I have done, all the hurt I have caused. I wish I could. But now that it's all said and done, what else can I do?

"I mean, seriously, what can I do?"

Nothing, I suppose, but to make that three-hour drive to see his kids as often as possible.

Nothing, but to care for his heartbroken mother.

Nothing, but to continue making the positive steps in his therapy and counseling.

Nothing, but to handle as many gambling interventions as he can squeeze into a seven-day week, hopefully to rescue one young innocent soul from following in his messy footsteps.

Nothing, but to swallow his pride, open his heart and reveal his soul to tell his story for all the world to read.

You see, when the clock hits zero and God writes Art Schlichter's final story, all of those nothings will amount to something substantial.

—Jeff Snook

BUSTED

Chapter one

LOCKED IN "THE SHU"

God, I'm tired. I'm tired of prison. I'm tired of being shackled and chained. I'm tired of being told what to do and when to do it. And most of all, I'm tired of not being able to see my daughters, to hold them and hug them and to tell them I love them. Please watch over them God. Take care of them. Help them be happy. Wrap your arms around them and show them the way. Take care of my mom, too. You know she's a good woman. She's someone who deserves happiness. You have to keep me from going insane in here. Please help me survive this place. Please keep me from killing myself. I don't want to go out this way. Please God ... please don't let me unscrew that light bulb.

It's late January, 2005, and my life has come to this. I'm praying about a light bulb—a stupid, stinking, meaningless 20-watt light bulb.

Hanging over my head, it's my constant companion. There are days it's the only light in my life. Other days, I'm sick and tired of staring at it. It just dangles there as if it's taunting me. Then there are the worst days, the days when the emotional stress of being imprisoned in this hell-on-earth are too painful for me.

Those are the days I want to unscrew it, break it into pieces and use a shard of it to slice my wrist.

I know that shattered light bulb could be my deliverance. It could be my only way out of this dungeon. Maybe I'll bleed to death all over this concrete floor before they can get to me. Then God can take my soul out of here. I can't walk through those steel bars, but He will take me far away from this miserable existence.

Weeks ago, I was living in a detention camp, the lowest level of incarceration there is in the American correctional system. I had a nice bunk, good food, I worked in the yard, I felt the warmth of the sunshine. Then I bet on an otherwise meaningless college basketball game. I needed one team to beat another by more than 20 points. The team I bet on won the game 80-60.

Typical.

I'd lost again, the latest in a lifetime filled with loss.

When the corrections officers discovered I'd gambled again, they chained me, shackled me, and threw me in here, The Hole—solitary confinement.

On the inside, we call this horrible place *The SHU*—Special Housing Unit. *This* SHU is the absolute most horrible, darkest, dirtiest place I've ever seen.

The corrections officers, or "hacks" as we call them, tell me I'll be deadlocked in this dungeon, deep in the bowels of the Indiana Reformatory near the town of Pendleton, for twenty-three hours a day for the next six months. Pendleton's a depressing concrete compound built in 1923. It once held John Dillinger. I'm housed in the most horrifying wing, locked in a six-by-eight feet cell, shut off from the rest of the prison ... and the rest of the world.

I have nothing but a steel toilet, a tiny steel sink, and a wafer-thin pad that separates me from the cold concrete floor.

And my light bulb.

I've spent ten years of my life in more than forty prisons. I've seen the beatings, the rapes, the common atrocities of prison life, but I've experienced nothing like this. This place is agony. This place is mental torture. This place will drive me insane if I'm left here for very long.

At night I can hear the rats running through the walls that are covered with messages and pictures drawn by the captives who preceded me here. Someone drew a perfect Jesus, his hands spread wide. I look at Him every day. A naked woman stares from another wall. Gang signs are all around me, but I can't decipher them.

I'm locked down with no interaction with anyone, other than the inmate to my right. He's been held in solitary for 17 years and surely is certifiably insane by now, if he wasn't when he was free. They tell me he killed an entire family years ago and recently stabbed somebody in prison. He'll never see the outside of this place.

When the hacks walk by his cell, he sometimes throws his own shit on them. On the days he behaves, they allow him outside his cell to roam the walkway. Somehow, he's become a living sports encyclopedia and he knows every statistic from every game ever played. He stops in front of my cell and recites them to me.

I figure he must be about my age, even though he appears to be in his 60s. They tell me he has AIDS. He smells like death, but everyone smells bad in here, including me. The chemical they gave me as deodorant burns my skin, so I never use it. The entire place smells like a mix of feces and body odor.

I don't experience much physical pain other than intense hunger and thirst. I've come to appreciate the slop they slide through the bars to feed me at four in the morning, ten o'clock, and three o'clock. Its arrival is how I tell time. I surely can't judge time by my stomach because I'm hungry around the clock. Sometimes I shake involuntarily from the cold. The thin, dusty blanket they give me wouldn't keep a mouse warm at night.

The emotional pain is much worse. It's so boring in here. Time stands still. The only thing that keeps me surviving from one day to the next is looking forward to the mail each weekday afternoon. I stash the letters from my mom and my children under my mat—my prized collection of pain and sorrow stuffed into tear-stained envelopes.

I write my mom and my kids almost daily, but there's never much new to say. It just gives me something to do. In my mind, writing them somehow helps me stay connected to the outside …

Mom, I hope this finds you well. I'm still in the hole. I haven't left my cell since last Friday for ten minutes to get some soap. They feed me the slop through the hole in the door. It's pretty primitive. This is my fourth winter without seeing sunshine. I can't wait for you to bring the girls to see me, but don't know when they will allow me to have visitors. I can only imagine how big the girls are getting. Mom, I can't take much more of this. It's tough sitting in here thinking about all I have lost. My freedom. My family. My integrity. The money. It all depresses me. I'm mad at myself. I can barely live with myself for doing the things I did. I can't live with the guilt for all I have done in my life. I worry constantly about you and the girls. I love you Mom. I miss you. Be safe. Love, Art.

I have no real possessions now, other than utter despair. I've lost virtually everything in my life and now my hope is slipping away, too.

All I have is time, seemingly endless time.

Time to sleep. Time to cry. Time to think of what I did to deserve this place. When I sleep, I lie on the dirty pad with my head resting on a tiny plastic pillow at the base of the toilet, with my feet toward the steel bars. If I would lie the other way, I'd risk someone reaching through the bars and bashing my head during my sleep.

But when I sleep, I can dream. And when I dream, I'm free. There are times I pray that I wake up and discover this was a just a horrible nightmare. Those prayers never work. Those are the mornings I'm the most depressed. Those are the mornings when I want to unscrew that light bulb.

I never stop wondering, "How did it come to this? What happened to me?" How did I become known as State of Indiana Inmate 954-154?

If only I could go back forty years to be Art Schlichter, the carefree kid growing up on a farm.

If only I could go back in time to when I had the world at my feet …

Chapter two

JUST A HAPPY FARM BOY

I like to tell people that a day didn't pass during my childhood in which my father didn't whip my ass. That's an exaggeration, but Dad believed in laying the wood to me when I misbehaved.

The discipline sequence in the Schlichter household went something like this: Mom told on me for whatever mischief I'd orchestrated and then Dad later whipped me for it. To complete the cycle, Mom would then come back into the picture to kiss me, hug me, and hold me as I cried my eyes out.

My father, John Max Schlichter, a third-generation German immigrant, was a real country boy who loved farming and sports. His father also had been a farmer. Dad grew up outside of Washington Court House, Ohio, but his school didn't offer any athletic programs, so his parents paid his tuition in order for him to attend school in town and play football.

And that's where he met my mother, a cheerleader at the local high school.

Mila Weatherly was a *city* girl, or at least a small-town girl, very petite and from those early pictures, I could tell she must have been the prettiest girl in town. I think she still is.

When I came along on April 25, 1960, their third child, my parents decided to honor each of their fathers by naming me Arthur Ernest. Mom's father's name was Alfred Ernest "Hap" Weatherly and Dad's father's name was Arthur Claire Schlichter. I could have been named Alfred Claire, as my parents joked to me over the years, so I'm glad I got the name they gave me.

By the time I was born, my sister Dawn was four and my brother was two.

My brother shared my father's name, but he went by John while Dad went by Max.

Don't get the idea that I didn't have a happy childhood simply because my rear end normally sported a welt or two. That's just how Dad grew up with his father and he passed the butt-whipping tradition down to us, or specifically, down to me.

Even now, I can honestly say that I probably deserved every beating, simply because I was an ornery kid. But Dad was a big man, so believe me, my tender backside felt each and every one.

Sometimes I carried jacks in my back pocket, those four-pronged pieces of metal that kids played with back then. One time, Dad starting whipping me with his bare hand and he let out a loud yelp. You know that familiar line fathers use before they administer a whipping?

"Son, this is going to hurt me a lot more than it hurts you." Well, that time, it was accurate. Those sharply-pointed jacks got the better of his hand.

The bottom line is this: I was happy. Very happy.

Our family farmed in Fayette County in the southwest part of Ohio, on a few thousand acres of land as flat as the surface of a pool table. Our house was located between the small towns of Madison Mills and Bloomingburg. On several days before school from the fourth grade through the eighth, I would ride my bike a mile and a half to meet my buddy Fred Melvin at the corners of Harrison and White Oak roads. Then we would race the final two miles into Madison Mills, just a tiny place with about thirty houses, a country store, and a grain elevator.

The big city to us was Washington Court House, the seat of the county located almost exactly halfway between Columbus and Cincinnati. Its population was about 12,000 and it was where we shopped, filled up our gas tanks, and got our haircuts. It was the nearest town with restaurants such as McDonald's and Pizza Hut.

Our life was a typical Ohio farm life. We raised hogs, cattle, corn, wheat, and soybeans and looking back, it was a simple, country life based on family and hard-working values. And of course, sports were our recreation. The heart and soul of the family, our mother Mila, was the person who held it all together.

My mother was the dearest, most-caring person I've ever known. She still is. I always said Dad never would have made it without Mom. She handled the cleaning, the cooking, and drove us around town while Dad handled the farming.

My dad's office away from home. We spent many hours riding and talking on the combine in the fall.

The thing I remember most: She was the conscience of the family. She knew right from wrong and tried to teach us the same. She possessed the soft, sentimental, sensitive, caring traits that her father had. She never said a bad word about anybody. My mom has always possessed a kind heart and a good soul. I figure that's where I got my sensitive side, because I know for sure I didn't get it from Dad.

"Arthur," he once told me, "in his entire life, my father never told me that he loved me."

Maybe because of that, Dad did tell us that magical line a time or two, but not as often as Mom did.

Dad was six-foot-three and probably 250 pounds when I was growing up. He later topped out at over 400 pounds as he grew older.

He had been a pretty good athlete in his day, becoming a highly recruited offensive tackle when Washington Court House High became the number one-ranked team in the state in the 1950s. But he sustained a head injury during his senior season and doctors told him he shouldn't play college football or he would risk serious injury.

Dad had poor eyesight and wore big thick glasses. He also had a bad right hand from an accidental gunshot wound while hunting. It was somewhat crumpled up like a claw. Still, he was strong, the strongest man I knew. He was strong enough to break the steers by tying a rope around them and over-powering them until they settled down.

One time, however, Dad bit off more than he could chew with this giant steer. I forget its name, but Dad believed that steer was a solid candidate for grand champion at the county fair. As he struggled to break him one day, I looked out the window of the house to see this huge steer and Dad tied together, flying by my eyes at about ten miles per hour.

The steer pulled Dad, who hung on for dear life, knowing if he let go of that rope that the steer would be off into the woods and he'd never get him back. I sprinted out of the house, just as the steer dragged Dad into the bean field, the two of them mowing down a wide row of fresh beans.

It took about five minutes, but the steer finally wore out and stopped. When I caught up to them, they were face-to-face … Dad covered in beans and the steer standing there staring at him, as if conceding the fight. Dad hooked him up to a tractor and slowly walked him back to the barn.

The first family portrait I can remember.

I knew then that big steer would have to rip Dad's arm off for him to get away. Dad wouldn't let go. And I also realized that my ol' man was one strong dude.

Another time the same steer took off, leading Dad into a large hole. It stopped in its tracks, unable to pull him out of that hole. I think it about broke the poor steer's neck.

In the end, not only did the steer *not* get awarded grand champion, it didn't even place at the fair. Naturally, Dad was pissed off. He had gone through all that trouble, about lost an arm in the process, had fallen into a hole and hurt himself, and the steer didn't win a thing.

Dad's poor vision sometimes resulted in a laugh for John and me. One day, Dad hopped off the tractor and was walking to his truck when he spotted a groundhog. He figured he would give that groundhog a swift kick (groundhogs are not exactly a farmer's best friend), but as he wound up to give it the boot, he heard a spraying noise.

Now there was nothing wrong with Dad's ears or his nose. He knew right away he'd made a huge mistake. He had kicked a skunk! Mom made him take off every bit of clothing and burn it before he was allowed back into the house that night. John and I had a good laugh that night, but I'm not sure Dad found it too funny.

While Dad had no problem thumping me for my misbehavior, John rarely faced such problems. He usually did the right thing and stayed in Dad's good graces. When he did get into trouble, I usually forced him into it one way or another. And if I hadn't, Dad figured I had.

Like the time we were playing on the Rogers Farm, a huge spread where Dad often took us because he tended to the horses and cattle there. We often played in and around a huge cinder-block-lined trough which held water for the cattle.

Well, John also had bad eyes—a Schlichter trait I guess since I've worn contacts or glasses my entire life—and he had to undergo a couple of operations on them. He'd just come from the eye doctor and one eye was covered with a big patch. We were sailing our boats in the trough when suddenly John leaned over to grab his boat and fell into the tank face-first, eye-patch and all.

We both got our asses whipped for that one. John claimed I'd pushed him, but I really didn't. It probably was the one time I caught hell from Dad when I was completely innocent. But I'm sure there are other times I got away with something, so I guess it evened out.

Something else happened at the Rogers Farm that affected me for years. In fact, I still think about it once in a while.

One day I ran into the barn to pet the horses and there he was … one of the hired hands just hanging there in front of my six-year-old eyes, all the life gone from his body. He had committed suicide.

I shot out of there as fast as I could run.

"Dad! Dad!" I shouted. "He's hanging in the barn!"

I can't remember the man's name, but to this day I can still see the poor guy hanging there with that noose around his neck.

When it came to working the farm as we grew older, John was the better farmer and had all of the mechanical skills. He was in Future Farmers of America and all of that.

Me? I could bale hay and drive a tractor, but that was about it. Well, I did like the pigs. I actually considered them my friends. I was a big Cosby

Picking up wood for the fireplace at grandpa Hap's home.

fan and I would give the pigs names such as Fat Albert, Old Weird Harold, and Russell. I would feed them, wash them, and take care of them before Dad would take them to the market to get butchered. He then paid me half of that money for taking care of them.

Other than that, however, you could say I was farm-illiterate, if there is such a thing. My contribution was being the go-fer, and sometimes, I even screwed that up.

Once Dad told me to put oil in the car and I poured it where the antifreeze was supposed to go. The car smoked like crazy after that.

Dad would pay me to pick up rocks in the field, because the larger rocks damaged the planter and the combine. I mean, any idiot can manage picking up rocks, right? So he paid me a penny a rock. My goal was to pick up a hundred rocks each day to earn a dollar.

While Dad and John farmed, I really just wanted to play ball. One day Dad said to me, "You love sports so much, just go work out and practice."

So I did.

I would practice sports for seven or eight hours a day. That was like a pardon from the prison farm for me. It was great at the time, but looking back, I realize Dad had an ulterior motive. I know that he saw the potential in me, because in seventh-grade basketball I averaged something like 45 points a game. In baseball, I was pitching no-hitters and striking out 15 or 16 batters each game.

Organized football in Washington Court House started in the fifth grade and if you weighed less than 95 pounds, they put you in the backfield. If you weighed 95 or more, they stuck you on the offensive line.

Fortunately, I weighed 90 pounds and could already throw the football pretty well. I didn't want to play on the line.

Of the coaches who had the first two draft choices, I liked a man named Paul Johnson, a nice, easy-going coach and a family friend who told me he would take me if he had the first pick of the league draft for all the fifth-graders in town. John had played on his team a few years earlier, and when I watched his practices, I also noticed another coach at the other end of the field, working his team to death.

His name was Fred DiDomenico, and he was our family insurance agent and an ex-military guy. Judging by those practices, something right out of the *Junction Boys,* I figured he was tougher and meaner than a rattlesnake. When the telephone rang that Monday, it was our insurance man and he hadn't called to talk about insurance.

"Arthur, this is Coach DiDomenico," he said. "I just drafted you for our football team. Be ready for our first practice, this Saturday morning."

I hung up the phone and turned to Dad.

"I guess I won't play football," I told him. "Basketball's my favorite sport anyway."

"Fine, if you change your mind, let me know," Dad responded.

By Saturday, I had changed my mind.

I attended the first practice and discovered that Coach DiDomenico wasn't so bad. He was the best coach I could possibly imagine for a fifth-grader who knew little about the game of football. By the next season, we had a team that was unbeatable, scoring 50 and sometimes 60 points in a game.

Dad once told a sports writer that he knew when I was very young that I would turn into a collegiate or even professional athlete someday, but *I* certainly had no idea. I know he gave me a lot more of his time than he did the other two kids and it often made me feel sorry for John and Dawn.

I guess Dad was living vicariously through me even at a young age. He was so proud of me when I excelled in sports, and I sensed it, wanting to succeed as much for him as I did for myself.

One time he even told me, "Arthur, I love you more than your brother and sister."

Can you imagine telling one of your kids that? Because of that, I always tried to make John feel special, even when we were fighting like the fiercest rivals. I usually bought him extra Christmas presents and when he competed in school sports, I wanted him to succeed more than I wanted success for myself. Later, I was his biggest supporter and fan and I like to think he was mine, too.

Anyway, there were no kids around to play with, so John and I played with each other. We did virtually everything together—fished, rode our bikes everywhere, played in the hay—and I can honestly say that we were best buddies as much as we were brothers.

Mostly, what we shared was a love affair with whatever game we were playing at the time. He and I faced off against each other daily in basketball, baseball, football, or even ping-pong.

I know this is one indisputable fact: Competing against him all those years helped make me the athlete that I became.

Dad had maintained a giant haymow on the second level of the barn, where John and I spent most of our free time playing basketball. The more hay Dad used, the bigger our court became. We battled one-on-one there for years, spilling a lot of blood and sweat all over each other and that hay.

John always was bigger than I was, but he never took it easy on me. Never. He was a good athlete, but not a great one. He had great eye-hand coordination, but he wasn't as quick as I was.

These days, you hear young kids dreaming of becoming the next Derek Jeter, Peyton Manning, or Michael Jordan. The thing is, John and I never dreamed that way. We never dreamed of playing football at Ohio State or basketball at Indiana when we were young. So you know that we didn't dare dream of playing professional sports. We just never talked that way or thought that way.

We idolized guys who played at our high school. Dad was the P.A. announcer at the high school stadium and we attended all of the football games, so when I got to visit the locker room, that was a huge thrill for me. I can still remember the high school football and basketball stars, such as Carl Gatewood, Dave Bihl, Steve Bowers, Doug Ford, Eddie Summers, Jeff Blake ... I always thought, "This is the ultimate. This is what I want to be." I dreamed of following those guys. I just wanted to play football for the Miami Trace High School Panthers.

As I got a little older, I dreamed of playing basketball for the University of Dayton. Dayton was coached by Don Donoher and I loved that guy. John and I once attended his basketball camp and from that point on Dayton Flyer basketball was the big time as far as I was concerned. We were just farm kids who played basketball in front of the cats and raccoons as we dribbled around the haymow. So when we stepped foot on that floor at the University of Dayton

Arena, we were in heaven.

While my life was all about sports, John had other interests.

He was somewhat shy, so when he landed the lead in *The Music Man* during his junior year, I was shocked, seeing him stand up there on stage singing in front of all those people. The funny thing was, I had never, ever heard him sing before. I just sat there in amazement, wondering what the heck happened to my shy brother.

Dawn, John, and me, in the '60s.

He was even shy and straight-laced with the girls.

I'll never forget a double-date when I was a freshman and he was a junior. There I was in the backseat, kissing and hugging my childhood sweetheart, Sandy Hughes, while John and his date sat at opposite ends of the front seat.

As for my sister Dawn, I always thought she got the short end of the stick when it came to Dad. There were two boys and a girl in our family, and Dad loved athletics so much that I don't think he ever paid much attention to her. It may have scarred her a little, as I think about it now.

What's more, I know John and I—probably just me—amounted to one big pain in the ass for Dawn. She didn't get much privacy with us around, and part of that was because we lived in a small house. Her date would bring her home and they would sit in the car kissing, while I peeked through the window to see what she was doing. Of course, I then ran to tell Mom and Dad about what I saw.

I would play stupid jokes on her all the time, like hiding under her bed when she got home. Then I would reach out and grab her leg and she would let out a scream. One day, Dawn agreed to play catch with me. I threw the football, it broke her finger and she never played with me again. She still tells that story.

Her loves were music and horses. She made me go to all of her musicals in which she usually landed the lead part. Her pride and joy, though, was a horse named Pansy, a good-looking horse that I loved to ride bareback. I'd hop on that horse and head off a hundred miles an hour through the field as the dirt flew. John, not a risk-taker by any means, used a saddle. Once, John hopped up on Pansy and the saddle must have cut loose. As he took off galloping, John slipped clear underneath him.

I can still see him hanging on for dear life as he rode pretty much upside down. He just about got trampled to death, but I stood there laughing my head off. I remember seeing him in the bathtub covered in bumps and bruises that night. He never got back on that horse again.

My brush with death as a kid had nothing to do with me getting into any monkey business. In fact, I was helping Mom when it happened.

It was the morning of July 29, 1972, just before my seventh grade year, and we were getting ready to take our 4-H steers to the county fair. We had just moved down the road, into the ranch house Dad had built, at 7320 Myers Road. Fresh tar covered the roof, but it had dripped down to the cement in the garage. John and I had tracked it into the house, all over the linoleum floor.

Well, you know how most moms would react.

"John, Arthur … ," she told us, "go get some rags and gasoline … you're cleaning this floor!"

For some reason that day, I wore nothing but a pair of cutoff jean shorts. No shirt, no long pants, no socks or shoes. No common sense.

We were down on our hands and knees, scrubbing away at this tar while Dad and Dawn watched television in the living room. John had set his can of gas on the dryer, which happened to be running at the time. Suddenly, as he stood up, he bumped it with his elbow, sending the gas flying into the hot dryer and … BOOM!

The explosion blew out the entire side of the house and sent Mom flying out the back door. Miraculously, she wasn't hurt. I went straight up into the air as my can of gas caught fire. When I came down, the flames shot straight up my back and instantly, I was engulfed.

I started running around in a circle like a dummy, instead of rolling to put out the flames covering my shirtless body. John also was on fire until Dad jumped off the couch and got him down on the ground. Fortunately, Dawn came running to me and tripped me to get me down. She probably saved my life, but the damage was done. I was burned all over my hands, back, arms, and on my ankle.

In a full panic, Mom ran to the garage and pulled out our big Mercury Marquis as Dad stayed behind to put out the fire. As we headed to the hospital, I screamed in pain from the backseat and John from the front. I remember Mom was so panicked that her tiny foot slid up and down on the gas pedal. She could barely reach the pedals in that big car under normal circumstances anyway. We were just creeping down the road as the car jerked back and forth to the rhythm of Mom's nervous foot.

Luckily, a few miles from the house, a sheriff's car was about to pass us when she flagged it down. The deputy loaded us into his car and sped off to the hospital.

I had third-degree burns on my back and second-degree burns on my arms and legs.

The worst part of it all was the treatment, which was the most intense pain I'd ever experience. The doctors would give John and me a shot of Demerol, but wait for it to wear off before giving us another. Then they'd take us into this cold room and scrape off the skin every two days. I know I cried like a baby each time.

During my football career years later, when medical staffs wondered how I could play with broken bones, I'd tell them it was because of those burns I experienced as a kid. Nothing, and I mean nothing, ever hurt like those burns. A broken ankle or separated shoulder seemed like a hangnail next to that.

While we healed, Dad wouldn't let any visitors into the room for fear of infection. The fair was happening that week, so it seemed to be routine for our friends to visit us after going to the fair. They would stand outside of our room, peer through the glass and wave at us, just as if we were caged animals on display at the zoo. I wondered if they made an announcement each night as people exited the fair: "Hey everyone, go see the Schlichter boys in all their glory, burned from head to toe!"

We were in the hospital for several weeks, sharing a room, but I believe John could have been released sooner. I think they kept him there to keep me company.

They tell me that I pestered the doctors with one simple question, "Will I still be able to play sports?"

I still have those burn scars today. Thank God Dawn had the awareness to trip me and put out the flames covering my body. If not, I may have died right then and there at the age of 12.

Sis, I know it's been about forty years, but I'm apologizing here and now for breaking your finger.

Chapter three

MY FIRST LOVE

Football is the sport people associate my name with, but it wasn't the sport I loved the most. Basketball was my first love. And it wasn't even a close contest.

My fondest memories of growing up are of the wooden court in the barn, holding the haymow where John and I banged against each other one-on-one, and then from age 12, the barn out back of our house where I spent just about all of my free time.

Dad had installed a glass backboard in the barn. I knew if I could dribble on the warped floor of the barn, I could dribble on anything. There was no three-point line in the game back in the early '70s, but I drew one up at about twenty feet anyway to make our games interesting.

I lived in the barn for hours at a time, playing by myself, shooting and dribbling. I even did drills like toe raises so I could jump higher, but ultimately that didn't help much, because I never became a great jumper. I also hung a speed bag in there to make my hands quicker.

My family and friends knew where to look when they couldn't find me.

When I wasn't practicing basketball, I listened to it on the radio. I taped games that included my three favorite players and then listened to the tapes in the barn as I practiced.

I first idolized a guy by the name of Allan Hornyak, one of the greatest guards ever to play at Ohio State. One of my favorite sportscasters, Jimmy Crum, called Allan the "Bellaire Bomber" because he could shoot the eyes out from long range.

Then there was Donald Smith, a great player from the University of

Dayton. He played with Johnny Davis and Mike Sylvester on Don Donoher's team, which took UCLA to triple overtime in the second round of the NCAA tournament in 1974.

During my early teen years, I dreamed of playing basketball at the University of Dayton and I was a religious watcher of the *Don Donoher Show* on TV. To me, the Dayton Flyers were bigger than anything back then.

Finally, my all-time favorite was Nate "Tiny" Archibald, who was with the Cincinnati Royals at the time before the franchise moved to Kansas City and became the Kings. (I got all of the Royals' games on radio.)

I absolutely *loved* the guy. I memorized one of the tapes I played over and over until it became scratchy … *"Ladies and gentlemen, Nate Archibald is unbelievable, that little man. He never shows any emotion, ever. He never says anything to the officials. He never shows a bead of sweat…"*

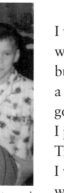

Christmas in the 60s, we each got something round.

Well, that was a problem for me, because I wanted to be just like Nate Archibald. He was a point guard and that was my position, but when I played basketball, I sweated like a hog. My goal one time was to get in such good shape that I would never sweat when I played the game, so I could be just like Tiny. I discovered that no matter how hard I worked, and no matter what great shape I was in, the sweat poured off of me and there was nothing I could do about it.

I knew I had *some* talent, because as I said earlier, I averaged about 45 points a game when I attended grade school and middle school in Madison Mills. By the time I was a freshman for the Miami Trace Panthers—kids in Fayette County attended one of two high schools, Washington Senior High or Miami Trace High—I had heard the other kids talking about me.

"He came from Madison Mills and they don't play anybody tough," or "He's just a scorer who shoots all the time," they'd say.

Nevertheless, I started on the varsity basketball team and averaged eight points per game and scored a high game of 16. Not bad for a freshman, but the seniors were really tough on me. They resented a freshman getting playing time, so they constantly harassed me.

When a freshman earns a starting spot ahead of juniors and seniors, a few parents of those kids resent it. And their resentment wasn't kept to themselves. They made their feelings toward me known.

Here's the way parents' night went for our family at the conclusion of my freshman season, when they announced our names in the gymnasium:

"Max and Mila Schlichter, proud parents of John and Art..."

BOO! BOOOO! BOOOOOO!!!

Our introduction had been drowned out by a chorus of boos.

I know they weren't booing John, one of the nicest and most-unassuming kids in town. It was directed at me, all because I took some senior's starting job away.

"Don't worry about it," Dad would tell me. "You let your play do the talking for you. I'll defend you when I have to. I'll be the bad guy."

It may have been a role he relished. I know my dad wasn't the most popular guy in town because he was outspoken, but he was my dad and I trusted his judgment and loved him immensely.

It wasn't just the parents who unleashed their disapproval upon me, either. I took some severe abuse and was treated very badly by many of the upperclassmen that year. I was stuck in a varsity locker room with kids older than me and I felt ostracized, because very few of them would talk to me.

And when they did, they usually made fun of me.

It seemed I was constantly teased then and it wasn't that good-natured, fun-loving teasing that goes hand in hand with athletics; it was the mean, nasty teasing.

Three years later, those same people and their parents were the same people cheering me, patting me on the back, acting as if they were my best friends.

My dad never forgot or forgave over the ensuing years, but I wasn't that type of person. I was easy-going and I cared about people and just wanted to be liked by everybody, a people-pleaser like Mom and her father had been. I guess that is why the ridicule bothered me so much emotionally.

Dad felt he had to be a people-pleaser only to four people: Mom, me, John and Dawn. Other than that, everyone else could jump into the Ohio River, as far as he was concerned. And he never softened or mellowed as he grew older.

As for me, it sizzled a brand into my head and into my heart, making me want to practice harder and to someday prove everybody wrong. It absolutely drove me to do everything in my power to succeed as I progressed through high school.

Miami Trace hired a new coach, John Wollums, before my sophomore year. He had coached Dayton Roosevelt to a state championship when he was younger. By the time he arrived to coach us, he was in his 60s and his heyday was long gone. He had this raspy, rough voice, so naturally, we loved to imitate him.

The first time I met him, he barked, "So you're Art? Well Art, can you shoot the rock?"

I mumbled something and he barked back at me, "Well! … Let me see you shoot the rock!"

We grew to love him, as well as all of his silly sayings and that raspy bark, but he got very nervous when the games were tight.

I came into my own during my sophomore year, averaging more than 20 points per game, making all-league and honorable mention All-Ohio. My brother started some that year as a senior and we both started in what was his final game. I scored about 30 points that night, which was a great memory even though we lost a close game to Portsmouth.

After I had a big game and we beat Lancaster 69-68 to start my junior season, Coach Wollums ran into the locker room and was all excited, jumping around hugging people.

"We're going to the state title!" he barked. "Twenty-five more wins and we're there."

We all rolled our eyes and headed to the shower.

When we played Cambridge, a talented blond senior by the name of Doug Donley was their star, but he had just broken his right arm and had a pin placed in it, so he had to shoot left-handed.

Well, Doug couldn't shoot left-handed. After we fell behind by about 15 points at the start of the fourth quarter, we decided to start fouling Doug. He would repeatedly miss the front end of the one-and-one bonus, allowing us to creep back into the game.

Finally, he grew frustrated with us hacking him, so he took a swing at one of our guys. The officials kicked Doug and our player out of the game. The problem was, we couldn't foul him anymore and we ended up losing the game.

That was the first time I ever met Doug Donley. I always told him later that if he hadn't gotten thrown out of the game, we would have won.

Our team motto became, "Fire and fall back" and that's what we did. There was no shot clock then, but we wouldn't have needed one anyway. We brought the ball across mid-court and fired away.

Another motto of mine was not quite the patented give-and-go. It was, "Give me the ball and everybody else go to hell." At least that's how my teammates jokingly described my offensive approach.

Even Coach Wollums had a similar version. During tight games, he would bark at the team: "Just get the ball to Art ... and get the hell out of his way!"

We never had a set offense, never played much defense and never fully understood the team concept. That probably is why we finished 10-11 that season. I was an exceptional basketball player, a player with some raw skills who averaged 24 points per game that season. I could dribble and shoot with the best of them, but I really didn't know *how* to play the game.

I was about to learn, however.

The school fired John Wollums following that season and the super-intendent had told Dad about this great coach from Frankfort Adena. His name was Ron Hall, whom Miami Trace had tried to hire two years earlier, but he turned them down cold.

This time, for whatever reason, he accepted the job, arriving before my senior season.

Ron was in his late 30s, a real smooth-talker, and a personable, good-looking guy. He was not very big, about 5-foot-9, but he knew the game of basketball better than anyone I would ever know.

On that Monday afternoon following my final football game, we reported to basketball practice, not knowing what to expect from this new coach. It didn't take long to find out. In a two-and-a-half hour practice, we spent about two hours in a defensive stance.

I thought, "My God, this is horrible!"

I absolutely hated it.

The best thing that happened to that team, however, was the blizzard of '78, a more than month-long event everybody in the state remembers as the worst snowstorm on record. We were snowed in, without school for three or four weeks. I had been exhausted from football season, so I slept in, rested, and became rejuvenated.

All the team members somehow found their way through the snow to the gym during the storm and we could practice about three hours each day because there was no school.

That's when we got better and learned Coach Hall's system.

He knew what he was talking about but it never registered to us then that defense was the key to winning games. We always thought you just had to out-score people. We struggled during the first few weeks of practice and I know it really was torture to me.

After we got beat by Wilmington, whose star player was Gary Williams, Coach Hall got right into my face in front of the entire team.

"You'll never be a real basketball player, Schlichter!" he screamed. "You know nothing about the game! You're selfish!"

Nobody had ever gotten in my face like that.

That night, I told Dad, "I'm quitting. I don't need to play for this guy. He's mean. He's crazy."

"You're quitting nothing," Dad shot back. "We don't quit, I don't care how bad it is. You just gut it out!"

Sure enough, we started winning games, but my shooting had been somewhat ugly. I think we were 7-1 when we faced Chillicothe, whom Coach Hall wanted to beat badly because he once coached there. In that game, I took a poor shot from the corner, which he didn't like one bit, so he pulled me out and sat me on the bench. Nobody had ever done that to me before, but I guess right then and there I became a disciple of Ron Hall.

My scoring average dropped to 18.4 points per game as a senior, but that served as evidence that his team-first concept had finally sunk in through my thick skull.

When Coach Hall wasn't sticking his proverbial foot up my backside, opposing players were getting in my grill.

When we played Washington Senior High, it seemed that they always tried to provoke me into a fight. But I would take the Tiny Archibald approach: I just backed off and remained calm. Never let them see you sweat, right?

Unlike three years earlier, there was nothing but total respect given to me on parents' night before our final home game. Dad, Mom, and I were introduced to thunderous applause and I felt total admiration from everybody. I believe it was a vindication for Dad, too.

We continued to improve as the season progressed, winning several close games. As the district tournament started, we won the first game by one point, then beat Lancaster by 20 before beating Chillicothe 43-42 in the finals.

We had played man-to-man defense all year, but to illustrate Coach Hall's genius, he had taught us a matchup zone throughout the season, but we had never used it before the tournament. We threw that matchup zone at teams during the tournament and just stifled opponents with it.

We defeated Walnut Ridge in triple overtime in the regional finals at the Columbus Coliseum to reach the state tournament, a place no Miami Trace team had ever been before.

Before my sophomore year at Miami Trace.

As most Ohioans know, the state tourney was played then at St. John Arena on the Ohio State campus. Every kid who played high school basketball dreamed of playing on that sacred floor where Jerry Lucas, John Havlicek, and one of my idols, Allan Hornyak, had played.

I know I had dreamed about it, too. I just never thought it could happen.

Our opponent, Kettering Alter, was led by John Paxson (who later played at Notre Dame and alongside Michael Jordan with the Chicago Bulls during their first NBA championship run) and sported a lineup that went 6-6, 6-5, 6-4, 6-4 and 6-3.

At 6-3, I was the tallest guy on our team.

I will never forget Woody Hayes watching the entire game while standing right outside the tunnel where the teams came onto the court. I scored 23 points that night, but we lost 63-53 to finish the season with a 22-3 record. Nevertheless, I still think our tournament run was the greatest thrill I ever had playing high school sports.

I ended my career as Miami Trace's all-time leading scorer with 1,345 points, but I realize now it was Ron Hall's coaching and leadership, not my scoring, which took us that far. It's just too bad that it took him a whole year to break us.

He quit coaching a few years later but remained a teacher at Miami Trace for the next twenty-five years.

"I just got burned out quickly," he told me.

I think Ron was miserable when kids didn't buy into his coaching system and I was one of those guilty kids who didn't buy in right away. When I returned to Miami Trace to play pickup games while I was at Ohio State and even later, I always tried to talk him into returning to coaching.

"Ah … no … I don't think so, Art," usually was his answer.

I can look back more than thirty years later and say he taught me more about basketball, and sports in general, than any man I've known.

He was absolutely right. I knew little about the game and I was a selfish basketball player when my senior season began.

By the time it ended, Ron Hall had given us one of the best years of our lives.

Chapter four

THEY TELL ME I'M
A SUPERSTAR

During one of my basketball games early in my senior season, I glanced up to the stands to see three of the biggest legends of college football sitting in the same section—Joe Paterno, Bo Schembechler, and Woody Hayes. All were within speaking distance of each other.

Up in the balcony sat Don Donoher, the University of Dayton basketball coach.

That picture accurately symbolized my future. Football would be front and center and become my meal ticket while basketball would fall into the background, the true love whom I would never marry.

Sure, I could have had a major-college hoops scholarship waiting for me somewhere if I had wanted, probably with Donoher's program. I may have been a farm boy, but I was not a dumb farm boy. After all, I was never going to be the next Tiny Archibald. There wasn't a high demand for relatively slow, Caucasian point guards in the NBA.

Football would pave my path to college stardom and perhaps even a professional career someday and I had to face that fact.

Just as I made the varsity starting lineup in basketball as a freshman, I did so in football, too, but as a cornerback. I was quick and could hit, but I was scared to death playing varsity as a freshman.

And I was probably the most unpopular starting player among teammates on any high school team in the state of Ohio. Or at least it felt that way.

Even today, what I experienced as a freshman bothers me. I think it also contributed to my insecurity. The seniors, just as they did during basketball season, heckled me all the time. The seniors' harassment resulted in another

John and I, in our baseball uniforms. It was my first team sport—Madison Mills Mosquito League baseball.

major decision for me—I went out for track instead of baseball during the spring of my freshman year.

I had been a pretty good pitcher until then and I believe I could have had a future in baseball if I had wanted it, but most of those aforementioned seniors played on the baseball team and I did everything I could to get away from them.

I also knew that track would help me become faster for football. Plus, the track coach was Fred Zechman, our football coach with whom I had a great relationship.

Immediately, I high-jumped 5-foot-10, even though I didn't have any idea of the proper technique or fundamentals.

During our first meet, at Hillsboro, Coach Zechman stuck me in the second heat (for the slower guys) of the 440.

"Okay," Coach Zech told me. "You will sprint for about 100 yards and then just pace yourself for about 240 and then over that last 100, you will sprint and gut it out to the finish line."

"No problem," I told him. "I can do it."

At the starting gun, I started sprinting as coach had directed. As I got to about 100 yards, I was out of wind and shifted down. The problem was, nobody else shifted down and they blew right by me like I was standing still. I caught rigor mortis coming down the stretch and staggered home, running a 60.2 seconds—a very slow time for a high school 440.

Then I walked away from the track and puked my guts out.

Coach Zechman and Dad were sitting in the stands laughing at me. When they finished their good, ol' belly-laugh, Coach Zech walked over to see how I was doing.

"Okay, you've got 45 minutes to get ready for the mile relay," he said.

At that moment, I wondered what the heck I had gotten myself into. I wasn't in good shape to begin with and I hated running, even later in college. I started thinking that maybe the seniors' harassment wasn't so bad after all and that I would rather be standing on the pitching mound right now.

I ran the mile relay, walked away from the track and puked again. If there would have been a vomiting event, I would have won a gold medal.

Anyway, my track experience improved and I eventually high-jumped 6-foot-6. Still, the baseball coach tried to get me to come out every year. I turned him down every year.

But I honestly believe that track experience helped me become faster in the long run, giving me the edge I needed when running from linebackers and defensive backs.

I became the starting quarterback as a sophomore while John, a senior tight end, became my favorite target. At about 6-foot-4 and 200 pounds, he wasn't fast by any means, but he had great hands and could catch anything.

What haunts me is that John never scored a touchdown during his entire career. I thought he was headed to one against Hillsboro, after I threw a short pass to him over the middle as he suddenly broke into the clear. As he galloped toward the end zone, I started hopping up and down, anticipating a celebration between the Schlichter brothers in the end zone.

However, he got caught from behind and was tackled at about the one-foot line. I was so mad at him for not scoring that I ran up and hit him harder than the guy who tackled him.

Not hooking up for a fraternal touchdown is still one of my biggest regrets. I believe it would have been special to John, as well.

We finished 9-0-1 that year, tying Gary Williams's Wilmington team. Gary played quarterback, running back, receiver … he did it all. I hadn't played well in that game before getting knocked out of it with a concussion.

I couldn't imagine having had a better head coach than Fred Zechman. I believed in everything he did and said. He believed in me, too, and that's all any athlete really wants from his coach. You want to excel for a man like that.

First, John had been my leading receiver the year before and he caught only fifteen passes, so what does that tell you about our offense? It was mostly a running game—a simple attack.

But Coach Zech, who always had been a great motivator, became a serious student of the game and started studying other offenses. Dad also became very close to him and we knew he had aspirations of taking his career as far as he could, wanting to move up to the college ranks when he received the opportunity.

That next spring and summer before my junior season, he put in the run-and-shoot and now we had a trap series, a buck series, and a drop-back series, too. To learn this new expanded offense, we practiced a lot in the gymnasium during the off-season when we weren't allowed to, running through the plays and blocking assignments.

I think somebody in the school must have told him to knock it off, so then we sneaked off to our farm and practiced behind the cornstalks where nobody could see us.

I am sure Zech would have been punished if anybody found out about our covert practices, but he only wanted us to get better. And we wanted that, too. I'll bet I spent almost every day of those final two summers with Fred, throwing the football.

About that time, Dad came to me and said, "Arthur, you have an unbelievable gift that God gave you. It's now up to you to make the most of it. You can either work your butt off to get the most out of it, or you can live on your talent and waste it. It's up to you."

Not that I needed to hear those words to work any harder, but after hearing them, I may have stepped it up a notch. I threw at least 500 passes each day during the summers and worked on my agility and strength. A teammate and good friend, David Creamer, caught my passes almost every day. David was about 5-foot-9 and 175 pounds, but pound for pound, he probably was the best player on our team by the time we became seniors. He later played for Terry Bowden at Salem College in West Virginia.

Dad also installed a net at home for me, a target stretched between two telephone poles, when nobody was around to play catch with me.

With our new multi-faceted offense, we became unbeatable during my junior season, winning all 10 games. I rushed for 525 yards and 10 touchdowns and passed for 1,685 yards and 16 touchdowns, but I never once believed I accomplished those numbers alone.

Our offensive line was very effective. Our guards were not big but they were the key to the offense. They would pull on about every play and cut down the defensive ends like they were cutting meat. It was fun to watch.

Miami Trace was the smallest Class AAA school in the state back then. There was no state tournament as there is now and only one team from each region advanced to the playoffs. Unfortunately, we were stuck in the same region with highly-publicized Cincinnati Moeller, coached by Gerry Faust, who later left for Notre Dame. Moeller also never lost a game and played against all the top Cincinnati schools, so we never got to go to the state playoffs.

I really think we could have beaten any team in the state, including Moeller.

Street and Smith's was the annual pre-season college football magazine, which listed the top high school players in the nation in the back of each edition. My goal in life was to be listed in that magazine.

During the summer leading into my senior year, I would sneak in the back of Risches' Drug Store in Washington Court House almost daily, and tip-toe behind this big rack of books to the magazine stand to see if it had arrived.

Finally, one day I saw it and opened it so quickly that I almost tore off the pages. There it was: *"First-team, quarterback: Art Schlichter, Miami Trace High School, Washington Court House, Ohio."*

That's the day I thought I hit the big time. I could have died a happy farm boy right then and there. I didn't care about going to Ohio State, Penn State, or Michigan. I just wanted to be mentioned in *Street and Smith's*.

That's when I started to believe, "Maybe I am as good as they say I am."

We ran the table again during my senior year, not having one close game. The closest was 34-6. Our offense's evolution over those three years was like progressing from Earle Bruce's system to Bill Walsh's.

We even thumped Gary Williams's Wilmington team.

Gary was a phenomenal player. Once we ran a waggle play where I faked to the running back who ran around left end as I continued running around right end. Gary first went for the fake, almost tackling the back as I rambled down the other sideline with a clear path to the end zone. I was brought down at the three-yard line, got up, and realized that Gary had made the tackle. He had run from one side of the field clear across to the other to catch me. It was the most unbelievable defensive play I ever saw.

We really dominated our opponents. During our homecoming game, we scored a touchdown to make the score 78-0 in the middle of the fourth quarter.

We told our kicker, Scott Grooms, who later played quarterback at Notre Dame, to intentionally fall down during the attempted two-point conversion.

Why?

We were the class of '78 and we all thought that it would be pretty neat to win our homecoming game 78-0. So we purposely didn't score again.

It wasn't as if I was throwing the ball 30 times per game, either. We were so efficient running our offense that nobody could stop us and we always jumped to a huge lead, so there was little need to pump up my passing statistics.

I completed 108-of-190 passes for 1,794 yards and 21 touchdowns as a senior, and rushed for 539 more yards and scored 13 touchdowns. Those aren't eye-popping numbers by today's standards, but I probably played the equivalent of no more than five or six full games because I rarely played during the fourth quarters. My favorite receiver, Bill Hanners, who also was my closest friend, caught 50 of those passes.

What fans around the state and recruiters around the nation noticed was our eye-popping team production. We had averaged 52.3 points per game during my junior season and 60 points per game during my senior season. You gain attention when you're putting numbers like that up on the scoreboard.

That team did things that people in the area still talk about today. And they'll talk about it fifty or sixty years from now.

I was putting on a show even prior to kickoff. I would warm up by throwing 75- or 80-yard passes standing and then sit on my butt and throw it 50 yards just to loosen up my arm.

I know it sounds boastful, but that grabbed people's interest.

The *Columbus Citizen-Journal* quoted Pittsburgh Coach Jackie Sherrill: "I saw Joe Namath at Beaver Falls (Pennsylvania) High. I saw (Kenny) Snake Stabler during high school in Alabama. But Schlichter is the best I've ever seen in high school."

We beat Washington 48-12 that night as Woody Hayes watched from the stands and after the game I cried my eyes out like a little baby. All of us cried that night, including Zech.

We didn't want it to end. I knew—we all knew—that life would be changing for everybody in the family. It was very surreal. Somehow, some way, I may have known that the best times of my life were ending.

To summarize my high school athletic career: We never lost a football game of the thirty in which I was the starting quarterback; I set all of the school's passing records (4,387 yards) as well as the total offense record (6,041 yards); and I was named the UPI's Player of the Year in Ohio. We also advanced to the state basketball tournament for the first time in school history and I finished as the school's all-time leading scorer.

I also became the first male athlete at Miami Trace to earn twelve varsity letters and I was very proud of that. Nobody has done it since.

Where I would earn my next letter was the question to which everyone wanted to know the answer.

Recruiting didn't start as early as it does today, when the top sophomores and juniors are being recruited by all the major football programs. My recruitment started the summer following my junior season when I met Bo Schembechler.

Here's how the meeting was arranged: A lawyer in Columbus by the name of Scott Knisley had been Bo's roommate at Miami of Ohio and they remained good friends through the years. My grandma's brother's daughter, Carol June McDonald, and her husband Mackey, ran Scott's farm in Bainbridge, Ohio. So one day during the summer of '77, Bo flew into this little airport down in Bainbridge, where we talked for several hours.

My MVP trophy, Ohio H.S. North South All Star game, 1978.

Today I figure that clandestine meeting had to be illegal according to NCAA rules, since it occurred in the summer between my junior and senior years. More than anything else, it shows how badly Bo wanted to get a jump on Woody.

By the time he flew out of the airport, I had decided, when the time came, I was going to sign with Michigan. I was in awe of Bo. He was larger than life to me.

Bo's mistake was bringing me to Ann Arbor for the 1977 Ohio State-Michigan game. We drove up there for my official visit and I was leaning toward becoming a Wolverine.

I met with Michigan basketball coach Johnny Orr and his assistant, Bill Frieder. They seemed like the odd couple. Johnny was a big, tall bald guy and Frieder, whom Bo would fire years later when he accepted the Arizona State job, was a little guy. Anyway, Bo didn't have a problem with me playing basketball because he had had other guys who played basketball.

On that Saturday, November 19, 1977, we sat directly behind the Michigan bench.

What struck me was how obnoxious the Michigan fans were to the Ohio State fans. I know now it goes both ways, but it really left an impression on me. I watched the game through scarlet-and-gray eyes, realizing I was an Ohio boy at heart. It was probably the wrong game for Michigan to invite me to because I had been an Ohio State fan my whole life and it made me realize I wasn't about to change. Midway through the game, I leaned over to Dad and whispered, "I don't think I'll be going to Michigan."

I spent much of the game looking up at the press box watching Ohio State offensive coordinator George Chaump who appeared about to fall out of the box at any moment. At other times, he looked ready to jump. I remember Rod Gerald fumbling near the end of the game, clinching Michigan's win.

The score was 14-6 and afterward I was invited to Michigan's locker room. I stood next to quarterback Rick Leach, who had scored the winning touchdown. While he did his post-game interviews, Bo approached me.

"That could be you in a few years," he said, smiling wide.

That day was the defining moment in my decision-making process.

Besides Ohio State and Michigan, my other visit was to Penn State.

To get to State College, Pennsylvania, we had to fly to Pittsburgh and then drive another three hours. That got me thinking how hard it was to get there. It seemed to be in the middle of nowhere. The weather was bad that weekend and it was a dreary place.

Fullback Matt Suey was my host that weekend and I thought he was a great guy. We went to some parties and saw the nightlife and I recall thinking, "This isn't me." I wasn't into the party atmosphere by any means.

Plus, I had a girlfriend back home and I considered how long it would take me to get home to see her during my free weekends. I knew then I wouldn't be a Nittany Lion, which disappointed Mom because she loved Joe Paterno. Hey, I loved Joe. He was so down to earth and harped over and over on getting an education. That impressed me.

Other than that secret meeting with Bo, and some things Miami Coach Lou Saban promised, there was little illegal recruitment of me.

"You come to Miami and we'll fly your parents in for free to see you play," Saban told me. "They'll have a real nice place to stay for free."

From the beginning of my recruitment, I believe most all of the college coaches saw that we were good, honest farmers and that wasn't the route to go with us. Dad surely wouldn't allow anything illegal to go on with me. All things considered, when it came time to make a decision, becoming a Buckeye appeared to be a foregone conclusion.

The first time I ever attended an Ohio State game was during the Archie Griffin-Cornelius Greene era in the early 1970s when Dad and I sat up in the upper deck, or "C Deck" as Buckeye fans know it. I was scared to death because I always hated heights.

Of course, we had much better seats when I attended every Ohio State home game in '77, the season when I fell in love with the Ohio State Marching Band. When I saw the band make that field entrance in the opener against Miami that year, I had a serious case of the chills.

I thought, "This is unbelievable. I want to be a part of this." Unfortunately, during my four years at Ohio State, I never saw the band perform on the field before, during, or after a game because we were always in the locker room.

It seemed like George Chaump, Woody, and Dad negotiated my recruitment throughout my senior year and into the winter. How would the offense change? Would I start from the beginning? If so, what would happen to Rod Gerald who would be a senior during my freshman season? What about playing basketball?

Coach Chaump was the main man recruiting me the entire time and I grew very, very close to him. He was an innovative and smart offensive coach but had been oppressed by Woody's stubbornness to stick entirely with the running game.

George saw this as an opportunity to change. He had envisioned a new beginning for the offense if I came to Ohio State. And it would be a new beginning for him, too—a new breath of life. He had great ideas for the offense and just needed a reason to talk Woody into changing.

I was that reason.

I believe Woody was intrigued by it, too. Part of him loved running the ball to beat people and part of him was intrigued by trying to not only throw more but to throw successfully. He was coming off of two straight losses to Michigan and I think he knew he had to pass more to beat Bo.

Woody often came down to our high school and stood by his old El Camino to watch our practices. He wasn't allowed to talk to me, so he never moved away from his car. The fact is that Woody didn't need to talk to me much. He knew everything about my family and me. And I mean *everything*.

Johnny and I at Miami Trace, in 1976. He was my favorite receiver.

He had done his homework.

Coach Zechman would wander over to talk to him during practice, but he never got within a long punt of me when he wasn't allowed to. Coach Zech, Dad, and I really wanted to work a package deal somewhere. In other words, we wanted Coach hired as an offensive assistant at whatever school I chose to attend. Accomplishing it was another matter.

In the end, the speculation of where I would sign built like a bubbling volcano through the holidays, and the phone calls to the house were incessant. Remember, this was early during my senior basketball season, occurring simultaneously with my battle of wills with Ron Hall, who wanted me to think of nothing but basketball.

So I had a lot going on in my life, all leading to one pressure-filled decision that I knew I had to get right. The outcome would affect my life forever.

Finally, I made my official visit to Ohio State early in January, just a little more than a week after the Buckeyes' 35-6 loss to Alabama in the Sugar Bowl. On the morning of the game on New Year's Day, Alabama Coach Bear Bryant called me, getting in one last recruiting pitch. No matter how charming the Bear was, I never considered heading south to attend college.

Doug Donley, the same guy from Cambridge whom we had fouled repeatedly in that heated basketball game a few years earlier, was a freshman receiver and my host for the weekend in Columbus. We went to an Ohio State basketball game and I was surprised that everybody there knew who I was.

"We need you," fans would shout at me.

"You're meant to be a Buckeye," others told me.

"We'll change the offense for you," was another line.

Doug and I went to a late movie while Dad spent the night with Coach Chaump and Woody.

The next morning, as we rode an elevator heading to a brunch with the coaches at the Ohio Union, Dad looked at me and said something that shocked me.

"I think it's time, Arthur," he said.

"What?" I asked him.

"Time to tell Ohio State you are coming here," he said. "They've made a promise to me that they'll change the offense, you'll start from the beginning, and they'll move Rod Gerald to wide receiver, because that's where he would play in the pros anyway. You do want to come here, right?"

"Yes," I told him. "This is where I want to go."

There were other recruits at the brunch that day and after a little time passed, Woody pulled me aside and took me to a private booth. I think he was about to try to close the deal with me, but I was an easy catch.

"Coach, I'm ready to commit," I told him.

"Are you sure?" he asked me.

"Yes, I'm sure."

"Well then, will you shake my hand on it?" he asked.

I extended my hand, prompting him to stand and start whooping and yelling. He gave me a big hug and had tears in his eyes.

"You will never regret this decision," he told me.

We agreed then to keep my decision private so I could hold a press conference a few days later at my high school. It's a common practice now, but nobody did that back then.

Immediately before the press conference was to begin, I called Bo Schembechler and Joe Paterno to give them the bad news. I really hated making both calls. Paterno was very nice about it and wished me luck, but Bo ... well, he wasn't happy.

"Well, I don't agree with your decision!" he snapped. "You'll regret it someday!"

It was just like Woody and Bo to disagree.

In the end, the decision really was easy.

First, I was an Ohio boy and I always wanted to be a Buckeye, dreaming of being a part of that rich tradition and playing in that huge stadium. Second, it was close to home and my family could share in it, easily. I also knew I would get a real chance to start as a freshman, which wouldn't happen at Michigan with Leach returning. Woody would allow me to play basketball, which was fine with Eldon Miller, the basketball coach. The clincher was that I learned Woody told Coach Zechman that he would bring him on the Ohio State staff to fill the next offensive opening he had. Dad and I realized Woody was the

Senior picture, class of 1978.

legend, but we loved Coach Chaump as a coach and as a person. He had great morals and was a good communicator. He loved people and I never saw him lose his temper. He was a real gentleman.

When I walked into the press conference at my high school on January 12, 1978, I couldn't believe so many people actually showed up, but there was a massive crowd. All the networks from Dayton, Cincinnati, and Columbus were there. I had bought a new sweater and pants for the event.

As soon as I announced the words, "I plan to attend The Ohio State University…" there was a loud cheer from the audience. I think even the media was cheering. Now the whole world knew I was about to become a Buckeye and all the pressure lifted off of my shoulders. Now there would be other pressures—to live up to this type of hype.

"Art is the best high school quarterback I've ever seen," Coach Chaump told the press.

Dad and I attended many of Ohio State's spring practices to get a feel for the offense. Coach Chaump would call us every morning and ask, "Are you coming?"

Some days we did and some days we didn't, but the players loved it when we showed up for one reason—Woody was a mellow softy when I watched practice.

"Man, you have to come every day," backup quarterback Greg Castignola told me. "Don't miss a day. When you're here, the old man never yells or screams. When you're not here, he is a maniac."

I had never seen that side of him and I figured out later that he didn't want me to see that side of him just yet. He always had been so soft-spoken, calm, and sweet when I talked to him.

One Saturday, Coach Chaump called and we told him we wouldn't make it to Columbus because we were working on the farm. But it started raining, so we changed our minds and decided to head to Columbus. They were holding a scrimmage inside the stadium. The gatekeeper recognized me and let us in, so we stood under the overhang of the stadium to stay out of the rain. None of the Ohio State coaches could see us.

There had been a few fumbles when suddenly I noticed Rod Gerald back-peddling out of the huddle as Woody chased him. Rod wouldn't let him catch him, although Woody was trying his hardest to grab him. Frustrated, Woody ran over to assistant coach Mickey Jackson and started hammering him with his fists. He was screaming like a maniac. He ripped off his glasses and stomped on them. He then ripped off his hat and stomped on it. He went berserk, just as Castignola had told me he did so often.

I looked at Dad, my eyes wide open.

"Holy shit!" I exclaimed. "I have never seen anything like this!"

What happened to that sweet, calm, old man who had recruited me?

There were clearly two sides to Woody Hayes. Over the next nine months, I would see each side intimately.

Chapter five

FINALLY, I'M A BUCKEYE

I cried like a baby the day I graduated from Miami Trace High School. I never wanted those days to end, because I realized everything from now on would be more like a business and less like a game.

I loved my high school coaches, especially Ron Hall and Fred Zechman, and the assistants, Bill Beatty, Gary Kellough, Terry Enochs, Doug James and Dick Hill, and how it all had worked out for me athletically. I loved my high school. And I loved my hometown and realized I'd be leaving it, perhaps forever.

I dreaded saying good-bye to my family, my friends, and my dog before leaving for Columbus. Even though I'd be living only forty miles up the highway, I just figured I would feel lonely at a school as big as Ohio State.

In many ways other than football, I wasn't prepared for college. I had used my knowledge to get by in school, but I'd never applied myself to study and learn the way I should have. I knew classes and exams would be much more difficult and that scared me.

I also knew the pressure would be greater. The stakes would be higher. The stage would be brighter.

If I succeeded, it was expected.

If I failed, the naysayers who still existed in my hometown would tell everyone, "I told you so."

The day I left home, I loaded my car and headed out to I-71 to drive north to Columbus. A few miles down the road, I almost had to pull over because I couldn't see a thing—my eyes were filled with tears.

Arriving in Columbus, everything seemed new and different. I didn't know the campus very well and the size of it intimidated me. I knew how to get to the football facility and to the stadium and that was about it.

The first thing I noticed was how small the dorm rooms were at Smith Hall. Our house wasn't big by any means, but the dorm rooms were no bigger than our closets at home.

My mom had requested to the coaching staff that I room with somebody who was neat, prim, and proper, so Woody picked Jim Houston.

Jim's dad had played at Ohio State and later with the Browns, and he was just the opposite of me. Academics were important to him and he wanted to be an accountant. He was a real bookworm and didn't come across as a jock at all.

Sure enough, during that first week, our dorm room was immaculate, but by the end of the first quarter, we had stuff everywhere. I remember my mom had brought us a strawberry cake during the first week of school. After the school year, as we cleaned up nine months' worth of trash, papers, clothes, and food cartons, there was the cake pan, filled with moldy strawberry cake. I guess Mom's plan didn't work, because Jim didn't make me a neat freak. I had turned him into a slob.

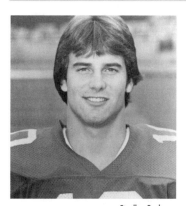

Finally a Buckeye.

The hype surrounding my signing created a buzz in central Ohio that was undeniable. I think it stemmed from the possibility that Woody finally planned to throw the football more. It's something he'd been reluctant to do his entire career, dating to his days as head coach at Miami of Ohio.

After all, his teams had won national titles at Ohio State in 1954, '57 and '68 with his usual pound 'em, three-yards-and-a-cloud of dust running game. In the '70s, behind two-time Heisman Trophy winner Archie Griffin and fullback Pete Johnson, it became seven-yards-and-an-Astroturf-burn.

And now I was supposed to be his new toy, albeit his first true passing-quarterback. Rex Kern had led the "Super Sophs," as they became known, to Woody's previous national title in 1968, but he was known as a great runner and a good passer. Still, even Rex would tell you that Woody didn't throw enough to satisfy him.

During my first few weeks in Columbus, people weren't sure they recognized me when I went to a movie or out to grab something to eat, because my face had not been on television that much.

"Excuse me," they would ask. "Are you Art Schlichter?"

It was *the* question during the early part of my freshman year.

My first memory of Ohio State football was walking into that locker room the first time and seeing the brand new pair of white Pumas with the red stripe on the side, sitting in my locker. Everyone loved those shoes, before Nike made its global impact on the athletic world.

Right there, seeing those shoes, I was in heaven.

The first day I put on the home scarlet and gray uniform I had dreamed of wearing, I was sick as a dog. My wisdom teeth were severely impacted and I felt as if I was going to die.

I sat in the locker room at Ohio Stadium waiting the start of picture day, always a huge fan attraction, as other players mingled outside on the artificial turf. I wanted to throw up.

Mom appeared at the locker room door.

"You need to suck it up and get out here, Arthur!" she demanded. "Get out here and get your picture taken! All of these people are here for you!"

I knew Mom was right and I rarely saw her this mad.

So I strolled out of the locker room in pain, marking my official arrival as a Buckeye, and was swarmed by cameras. I looked over to see Tom Cousineau, an All-American linebacker, with a few people around him. I saw Rod Gerald, the returning starting quarterback, with a few people around him. And I noticed Ron Springs, the starting tailback, with a few people around him.

It seemed that just about all the media had circled me like wolves surrounding a wounded calf, and at that moment, Ohio State football suddenly seemed a little bigger than even I had expected.

I was overwhelmed.

I had my picture taken over and over, my smile hiding my painful wisdom teeth, which were pulled later that day. My recovery would be no picnic, either. I couldn't practice right away and I was supposed to take it slow, but I realized every practice I missed would make it that much tougher to win the starting job.

Over the summer, I thought I'd learned the offense pretty well thanks to some special meetings called just to break me in, as George Chaump and Woody took turns teaching me their specialty.

Woody's specialty was the Robust, a full backfield of three running backs in the T-formation.

Chapter five

Today, that offense is as obsolete as a typewriter, but through the '60s Woody used it almost exclusively. Once Archie came along, from 1972 through '75 George had convinced him to switch to the I-formation. Still, Woody saved the Robust for when the offense entered the red zone or faced short-yardage situations.

I sat there for three hours one day as Woody, entering his 28th season at Ohio State, went over every detail of every play of the Robust—all the running plays, all the passing plays, how they were supposed to be blocked and how the opposing defenses would try to stop it.

As I sat there taking notes, I could tell he was proud to be working with me. Woody was not only proud to have signed a passing quarterback, it seemed to me that he was proud to have out-foxed Bo to get me. He loved to beat people, not only on the field, but also in recruiting, just to stick it to them.

I could tell that I was his new baby.

When Woody finished, George came in the room to teach me all about the passing game.

I grew to love George Chaump, but it was obvious to everyone that he wasn't always on the same page with Woody. If it would have been up to him, Ohio State would have been throwing 30 passes per game.

By the time I arrived, George was entering his 11th season under Woody and I'm sure he saw this as a new beginning for himself as well.

During those early practices in August, Woody would be down at the other end of the field, working with the defense. George would be running the offense. There would be days when I threw three or four interceptions and George had the film staff edit them out of the film as if they didn't happen, so when Woody watched it later, he'd be satisfied with the new and improved passing game. Therefore, he'd be willing to rubber-stamp more passing plays. At least that was the way it was supposed to go, the offensive staff figured.

Well, one day, Woody grabbed the film and started watching it before they could edit out my interceptions.

He ran the film. Interception. He ran it back. Interception. He watched some more. Interception. He turned off the projector. He hadn't uttered a word to that point. He just sat there.

Suddenly, he snapped.

"Turn that goddamn light on, you sons-a-bitches!" he screamed.

Then he stood up and threw the projector against the wall.

"I will teach you about the passing game!" he said, pounding his fist on the table.

Then he pounded his head on the table, saying, "You never throw late over the middle!"

He repeated, "You NEVER throw late over the middle," as he continued to pound his forehead on the table.

Then he yelled, "You never throw a long pass short!"

"You NEVER throw a long pass short!"

"George!" he said. "Get up here and do this!"

He actually wanted George to pound his head on the table with him and repeat those phrases.

"Woody, I'm not doing that!" George responded. "I'm not pounding *my* head on the table!"

I thought back to the first time I saw Woody go off, chasing Rod Gerald out of a huddle the previous spring. Now I was seeing it up close.

———— ⬤ ————

From the beginning of practices, Gerald treated me like a king. He really helped me out, even though I was in the process of taking his job. I have nothing but great things to say about Rod. Springs, also a senior, was good to me, too.

It was the offensive linemen who gave me a rough time. It was like high school all over again, but not as cruel. They just rode me hard that year, especially early on, before I ever played a game.

While the media and fans speculated who would start at quarterback for our season-opener against Penn State at Ohio Stadium, the topic evolved into the biggest issue in the state, like a champagne bottle whose cork wouldn't pop until kickoff on game day.

Would the highly-recruited freshman win the starting job?

Or would Rod Gerald, the two-year starter, keep it?

I knew the answer after the first week of practice. It was just assumed, if not ever spoken, since I was practicing with the first team while Rod had been moved to receiver. Of course our practices were closed to the public and to the media, so only coaches and players knew it and they were sworn to secrecy. I told a few people—Coach Zechman, my parents and my buddies—but it never got out in the media. I could never have done that today without it becoming public knowledge.

I returned home because Miami Trace was retiring my number 10 the week before our first game. I was so happy just to get home for a weekend, to get away from the pressure I felt mounting on my shoulders. Everybody wanted to know how I was doing and if I was going to be the starter.

That was the first time I felt like a celebrity. People ushered me here and there and kids approached me for my autograph. There must have been thousands of people at the stadium and it seemed every one of

Woody Hayes, standing in front of our 1978 team on Picture Day.

them came up to wish me luck. It was crazy. I stood there on the field that night, as they retired my number. Once again, I cried my eyes out.

When I returned to Columbus, the hype continued to build throughout the week of the Penn State game. It was Joe Paterno versus Woody Hayes, who had won both previous meetings, in 1975 and '76. The game would be televised nationally by ABC. Penn State, which had beaten Maryland in its season-opener a week earlier, was ranked fifth. We were ranked sixth.

And it would be my college debut.

I was so nervous before the game that I couldn't sleep. I fell asleep exhausted. I woke up exhausted. I guess it was from all the excitement, the pressure, and the expectations.

Finally, September 16, 1978, had arrived. I thought we had a great offense installed and a great game plan ready for Penn State. It was some pro-style, five receivers at times, and some I-set. I envisioned a 200-yard passing day and a big victory.

Just before the game, however, offensive line coach Alex Gibbs, who had Woody's ear, convinced him that his line wouldn't hold up if we sent so many receivers out at one time. Against George's wishes, Woody scrapped much of what we had done successfully for a month in camp and tried to simplify things.

Our plan now was to send two and three receivers out at the most, even if seven defenders were dropping into coverage.

Woody and Alex Gibbs were satisfied with the change. George was absolutely furious, and I was confused.

On the bus ride over to the stadium that morning, Jim Savoca, a senior offensive lineman, a real big rough guy who looked gruff and never shaved, leaned over and something fell out of his pocket. I looked down. It was a cigarette! Here I was, a clean-shaven, non-smoking, non-drinking, naive freshman about to start the biggest game of my life, in fact the biggest game in college football that weekend, and one of my offensive linemen had a cigarette fall out of his pocket.

I write it off now to the period of time, the era when most of the guys drank and some smoked, but it didn't exactly inspire confidence as I was about to drop back behind that offensive line all day.

It had rained before the game and then it became very hot and humid, reaching well into the 80s. The entire fall had set high temperature records throughout Ohio. Anytime it rained, or the field was wet, I worried about whether I would be able to grip the football. Woody always had watered down our practice field in order to prevent injuries, but it made gripping and throwing the football more difficult. I had small hands for a quarterback and I worried constantly throughout my career about my ability to grip the football.

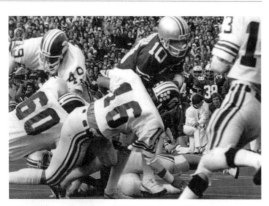

Scoring against Michigan State, one of the 35 TDs in my career.

We received the kickoff and just as Rod Gerald and I ran out to the field to the huddle before that first play, most of the 88,202 fans at Ohio Stadium erupted into a huge roar.

When we broke the huddle, they had their long-awaited answer: Rod spread out wide to the left and I was behind the center, about to take my first snap.

The coaches had called for a pass on my first play. It was a quick out to the right sideline to Doug Donley, a relatively easy throw. I took a quick, three-step drop and fired it for an eight-yard gain, as the crowd roared even louder.

It was the first pass of the 951 I would throw as a Buckeye.

Just as Donley tapped his feet down inbounds, I thought this college stuff was going to be easy.

A few plays later, I threw a long pass down the right sideline to Rod, who caught it and started to fight for that extra yard when he got hit from behind at Penn State's 15-yard line. His fumble ended our first possession.

As it turned out, that was as close as we'd come to scoring all day. I often wonder if we had punched that drive in, if that game, if that season, would have turned out differently.

Thanks to Gibbs's suggestion that Woody scale back the passing game, there weren't many receivers open that day and once we got behind, I started forcing many of my throws into double-coverage.

In a game that would go down in infamy in Ohio State's history books, I threw a school-record five interceptions, a dubious record that still stands. Penn State defensive tackles Matt Millen and Bruce Clark, each of whom would be starting in the NFL a year later, took turns making my debut miserable. Sometimes they arrived in the backfield simultaneously. My body just represented their meeting place.

As I threw one pass, Millen caught me with his helmet in my ribs and pile-drove me into the ground. And then he let me know about it, too.

"How's that feel, freshman?" he scowled. "Stay down! Don't get up!"

I'm sure that part of his anger stemmed from the fact that Penn State recruited me hard and I turned them down, so I'm sure they used that as motivation leading up to the game.

I took a real beating which I felt for days following that 19-0 loss. I had never taken a beating like that before, or after. I knew I had a long way to go to become a college quarterback.

Following the game in which I completed 12-of-26 for 182 yards, I felt as down as I'd ever felt. Mark George, one of the student managers who would later become my roommate, called out to me in the locker room after most of the guys had left. "Art, Coach Hayes wants to see you."

I remember thinking, "Oh my God, he's going to beat the shit out of me."

I limped into his tiny office in the bowels of the stadium and there stood 66-year-old Woody Hayes, naked as a jaybird. Woody had the strangest body I'd ever seen. It was never a pretty sight to see him stark naked, especially after the most disastrous game I'd ever played.

"Let me tell you something," he started. "Don't let this get you down.

Don't listen to any of those goddamn critics. By the time you leave here, you'll be the greatest quarterback to ever play at Ohio State!"

I left the stadium that day feeling a little better, knowing at least my head coach, if not my teammates or our fans, still had confidence in me.

Still, after I attempted only seven passes the following week against Minnesota and then only nine against Purdue, I knew Woody's confidence in me didn't translate to the game plan.

I scored my first two touchdowns as a Buckeye during that 27-10 win over Minnesota. Then we held off Baylor 34-28 at home, but I threw another interception, this one to a future NFL star linebacker named Mike Singletary. The following week I threw my first touchdown pass, to Donley, and rushed for 100 yards, but we tied SMU 35-35.

On the final play of the game, I took a huge hit and separated my shoulder, an injury that would bother me for the remainder of the season.

We lost at Purdue 27-16, but suddenly, the coaches were letting me throw a little more. I completed 20-of-34 passes and totaled 384 yards of offense (289 passing, 95 rushing), one of the best games of my entire career, but our 2-2-1 start was Ohio State's worst in 11 years.

Following that Purdue game we found a groove and ripped off five wins in a row to improve to 7-2-1 heading into the Michigan game at Ohio Stadium.

As the season had progressed, aside from the Purdue game, I had become more of a runner and less of a passer as the offense reverted back to where it had been throughout the 1970s. I also accumulated injuries like mosquito bites on a camping trip. I had a bursa sac on my right elbow that the doctors drained every week. My right shoulder was slightly separated and my right thumb was jammed. I was in constant pain for those four months of my freshman season.

There was a difference between playing through pain and playing while injured.

And if you're a real Buckeye, you're expected to practice through pain during Michigan week.

We'd studied all week on how to combat Michigan's blitz, to read the hot receiver, and go to him. It was very cold and wet that day and the ball was slippery, conditions I absolutely hated. After we kicked a field goal to take a 3-0 lead, we drove down inside the 20-yard line again, but I missed the hot receiver and then fumbled, and that ended up costing us.

Michigan held us without another point to win the game 14-3.

We were 7-3-1, Ohio State's worst season since 1971, and were headed to the Gator Bowl.

I had finished the season with 13 rushing touchdowns to lead the team in scoring, but my 21 interceptions were also a school record. I had thrown six touchdown passes.

We had played the season with an offense that was not meant to be throwing the ball and the odds were stacked against me when I did throw it. That's not to explain away the 21 interceptions and 49.7 completion percentage. Those are just the facts. I showed promise at times, such as in the Purdue game, that I would become a pretty good college quarterback, but I also displayed the immaturity that most freshmen show.

Taking a break from the action.

Over the years, I've read or heard that a few of the upperclassmen thought the '78 team was divided racially, due to the coaches' decision to move Gerald to receiver and to start me, but I never sensed it then. I never saw any evidence of it.

I was never into thinking along racial lines and even today, I don't think it's a fair discussion. The fact is, there were other problems the coaches had with Rod Gerald, but I'll not throw him to the wolves by disclosing them, even three decades later. But most of the people on the team, as well as the entire coaching staff, knew this was not a racial decision. Rod was very good to me, and I always appreciated him for that.

We had a few weeks until practice began for the Gator Bowl, so on the Monday following the loss to Michigan, I hit the court to practice with the basketball team for the first time.

My lasting impressions of that first practice were that the floor seemed much bigger than it did in high school and Ohio State guard Todd Penn was the quickest son of a bitch I had ever met in my life. I was about fifteen pounds overweight, I never had to run a wind sprint for Woody, and my legs already were tired from football season.

And Todd blew by me like I was standing still.

A few weeks later, I was back where I belonged, on the practice field, throwing a football.

There were plenty of malcontents on our team regarding the pending trip to Jacksonville for the Gator Bowl. The way I saw it, they just didn't care about the team and it was something I couldn't understand. I always dreamed of going to a bowl game, no matter where it was played. Sure, I wanted to play in the Rose Bowl as much as anyone, but I couldn't figure out those guys who didn't want to go play another game.

I thought then, "This is why you come to Ohio State in the first place, to play football, to play bowl games, to play on TV. Just because we didn't have an 11-0 or 10-1 record is no reason not to go to a bowl if you're invited."

During the late '70s, there weren't many bowls anyway, and the Gator Bowl certainly ranked in the top five or six of them. There were the top majors—Rose, Cotton, Sugar and Orange—followed by the Gator and perhaps the Fiesta, which didn't become a major player in the bowl scene until a few years later.

What excited me during our preparation was the coaches' decision to throw more than we had the entire season. We had plenty of time to work on the passing game, which is exactly what we needed. Those three weeks were when I improved the most and I finally felt comfortable as a college quarterback.

I knew absolutely nothing about our opponent, Clemson, before the game other than their 10-1 record and number seven national ranking. Their coach, Charley Pell, had left to accept the Florida job before the bowl, leaving assistant Danny Ford as the new head coach. I also knew they had some talent with players like Steve Fuller, Jerry Butler, and Dwight Clark, and they were very quick on defense.

Woody had done his raging best, or worst, for weeks to get us fired up for Clemson, but in Jacksonville, he turned it up a notch. He just seemed to be … well, contemptuous even by his standards.

"These Southern bastards kept your ancestors in slavery," he told our black players. "They killed my grandfather in the Civil War! Now is the time to get revenge!"

That night in Jacksonville, we started slow and trailed 10-9 at halftime after I scored on a four-yard run, but we had missed the extra point. Clemson took a 17-9 lead before everything started clicking for us offensively. We moved the ball consistently in the second half, but still didn't score a lot of points even when I got hot.

After I scored again on a quarterback sneak to make it 17-15, we failed on the two-point conversion. Then we got the ball right back and started what I believed would be the winning drive in the final minutes of the game. I had completed 16-of-19 passes for 205 yards by the time we moved to Clemson's 24-yard line.

My next pass would haunt me forever.

Facing third-and-five, we were in field-goal range when guard Jim Savoca, the same guy who dropped his cigarette in front of me three months earlier, brought the play from the sideline to me.

"Twenty-four tuba," Savoca shouted, relaying the call to me. "Coach said, 'Whatever you do, DO NOT throw an interception!'"

"Do not throw an interception."

Those words would ring in my ears for a long, long time.

It was a tailback delay, a simple play really. Ron Springs was supposed to circle out of the backfield and I was supposed to dump it off to him for the first down. We would then eat the remainder of the clock, score either a touchdown or Bob Atha would kick a game-winning field goal, before returning to Columbus with a pleasant off-season in store for us.

I took the snap, dropped back and shifted to the right, seeing Ron wide open over the middle. I always believed through the years that Clemson's nose guard, Charlie Bauman, got knocked down early during the play, but after seeing the film in recent years, he was blocked out of the play to my left.

I was looking at Springs. As I let it loose—it was just a soft toss—Bauman came back across to the right in front of Ron and the ball was headed directly to him.

I had been cautious about not throwing an interception the entire night and then this, this fluke play. If you watch the replay, you can see me practically hitting myself in the head before he intercepts it.

Once he did, he ran to our sideline, I tackled him and the rest is history.

After I made the tackle, I rolled over and stayed down because I had a cramp in my leg. Next thing I knew, all hell was breaking loose around me. I remember somebody holding me down and I think it was Doc Murphy, our team doctor. By the time I got up, people were everywhere, but I still had no idea of what happened. I walked back to sit on the bench just to get away from the mass of players gathered on the field.

"What happened?" I asked Donley.

"The ol' man slugged the guy!" he responded.

I couldn't believe it. The whole thing was so shocking, no matter how strangely Woody had been acting leading up to the game.

The ramifications of Coach Hayes's punch slowly sank in as that cold, foggy night grew into the next morning. By the time we got back to the hotel, I was upset—very upset. I met with Coach Chaump and he knew then it was all over. There was a time when it was expected that he'd have been the natural replacement for Woody when, or if, Woody had decided to retire.

Looking for room to run.

But nobody wanted to see Woody go out that way, most of all me.

Now there surely would be little chance for one of his assistants to replace him.

As our team flight approached Columbus the next morning, Woody's familiar voice came over the intercom.

"This is your coach," he said sternly. "I want to tell you that I will no longer be your football coach at Ohio State."

The whole thing was horrible. Imagine what a burden that was for an 18-year-old kid like me to carry. I tried my best to take responsibility for it and move on, but no matter what I accomplished later in my career, I'll always be known as the guy who threw the pass that got Woody Hayes fired.

The city of Columbus, in fact the entire state of Ohio, seemed to be under a dark cloud. It was all you read about. It was all people talked about. It was before ESPN existed, but the events of the Gator Bowl's waning moments topped the national news.

It was one of the saddest times of my life.

One of college football's biggest legends, the man beloved in Ohio, the man who recruited me and who had eaten Thanksgiving dinner with our family, the man who promised to change his offense for me, the man who told me three months earlier that I would become the greatest quarterback in Ohio State football history, would no longer get to do what he lived to do—-coach football.

And somehow, I had to live with that.

Chapter six

A ROSY YEAR

"What's your take on the coaching search, Art?"

The question seemed innocent enough and I wasn't about to shy away from it. I was on the road with the basketball team early in the new year when a reporter approached me, asking for my opinion on who should replace the legendary Woody Hayes.

My hope since that horrible night at the Gator Bowl was that George Chaump would be the answer to the question. I loved George, knew he was innovative, creative, and would have us throw the football more. I thought he would be a great head coach.

All these years I believed he never had received an interview for the job. Recently, I called him in Pennsylvania, where he still coaches high school football, just to catch up with him when he told me a story that shocked me.

"I interviewed for the job," he said. "Then I was told by the head of the search committee, a chemistry professor by the name of Harold Shechter whom Woody knew very well, that I was the unanimous choice and it would be recommended to the president that I be hired as the new head coach.

"I thought I had the job. Then the president, Harold Enarson, came in at the last minute and said, 'No, no, we're going in another direction.' I was never given a reason why they'd changed course. To this day, I still don't know what happened."

I was stunned to hear this. I could sense, even now, the enduring disappointment in George's voice.

Like everybody else at the time, I kept up with the coaching search through the newspapers and had read that Arkansas's Lou Holtz, who coached the defensive backs for Woody during Ohio State's last national championship season in 1968, was the leading candidate.

But when the reporter asked me the question that night, I answered honestly, "I don't really know anything. I'm thinking about transferring."

When the basketball team returned to Columbus the next day, the newspaper headlines captured those words: "SCHLICHTER CONSIDERS TRANSFERRING FROM OHIO STATE." Suddenly, I was bombarded by the media.

I was honest with reporters, telling them, "Hey, I came here to play for Coach Hayes. I am disappointed they'll not hire Coach Chaump. I think he deserves the job. Once they name a coach, I'll weigh all of my options."

As it worked out, Holtz stayed at Arkansas before Ohio State turned to the Iowa State coach, a man named Earle Bruce.

I didn't know anything about him, but once he was named to replace Coach Hayes, I seriously considered transferring. I know Dad was looking around a little bit for me behind the scenes, but I'd been busy with the basketball team since the Gator Bowl.

Soon after Earle was hired, he requested to meet with me in his office at St. John Arena. I walked in, not knowing what to expect.

"I want you to stay," he said. "We're going to do some very good things here and I want you to be a part of it."

He said nothing about what the offense would look like. I told him, "Thanks. It's nice to meet you," and I walked out, still uncertain of my future.

As he put together his staff, I think he believed I'd leave. Within a few days, I received a call from my high school coach, Fred Zechman.

"Guess what?" he asked. "I interviewed with Coach Bruce and he offered me a job."

Sure enough, Zech had been named our quarterbacks/receivers coach and all the "Schlichter transferring" talk died a quick death.

The question is, if Earle Bruce had not hired Fred Zechman, would I have left Ohio State? It would have been a tough decision, and I still can't answer it, but I know I seriously considered leaving until Fred was hired.

On February 10, a few weeks after my football future was settled, I saw my first significant action with the basketball team during the season's biggest game.

Scoring against the one and only Magic Johnson.

Michigan State, which came to town as the heavy favorite to win the Big Ten, was led by a sophomore point guard—Earvin "Magic" Johnson.

That night, St. John Arena was packed to the rafters to see us play against Magic.

Our team was down to eight guys because of injuries, when Eldon Miller sent me into the game as we trailed midway through the second half. The first time I touched the ball, the crowd roared, but I quickly passed it, just trying to get a feel for the game. No sense shooting right away, right?

The next time, I took my first shot and it went in as the crowd roared again. The next time I touched it, I made my second shot and the crowd went crazy. The next time down the court, I made a move at the top of the key, shot over Magic and Greg Kelser and the ball found nothing but net again.

Now, St. John Arena was a loud place to begin with, but it was in an absolute frenzy. Michigan State called for a quick timeout.

I was three-for-three and we suddenly were back in the game.

The next time I touched the ball, I was thinking our fans would blow the lid off the place if I started four-for-four.

I was all the way out by the five-second line, when I launched about a 25-footer. Michigan State's Ron Charles, who was about 6-foot-8 and had the longest arms you will ever see, knocked it into the stands.

The coaches had told me that I would guard Magic "until he scores." So the first time down the court, he posted me and I fouled the shit out of him. As the referee handed him the ball for his first free throw, he said, "Okay Magic, you got two shots."

I thought, "The referees respect this guy that much that they call him by his nickname?"

That didn't sound right to me.

About two minutes later, they had to sit me on the bench and give me some oxygen. I missed two more shots, finishing with six points, three rebounds and four fouls as Michigan State went on to win the game 73-57, but I always can talk about the time I scored in Magic's face. (Five weeks later, Magic and Michigan State won the national championship, beating Larry Bird's Indiana State team in the finals of the NCAA Tournament.)

A few days following the loss to Michigan State, we played at Minnesota against a great team led by guards Trent Tucker and Daryl Mitchell. I entered the game about midway through the first half and Minnesota had three fast-breaks in a row in which Tucker and Mitchell ran by me like I was running in cement.

Coach Miller took me out of the game and that was it for any significant playing time for the remainder of the season. I played in eight games that season, scoring 14 points and totaling three rebounds.

I still loved the game of basketball, but I realized my future rested across the street at Ohio Stadium.

In addition to Fred Zechman, Coach Bruce had named Glen Mason as his offensive coordinator, Wayne Stanley as running backs coach and Bill Myles as his tackles and tight ends coach. I liked Glen very much and I was excited heading into spring football, especially since I'd be working with Coach Zechman again.

But my relationship with the head coach was very different than it'd been with Coach Hayes. Earle Bruce arrived carrying the attitude, "I'm not going to give special treatment to any player—Art Schlichter included."

It seemed that he went out of his way *not* to communicate with me. Woody had been totally different. He'd call me into his office every week for a five-minute pep talk and I loved that about him.

Earle wasn't about to give me the starting quarterback job, either. I had to earn it all over again. So I went to spring ball and started the process of winning the job, just as I had the previous summer. Greg Castignola and Bob Atha were the quarterbacks fighting for the job with me and if anybody treated me badly over those first two years, it was Castignola.

During my freshman season, it was, "You're Woody's boy."

Then when I was a sophomore, it became, "You're Earle's boy."

I just grinned and put up with it, never responding to his cheap shots, but I give him credit for at least saying it to my face and not behind my back as others did.

Coach Bruce making sure I got the instructions.

Spring ball was a bloodbath. With new coaches, everybody tried to prove themselves. The hitting was fierce and the physical conditioning was brutal. Basically, we worked our asses off. I had some confidence coming out of the Gator Bowl, but now I had a new offense to learn and all the terminology was very different. I mean it was no Einstein offense. You didn't need to be a Rhodes Scholar to figure it out.

One guy who was happy about the coaching change was Gary Williams, my old high school rival from Wilmington. Gary, who signed as a defensive back, was all set to transfer until Woody was fired. For some reason, Woody just didn't like him much. In fact, he treated him like a dog. During our post-season banquet following the regular season, as Woody passed out our Gator Bowl watches, he insulted Gary in front of the team.

"You really don't deserve this watch, young man," Woody said, half-heartedly handing him the watch.

The final moments of the Gator Bowl changed Gary's future. Having seen what Gary could do while playing against us in high school, Coach Zechman promptly switched him to receiver, knowing that was the position in which he could become a star.

That summer, I threw to Gary and Doug Donley almost every day and played a lot of basketball to stay in shape.

Who knew what to expect as the 1979 season began?

We had a new coach, a new offense, even new uniforms with our names on the back of our jerseys.

We pounded Syracuse 31-8 at Ohio Stadium to open the season. Then we fell behind Minnesota on the road before rallying to win 21-17. We came back home to beat Washington State 45-29 to start 3-0.

We had some confidence brewing, but we all figured our next game, a nationally televised game against UCLA in the Los Angeles Coliseum, had the potential to make or break our season. The Bruins were coached by Terry Donahue and entered the game with a 2-1 record, but had destroyed Wisconsin the previous week.

It was only the third time that I played in such a marquee game, in addition to the loss to Michigan and that Penn State disaster. We were underdogs and struggled offensively for the majority of the game, largely because we were losing offensive linemen to injuries about every other play. We trailed 13-10 late in the fourth quarter, when UCLA missed a short field goal.

We had one last chance—the ball at our own 20 with only 2:21 remaining.

I entered the huddle and just blurted, "Okay, let's get this thing done. We've messed around all day and it's time for it to stop!"

They were giving up the out routes. I hit Donley on one and then another, at the end of which they grabbed his facemask, which gave us another 15 yards. Then Gary ran a corner route and I saw him flash his hand in the air, just as a defensive lineman broke into my vision. I let go of the football just as Gary came out of his cut. He had a guy blanketing him, but the football fell right over the defensive back's shoulder into Gary's hands.

It probably was the greatest pass I ever threw at Ohio State.

And it gave us a first-and-goal at UCLA's three-yard line.

After we ran up the middle for one yard, the coaches sent in "Play Pass 21," a play-action roll out which gave me a run-pass option. Tight end Paul Campbell had faked his block and slipped beyond the linebackers. He was wide open. In that case, there are only two things that you fear as a quarterback—overthrowing him or the receiver dropping the ball.

Neither happened. I dropped a soft pass into Paul's hands with 46 seconds remaining and we won the game 17-13.

There would be two plays that made our year and that was the first. The second would come a few months later in Ann Arbor.

After the UCLA game, I started thinking of our destiny, which I believed was a return trip to Los Angeles for the Rose Bowl.

We struggled to get by Northwestern 16-7, but then didn't have any close games over the next five, spanking Indiana 47-6, Wisconsin 59-0, Michigan State 42-0, Illinois 44-7 and Iowa 34-7.

That '79 team just had a special makeup, a real good chemistry that all championship teams need. We had some good seniors like Jimmy Laughlin, Tommy Waugh, Ken Fritz and Ernie Andria. They were all great leaders.

Ken, whose wire-service photo trying to hold back Woody after the Gator Bowl punch had been seen around the world, was a big ol' tough boy from Southern Ohio. He was really rough around the edges, but deep down, he had a big heart and I could see that. I think at first he wanted not to like me, but in the end, we became pretty close. Tommy was a great guy, too, a very undersized center, but he was tough as nails. Ernie also was very tough. I would've liked to have that entire offensive line for each of my four seasons.

The line really jelled that season and I give a lot of credit to the assistant coaches, Glen Mason, who coached the guards and centers and Bill Myles, who coached the tackles and the tight ends. They knew what they were doing.

Coach Myles, who came to Woody's staff from Nebraska in 1977, was one of my favorites. Bill also was the "announcement coach" to us, making all the team announcements on the bus rides and flights. He had this deep, Lou Rawls-type voice and he would end each announcement with *"...and be on time!"*

That bass sounding " *... and be on time"* rang in our ears.

Earle Bruce never warmed up to me that year. He wasn't mean to me, but it was a very business-like relationship. My communication with the coaching staff was through Coach Zech.

Fred was the coach who always reassured me, made me feel good, and gave me the confidence that I could succeed at the college level. We were starting to throw it a little more, too, which of course made me happy. So did winning.

By the time we reached 10-0, I had read a few stories with the theme, "Together, Zechman and Schlichter will never lose."

If we had added in my high school games, Fred and I had a record of 39-0-1. That 40th would be the most difficult one, at Michigan, which was ranked 13th.

We were ranked second in one poll and third in another.

As usual, it was a real dogfight. We trailed 7-6 at the half and it appeared it would be the usual low-scoring, hard-hitting, one-play-would-make-a-difference game.

For us, it was two.

First, facing third down at Michigan's 18-yard line, I threw toward Chuck Hunter in the left corner of the end zone, but the pass was tipped. I thought it was out of his reach, but Chuck stuck out one hand and stabbed it, pulling it in for the go-ahead touchdown.

Michigan scored again, however, to take the lead back. Almost four minutes into the fourth quarter, we trailed 15-12 and it looked like our Rose Bowl dreams would be squashed. Our defense had forced them to punt and I was thinking we were running out of chances offensively.

I said that two plays made our season...

Well, as I was preparing to run onto the field for our next possession, thinking of putting together another game-winning drive like the one that gave us the win over UCLA, Jimmy Laughlin broke through and blocked Michigan's punt. Todd Bell scooped it up and ran 18 yards for the game-winning touchdown.

It all happened in the blink of an eye.

The final score was 18-15.

We were 11-0, Big Ten champions and headed to the Rose Bowl to play USC for the national championship.

California, here we come.

I took a week off, then began watching films of USC's defense. The Trojans were 10-0-1, having tied Stanford 21-21 in the sixth week of the season. Game film quality wasn't as advanced as it is today, but I could see enough to tell they were really talented.

I just didn't have any clue then that Ronnie Lott would be a future Hall-of-Famer, or that Dennis Smith, Joey Browner, and Larry McGrew would become great NFL players. On offense, they had another Hall-of-Famer in Anthony Munoz, as well as Keith Van Horn and the Heisman Trophy winner, Charles White.

They were loaded.

I still believe that we came up with a pretty good game plan for USC. We expected them to come at us hard and blitz a lot, because they played a lot of man-to-man. That freed other people to rush the quarterback, but we had a lot of confidence in our offensive line. I thought if our line could protect me, Gary Williams and Doug Donley would get open against USC's man coverage.

We planned to flood some zones with multiple receivers and move the pocket around a little, too.

The most passes I had attempted in any game was 22, against UCLA and against Michigan, so we still weren't operating a wide-open offense by any means. I was excited that we planned to throw more and I had full confidence we'd throw it successfully, no matter how talented USC was. I had passed for 1,816 yards and 14 touchdowns that season, reducing my interceptions from 21 as a freshman to only six as a sophomore.

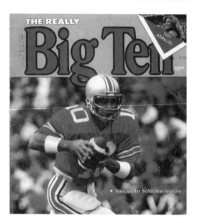

Making the cover of *Big Ten Magazine*.

As long as I live, I'll never forget running out onto that Rose Bowl grass before the game. It was as green as money, the sun was shining, the stadium full with more than 100,000 fans—it was the setting I had always envisioned. I don't think I ever realized how many people around the world watched the Rose Bowl every year. Back in 1980, it was the Granddaddy of Them All for a reason. The Orange Bowl and Sugar Bowl were big games, but they didn't compare to the Rose Bowl.

It was *the* bowl game, *especially* with Ohio State and USC, and all the traditions of both schools...*especially* with two undefeated teams... *especially* with a national championship on the line.

The game could not get any bigger.

And I could feel the pressure of it from the kickoff. Everybody could.

On our first possession, I worried about throwing an interception, and naturally I threw one on my first pass, although in my defense, the ball was tipped.

After that mistake, we moved the football the entire day.

The play of the game would come on the first play of the second quarter. Trailing 3-0 we moved to USC's one-yard line where we faced a fourth-and-goal. The coaches never hesitated, sending in an option play.

As I carried the ball down the line, I saw a gap and tried to lunge for the end zone, rather than pitch it to the tailback, but USC linebacker Chip Banks got me. Later, I realized if I had pitched it to Cal Murray, he probably would have walked into the end zone.

Down 10-3, just before the half, Gary Williams and I, rivals from our Washington Court House-Wilmington days, connected on a play I think put me on the map as a top collegiate quarterback.

It was called "84X-Go" and Gary blew by the safeties and was wide open. I threw a wobbly pass, but it hit him in stride. The 53-yard touchdown tied the game 10-10 at the half.

When I watched the TV replay of the game, I heard NBC's Merlin Olsen say after that play: "Schlichter threw that somewhat off-balance. Look at the power in his arm."

As Gary had shown all season, moving him to receiver was brilliant. He was a receiver for all seasons. He was big and strong and could block as well as any receiver in the country. He didn't mind hitting somebody.

On the other hand, Doug wouldn't knock you down, but he would shield defenders. Still, he was the fastest—not to sound racist—white man I ever saw. He ran a legitimate 4.3 in the 40 and that's unheard of for, well, a blond guy.

At halftime, we talked about attacking USC in the second half, playing to win instead of playing not to lose.

We had another great chance to score early in the third quarter but kicked a field goal. Then we kicked one more, taking a 16-10 lead. As the game wore on, we were getting guys hurt on defense, which was undersized up front to begin with. The linemen and linebackers who were on the field started to wear down, getting attacked play after play by USC's huge offensive line.

USC took possession for what appeared to be a final opportunity, at their 17-yard line. They were 83 yards away from winning the national championship. We were five minutes and 21 seconds away.

That's when Charles White took control of the game.

As USC marched down the field and White ripped off runs of eight, 10 and 12 yards, I had so many thoughts going through my head. First, I hoped we could stop them. Then I prayed for a fumble. When it appeared inevitable that they would score, I hoped they would leave us enough time to win the game.

None of the three happened. They used only eight plays, but left us only 1:32 on the clock. White rushed for 71 of the 83 yards they needed and scored from one yard out to make it 17-16.

We had a two-minute offense, but we probably hadn't worked on it as much as we should have. I threw four consecutive incompletions and the dream died right there on the 25-yard line.

I had passed for 297 yards on only 11 completions in 21 attempts, but that fourth-down option play at USC's one-yard line in the second quarter was the difference. If I had pitched it, we probably would have scored and won the game. Even if we'd taken a field goal there, we would've had enough cushion at the end of the game.

As I matured during my junior and senior years, I realized I probably rushed those final four throws at the end of the Rose Bowl. I would've liked to do them over again and hit my check-down receivers underneath, allowing us to move the ball down the field.

We had little time, but we had some timeouts, and all we needed was a field goal. I think we had the mentality on that final possession that we had to get a big chunk of yardage right away.

My first thought after the game was, "We got a young team, we'll be back here next year and have some fun by winning it." I know I cried in the locker room that day, as did many of my teammates. We were just so close to winning … and thinking of the missed opportunities made it even more painful.

I look back and realize now that was the one game that would have changed everybody's life forever. You just don't realize it while you're playing the game. It would have elevated us all to hero status, a lasting legacy as an Ohio State national championship team. The impact of a national championship in Earle's first year, I'm sure, would have changed his career as well.

It would remain the biggest game I ever played.

And losing it still hurts.

Chapter seven

WHO WANTS TO BE A CELEBRITY?

One of my favorite movies of all time is *The Natural* starring Robert Redford, because I could relate to his character in the movie. I identified with the line when he said that all he wanted in life "was to walk down the street and have somebody say, 'There goes Roy Hobbs, the greatest ballplayer to ever have played the game.'"

I knew what he meant.

Too, I had a weakness for women like he had. I didn't really care about fame, fortune, or anything that accompanied it, just as Roy Hobbs hadn't. All I ever wanted was for people in my little hometown to say, "There goes Art Schlichter, the greatest ballplayer to ever come out of here."

My dad, on the other hand, mapped it out for me to become a collegiate superstar, then a professional athlete, and eventually a sports legend (I made two out of three anyway). He always had the bigger dreams for me, the bigger goals, all rounding into the bigger picture.

Those things weren't on my mind.

Nevertheless, whether I wanted it or not, fame and celebrity were gaining on me like a runaway locomotive by the end of the 1979 season, especially after we beat Michigan to finish 11-0, win the Big Ten championship and secure a Rose Bowl berth opposite USC.

Life as the starting quarterback at The Ohio State University couldn't have been much better. For starters, I loved winning as much as anyone who had ever played the game. And we'd won them all for the Buckeyes' first unbeaten regular season in four years, before the Rose Bowl loss.

One of my proudest moments — beating Michigan and making the cover of *Sports Illustrated*.

I'd become, in all modesty, a huge name in the state of Ohio, even though that was never my goal. It just worked out that way.

I was voted to most All-American teams and would finish fourth in the Heisman Trophy voting that season (won by USC's Charles White), the highest finish for a sophomore in the 45 years of the award. This was 28 years before a guy named Tim Tebow became the first sophomore to win the Heisman.

Columbus wasn't a celebrity-driven town like Hollywood or New York. Woody Hayes was a celebrity in Columbus, during and after he was head coach. If you were a starter for the Buckeyes, you were a celebrity. That included the quarterback, especially the All-American quarterback of an undefeated team.

But my level of celebrity had reached heights even I had never imagined. It seemed that everybody in the state knew me, or wanted to talk to me, or have me talk to them, or just wanted to touch me or take my picture.

During the final week of November, I was pictured on the cover of *Sports Illustrated* for the second time in three weeks. The first time I shared the cover with four other players from the nation's top-five teams—Alabama's Steadman Shealy, Nebraska's Jarvis Redwine, Florida State's Jimmy Jordan and Houston's Dedrick Brown. The cover headline read: "Who's No. 1?" as each of us waved our index finger.

But it was the November 26 cover photo of me scrambling against Michigan that meant the most to those around me. I didn't know about it until Dad called me and told me when the issue hit the newsstands.

I can honestly say that it wasn't that big of a deal, unlike seeing my name in the *Street and Smith's* magazine two years earlier. It just went along with everything else that was happening and I didn't get too excited about it. But to Dad, it was huge. I think my family might have bought 100 copies. I know I never bought a single one. Today, I still sign those covers and see them on Ebay. In fact, I've probably signed about 200 of them in just the past year.

To put it in perspective, all the publicity and fame was surreal for me, I guess because I had very low expectations for my career.

The day after the Michigan game, I was invited to Beulah Park, the fall-winter horse track on the south side of Columbus, to be the guest trophy presenter to the winner of the featured race.

I was near the grandstand that day when I was introduced to a man named Perry Bayley, one of those old-time horse trainers who worked about eighteen hours a day in a barn. He seemed to warm up to me immediately, and he innocently mentioned, "I really believe my horse is going to win this race."

Hearing Perry's confidence and deciding immediately that he was a straight-shooter and genuine nice guy, I walked away and bet $100 on it. Sure enough, his horse won and I cashed the ticket for $600.

I thought, "Hey, this Beulah Park place is for me..."

I had already beaten a path to Scioto Downs, the local harness-track, plenty of times, but now, I had found a new betting playground for the winter months. That moment sucked me in to that track for the next twenty years. What I wouldn't give now for Perry's horse to have finished dead last that day.

Public appearances were common for me then. I was invited virtually everywhere in Ohio—to cut a ribbon at a gymnasium opening, to make a speech or present a trophy.

There's a certain feeling celebrities know when they go out in public. They can just feel people staring at them. I felt that every moment of every day at Ohio State. I still know that feeling, but not to the same degree as when I played for the Buckeyes. You learn to feel the eyes on you, even without looking, but I must admit that there is something about it that you always love. I don't know, but I guess it makes you feel special. As my career wore on and the recognition mounted, I would've liked some anonymity. I rarely had any of it.

When I went into restaurants, I was mobbed at my table for autographs and pictures. The thing is, I usually enjoyed meeting people, especially kids. I knew that an autograph or a smile or small talk would make their day and I was glad to do it. It was the grownups who were a bit too much.

I suppose I lived the life of a guy who had everything at his feet and I didn't know what to do with it. I would've been happy back on the farm, but I was sprung into this new way of life and it was like a runaway freight train.

At times, I just felt overwhelmed by it.

Even in the solitude of my dorm room, which should have been a refuge in which to sleep and study, it became very difficult to enjoy any privacy. A good night's sleep was out of the question.

Women would come up to my door at all hours of the night, wanting to meet me. They would knock at two or three in the morning. There were times I had a date in my room, but that didn't stop other girls I had never even met from knocking. You can imagine how that looked.

Other times, I would open the door, half-asleep, not knowing who was on the other side.

"I just wanted to meet you," some strange girl would say as I wiped the sleep out of my eyes, except she didn't always use the word "meet."

It sounds superficial and shallow, but it happened more times than I can count.

After my freshman year, my parents rented an apartment for me out behind the OSU golf course, a few miles west of campus, so I could have some privacy.

Hanging out with Mickey and Doug Donley at Disneyland, before the Rose Bowl.

As a student-athlete, the rules at Ohio State dictated that I live in the dorm, but I had figured my way around it. I would sleep in the dorm one night a week and at my apartment the other six.

This didn't help me grow close to my teammates, either, since they were together all the time and I was isolated in my home away from campus.

When it came to girls, I needed more discipline than I had back then.

I knew I could go into any bar in Columbus—although I hated bars and didn't drink—and walk out with the prettiest girl. I wasn't naïve enough to think it was my charm. I knew that there was an ego trip for them to tell people they were Art Schlichter's girlfriend.

This obviously made it difficult on the steady relationships I did have. I had dated a cheerleader steadily as a freshman and my longest relationship in college—with another cheerleader named Maria Ciminello—began near the end of the 1979 season.

I can't say that I didn't care for the girls I dated while at Ohio State. I did care for them. I can't say I was ever in love back then, because I probably didn't know what love really was. When Maria left me before my rookie season in the NFL, my heart hurt a little.

Dad influenced me a great deal. I never dated anyone without his approval. I think he had a vision of me being like Tom Brady is today, dating movie stars and models. So no girl was good enough for him.

I had just begun dating Maria by the time we arrived in California for the Rose Bowl when Jim Hill, the L.A.-based broadcaster asked, "Art, can you give me an interview?"

"Sure, if you can get me two tickets to the Celtics-Lakers game," I answered.

It was the first time Larry Bird and Magic Johnson—the same Magic over whom I'd scored that basket a year earlier—were facing each other in the NBA and I wanted to be there to see it.

"No problem," Jim told me. "I'll get a car to pick you up. How many tickets do you need?"

Jim sent a limo to L.A. to pick up Maria where the cheerleaders were staying, and then they headed out to Pasadena to pick me up at the team hotel. I'd never been in a limo. When it pulled up to the entrance of the Forum, we strolled out like movie stars, settling into prime seats, courtside.

The entire week leading up to the game put me on "cloud nine."

Dick Enberg, then with NBC, which was broadcasting the game on New Year's Day, walked with me to do an interview after practice one day and that was a thrill. I'd always admired Dick and his "Oh my!" calls on basketball and football. He was my favorite announcer. I'd studied sports announcers because I considered getting into the broadcasting field following my playing days.

He wanted to know everything about my childhood and my background because I grew up on a farm and I could tell he didn't know much about farming.

Then on the bus before the game, O.J. Simpson interviewed us.

"How are you feeling?" the Juice asked me. I know I gave some politically correct softball answer, even though I was anxious as a pig at a bacon factory. Little did we both know that O.J. and I would each run into our own set of problems, spend time in prison, and become two of the most infamous athletes in history…

The one goal I had the week of the Rose Bowl was to meet and date the Rose Bowl queen, just like Ohio State quarterback Rex Kern had done eleven years earlier. Rex, who also wore number 10, met the queen before the 1969 Rose Bowl, which the Buckeyes won 27-16 over O.J.'s USC team to win the national championship. Recently inducted into the College Football Hall of Fame, Rex and his Rose Bowl queen are still happily married to this day, living in California.

I did go out with the queen that week. Her name was Julie Raatz and I met her at Disneyland the day the team took its traditional trip to the amusement park before the game. We never got married, of course, but she called me years later and we had a nice conversation.

Anyway, to meet O.J. and Dick Enberg was beyond the wildest dreams of this farm boy. Following the loss to USC in the Rose Bowl, Dad and I went to the Santa Anita Park racetrack for a few days, to relax, and Dick invited us to sit in his box. He was down to earth and friendly. I thought he was one of the coolest guys I'd ever met.

I had no idea what I was doing with the horses back then, but it got my juices flowing, being there in that atmosphere. I figured if horse racing was good enough for a guy like Dick Enberg, then it would be okay for me, too.

Being a well-known athlete in Ohio gave me the opportunity to meet other athletes, such as Bengals quarterback Kenny Anderson and many of the Cincinnati Reds. I'd always been a fan of the Big Red Machine and the broadcasters who called the games on radio. Joe Nuxhall and Marty Brennaman, guys I grew up listening to, would have me on the air with them all the time.

I was invited into the Reds clubhouse many times and got to know Pete Rose, Johnny Bench, Tom Seaver, and the entire team. Johnny was from Oklahoma and always busted my balls about how the Sooners were better than the Buckeyes. And Seaver would talk about how great USC was.

But Pete loved Ohio State.

At about the same time, a book about my life was being released. There aren't many college kids who have a biography written about them, but it happened to me. A Dayton, Ohio, sportswriter named Ritter Collett, a good guy and a friend of the family, approached my dad about writing a book on my life and it resulted in *Straight Arrow*.

I think I still have a copy. Maybe it was goofy to most people, but to me it was a nice little book about how I grew up. I know people take potshots at the title since my troubles became public. I take potshots at the title, too, joking it should've been called *Broken Arrow* or *Straight Zero,* but at that time, I'd always tried to do the right things, for the most part.

I never drank alcohol or experimented with drugs like other college kids. I never even smoked a cigarette. I didn't believe in putting those things into my body. I didn't grow my hair long or get a tattoo. I always believed, and still do, that drinking and drugging were nasty things to do to your body. I was brought up to not abuse your body or put anything in it that would put you at a disadvantage and I lived by that. I just don't like the taste of alcohol and I never liked it. Diet Coke was my drink. Today, it's root beer. I drank alcohol twice in my life. I never hung out with the guys who were going to the High Street bars to go drinking. That wasn't my scene.

I remember *Playboy* magazine's All-American team of 1980, for example. The magazine gathered its All-Americans in Lake Geneva, Wisconsin, following spring practice, to shoot the annual pre-season issue. I remember walking into a hotel room that weekend to see a few of the players lying there with cocaine and booze all over the place. It wasn't the scene for me. I was happy playing golf with Cris Collinsworth and a few other guys on the team.

In other words, that *Straight Arrow* stuff was accurate in many ways.

The Columbus media often treated me like a king. Few may have known of my gambling issues while I was in college. Channel 6, the ABC affiliate, produced a show about my first three years. They played my highlights in slow motion to the song, "One In A Million," by Larry Graham and after my career, Channel 10, the CBS affiliate, produced a 30-minute show called "The Schlichter Years." It was a documentary of my career and the station hired people to play me in my early life, including a kid named Tobin Hoppes, from my hometown, to play me as a boy. The funny thing was, he was a left-hander and they had to teach him how to drop back and throw right-handed for the documentary.

Things like that made me feel that my own life was something that existed beyond me. I know I was starting to struggle with the celebrity issue and I began to isolate myself more during my junior and senior years.

All the while, I knew Dad was living vicariously through me. He was so proud of me. I wanted to win games, be an All-American, win a Heisman Trophy, and do all those great things for my dad as much as for myself. Mom loved me no matter what I did, or didn't do, on the field.

Raising money for charity with Dave Logan of WTVN.

But Dad, he was a different animal. As much as he was living through me, he still never had any usable advice as to how to handle celebrity. Nobody did. He just told me, "Be careful how you handle yourself," and things of that nature. There was no guidebook to read on the subject.

I soon discovered one place where I was left alone and it became my refuge.

Scioto Downs, the harness-racing track south of Columbus, was a popular place in the 1970s and '80s, with 3,500 seats packed nearly every night and hundreds more milling around. It was always a happening place—my type of place. Horse racing fans were there to watch the horses and to gamble, too, so they just didn't bother me. I was there to get away, look at the program, have supper, place a few bets, and relax.

I've always liked having private moments like those I experienced at Scioto. Other people love to go out to bars and restaurants, but I didn't. I didn't want to go to a bar because I didn't drink. I couldn't concentrate on a movie because everybody knew me and wanted to shake my hand or interrupt the conversation with my date.

The people I met at Scioto were my type of people.

I loved horse people, who make a living owning and training horses, rather than gambling on them. They're hard-working, honest people and I felt comfortable around them from the beginning, partly because I was raised on a farm. They're different from the people who go to casinos, play black-jack and try to make an easy buck sitting on their butts.

While my teammates and most Ohio State students would hang around High Street, the campus's Mecca for bars and nightlife, I would be 20 miles away in my element at Scioto.

I can remember the first time I saw the track as if it were yesterday. On any given night during the summers in high school, I would ask my buddy what he was doing.

"Going up to the racetrack," he'd say.

"The racetrack?" I would ask. "What's so fun about that?"

I had never even thought of going to the racetrack.

Then one day, he got me and my friends all fired up. There was a sure-fire way to make some spending money, he told us.

"Listen guys, they're are going to fix a race at Scioto Downs, and we can bet on it," he said.

I didn't know what a fixed race was, but my friend explained how it would go down. A guy was driving one horse and he and some other guys would work together to fix the ninth race that night.

"They're going to tell us the details after the seventh race, so we'll have time to bet on it," he told us.

"Ninth race?" I asked. "You mean we will have to sit there for eight races?"

Other than the possibility of winning some money, I wasn't too thrilled with the idea. My buddy said we would bet something called "trifectas," which he explained amounted to picking the top three horses in the race, and that we would "clean up big-time." He explained that we would bet on longshots, probably 20-to-1 or 30-to-1 odds. I did understand how the odds worked, but that was about it.

I got $300 out of my bank account. My buddy Scott got $200 and my friend … well he never had any money, so I don't know what he put into the pot.

By the time the eighth race finished, my buddy had received his tip before taking all of our money and darting to the betting window.

As the race started, it was raining so hard you could barely see the track. One of our horses was in the one-hole and that was the best place to be in harness racing, he told us. Another of our horses started on the outside. Sure enough, as we stood there screaming like the foolish teen-agers we were, our three horses came trotting around in a 1-2-3 finish just as he had been told.

"Oh my God!" I shouted. "How much will this be worth? Twenty thousand? Thirty?"

Well, the guy who owned one of the horses must have figured what had happened, because they were down on the infield arguing after the race ended, about the same time we were figuring how to spend the money. I think the trifecta paid about $200 per ticket and we had that several times over.

I know one thing. We never cashed the tickets that night because we were scared to death of getting caught. My buddy went back to the track a few nights later and cashed our tickets, and there was a big investigation, but I don't remember much about how it ended or if the public ever heard about it.

That was the first time I ever saw Scioto Downs. And it was that night when I lost my gambling virginity, other than a few nickel bets when I was a kid, playing cards with Uncle Jesse and my cousins.

By the time I visited Scioto while I was in college, people recognized me at the track's ticket window and probably wondered where I received the money to gamble. After all, I was an amateur athlete and not supposed to be walking around with thousands of dollars in my pocket.

But I was making speaking appearances for alumni groups like the Kiwanis and got paid anywhere from $100 to $500 a pop, which I'm sure was against NCAA rules back then. Then again, the coaches had not arranged it.

Anyway, I always had spending money. And spending money to me meant gambling money.

In retrospect, I know that fame overwhelmed me. I was still just a few years from high school and yet, I lost who I really was. I became something I didn't want to be. People think you're the greatest thing to walk the earth just because you can play football. And if you're not careful, you start believing it, too.

All of it has nothing to do with who you really are. It was a façade for me. During those college years I became isolated and grew into thinking that my job was to play football and my recreation was to gamble and chase girls.

I lost sight of who I was.

Maybe that's why I enjoyed doing charity work so much. I worked for Easter Seals, Multiple Sclerosis, the Columbus Police Athletic League and I was chairman for the Special Olympics in Springfield, Ohio. That was the most rewarding.

I remember this one little guy who had Down Syndrome—a short chubby guy who would run his butt off each year in the races. He loved me. He always came running up to give me a big hug. I knew I would make their day if I paid

WHO WANTS TO BE A CELEBRITY?

attention to them and spent time with them.

I held summer camps for quarterbacks and receivers at a camp in Springfield, which a local dentist, Ski Schanher, who also organized the "King Arthur Fan Club," had arranged for me.

Those are a few of the good things I did, but you never read much about it in the newspapers.

Why was I at Ohio State to begin with? I have more regrets about that than about anything. I rarely went to class.

I was a communications major, but I was horrible about studying. I wish I would've gone to class and taken care of what I needed to do, but I was lazy and I cut all the corners. I took the tests when I needed to or looked over somebody's shoulder if I had to. I did enough just to get by.

I was usually tired. I played football, then played basketball, then went right into spring football. I was worn out after my freshman year, so I just stopped going to school. I would go early in the quarter to figure out what I needed to do to pass and then I tried to get by as easily as I could.

The athletic department had tutors for us, too. I had a class or two each quarter in which I knew I could get a decent grade no matter what. Some professors were football fans and they'd make it easy. In one class, the professor gave out all the answers the day before the test and you just had to memorize them that night. I also had people write papers for me.

I was just hurting myself by doing all of these things. I know that now. I had a chance to get a free education and didn't take advantage of it. I've said it a thousand times—it's one of my biggest regrets.

Today at the Woody Hayes Athletic Center, there's a long wall of portraits of the Academic All-Americans. I never did anything to earn a place on that wall. My face is in the other section, for football achievements only. When I look at my publicity pictures from Ohio State, it's a lifetime ago.

Sadly, I can't remember where or when they were taken. I only can tell I had a full head of hair, a flat stomach and I was smiling. So I must have been happy, right? At least that's what everybody believed then.

Those pictures, as well as the *Sports Illustrated* covers, show an All-American quarterback, someone whom everybody believed had the brightest of futures.

I believed it, too.

Chapter eight

FRUSTRATION AND DISAPPOINTMENT

Hanging around Scioto Downs, I ran into some characters who liked to gamble on other things beside the horses. I became friends with a man named Frankie, who owned horses. One night, he invited me to sit in his box and he happened to mention his sports betting.

"I've won $40,000 betting on the Reds this year," he told me. "I usually bet five dimes a game."

"Five dimes?" I asked him. "What's that?"

"Five-thousand," he said, looking at me like I was the gambling neophyte that I was.

"Anytime you want some of my action, just let me know. In fact, I got five dimes on the Reds tonight," he said.

I glanced at my watch and quickly excused myself. I walked out to my car, turned on the radio and discovered the Reds were ahead 7-0. I practically sprinted back inside.

"Hey Frankie, I've been thinking … ," I said. "I'll take half of that bet you got on the Reds tonight."

And thus, it all began.

Driving home that night, I felt a high like I'd never felt before, at least off of the football field or basketball court. All that money just for picking the right team? Now that was pretty cool to me. By the next week, I had lost all of that money and another $1,000 on top of it.

That was the episode that jump-started me into betting on sports.

As the 1980 season approached, I was the leading contender for the Heisman Trophy and was pictured on just about every pre-season football magazine in the country. We were ranked Number One in most of the pre-season polls. And we were supposed to go back to the Rose Bowl. At least that's where I figured we'd end the season.

All the hype had gone to our heads, including mine, because we fell behind Syracuse 21-3 in the second quarter of our season-opener at Ohio Stadium, which was sporting new artificial turf.

"Damn," I thought, "I don't like this new turf very well."

We fought back, scoring 28 consecutive points to win the game, 31-21, but the warnings were right there in front of our faces.

A *Sports Illustrated* reporter came to town that week, producing a story on us following the Syracuse game. It was full of platitudes:

This fall Schlichter is also appearing frequently on television. An articulate communications major, he is one of five athletes—and the only undergraduate—showcased on NCAA TV ads stressing the value of higher education. The others include Colonel Pete Dawkins and Arthur Ashe. Meanwhile, Ohio State is using him to promote its academic side in a series of public television spots distributed around the state. "You probably know me as the quarterback of the Ohio State football team," Schlichter says on camera, before claiming that the university offers much more than athletics. Indeed, Schlichter is so well known in Ohio that a recent letter from Chicago, addressed only to "Art—the best athlete in Ohio—Bloomburg [sic]," was delivered in two days.

Already the pro scouts are buzzing around. "Schlichter is the best quarterback for the college game I've ever seen," says Dallas Cowboy personnel chief Gil Brandt. "I'm not saying he's going to be the best pro quarterback. We'll have to watch how he develops the next two years. He looks like the kind of guy you'd want to start a new franchise with and build around. Where he's really amazing is in the clutch."

Me? Stressing higher education? I rarely went to class.

Woody had always preached, "Don't listen to people who tell you how good you are. They'll make you soft. Don't listen to the praise. You'll get lazy."

He had a way of grasping the big picture in life, and the 1980 season would prove him correct as usual.

I probably did get a little soft following the Rose Bowl season. I thought I was working hard, working to get better, but now I realize I probably wasn't doing all the things, mentally and physically, to get better every day. What happened in the next game infuriated me.

Against Minnesota at home, I threw only 12 passes, completing five. We just ran the ball up the middle all day long. We won 47-0, so I said all the right things in the press conference when reporters asked me if I wanted to throw more. "No, as long as we are winning, that's what it's all about."

I left the stadium that day as frustrated and as angry as I'd ever been. We had so many great, skilled players with Gary Williams and Doug Donley receiving and me throwing, but we relied on the running game until it became boring and monotonous. When we had weapons like we had, I figured we should be firing them.

Earle Bruce, obviously, had other ideas.

As I rode in the car with Dad and Coach Zechman from the stadium to a restaurant after the game, I told them, "That's it. I'm out of here. I'm serious. This is my decision. I'm leaving Ohio State!"

Since classes hadn't started yet, I could transfer and still have two seasons of eligibility remaining somewhere else. I had no idea where I would go, but I was going someplace where I could throw the football.

Fred listened and let me rant and rave for a while because he understood my frustration.

"I tell you what," he said, "Give it one more game. I'll go in there this week and promote that we start throwing the ball."

The next game, I threw for a bunch of yards (271) and three touchdowns as we beat Arizona State 38-21. My feelings were soothed a bit and we were 3-0 again, so I missed the deadline to transfer.

Here was the scenario: We were ranked second in the nation (we dropped a spot after the season-opener) having won 14 consecutive regular-season games; I was the leading Heisman Trophy candidate; and I still wanted to leave.

I was *that* frustrated.

UCLA came to Ohio Stadium the following week, looking for revenge for our come-from-behind win on the West Coast a year earlier. The Bruins got it, shutting us out 17-0. Their big defensive end, Irv Eatman, knocked me out of the game with a concussion.

When I woke up, I glanced at the stadium scoreboard and saw three minutes remaining in the third quarter, so I approached Earle on the sideline.

"I'm going back into the game!" I told him. "Put me in the game!"

"No, you're not. Go sit down!" he told me.

"Look, there's three minutes left in the third quarter. Put me back in and we can win this thing," I explained.

"There are three minutes left—IN THE GAME!" he yelled back at me. "Go get your helmet and get to the locker room!"

My head was so fuzzy, I had no idea how much time was left and those old scoreboards at Ohio Stadium didn't list the quarters, but I had the sense to realize getting shut out was devastating. Not only were we not going to win the national championship, the Heisman hype was finished for me and people would see all the chinks in our armor. When you have the highest expectations and you lose, it's devastating.

With Fred Zechman as part of the offensive staff, and with us coming off the Big Ten championship, I just figured we'd continue to expand the offense and put in some great stuff. When it didn't happen, and we continued with our basic, run-first approach, Dad became very bitter.

He would rant and rave about the offense. His bitterness seeped into my thinking, affecting my opinions.

To show how Earle would shut the offense down once he had a lead, we jumped up on Illinois 42-14 as I completed 17-of-20 passes for four touchdowns. We never threw another pass. Next thing you know, the score was 42-42.

With Coach Bruce on picture day.

When it was all over, we had pulled out a 49-42 win, but Illinois's Dave Wilson had completed 40-of-69 passes for an NCAA-record 621 yards, which was the national story of the day in college football. It usually took me four games to throw 69 passes. Houston's David Klingler now holds the NCAA single-game record of 716 yards.

Other than Wilson's record day, I don't remember much about the six consecutive wins that put us at 9-1. I knew we weren't that great of a team, though. We had great talent, but little chemistry.

With Michigan coming to Ohio Stadium, a win would give us the Big Ten title again and another trip to the Rose Bowl and that was what was important. I played terribly against Michigan, completing only 8-of-26 passes for 130 yards. We had some balls dropped and no continuity offensively that day. We had lost our confidence early in the game and we played not to lose, instead of attacking to win, as usual.

One of my career goals was to beat Michigan at Ohio Stadium and that 9-3 loss ensured I'd never do that. In fact, in my two games against Michigan at home, we never scored a touchdown. That was a great disappointment for me.

After that game, Earle signed a contract with an up-and-coming shoe company, Nike, meaning we were no longer allowed to wear our Pumas, the only football shoe I loved.

That was a big problem for Doug Donley, who also loved the feel of the Pumas.

During the first practice leading up to the Fiesta Bowl against Penn State, Doug and I still wore our old shoes.

"You have to wear Nike. That's part of the deal," Earle told us.

"No, I'm wearing Puma," I answered.

"Okay, but during the game, you'll be wearing Nike," he told me.

We flew to Arizona, had a great week of preparation, and before the walk-through practice on New Year's Eve, Doug and I walked onto the field wearing our Pumas.

"GET OFF THE FIELD. YOU AIN'T PRACTICING IN THOSE SHOES!" Earle screamed at us.

He actually kicked his starting quarterback and senior receiver out of practice for not wearing the shoes that the school was contracted to wear.

The next day, New Year's Day, 1981, was the first time I ever "spatted" my shoes. Spatting is wrapping the outside of your shoes in tape to keep them secure to your feet. I wore my familiar Pumas, covering them completely with white tape. Then I took a red magic marker and drew the familiar Nike swoosh on the tape of each shoe to make Earle happy.

Later that year, he called me into his office and screamed, "I know you're on the take with Puma! I know you are on the goddamn take with Puma!"

"Me on the take?" I shot back. "You are the one on the take with Nike!"

The Fiesta Bowl played out like an old song in which I knew every line once again.

We just dominated Penn State in the first half by throwing the ball. I passed for 244 yards and three touchdowns—23 and 19 yards to Doug and 33 yards to Gary. We jumped to a 19-10 halftime lead.

Coming off the field, Earle gave one of those quicky halftime TV interviews that make you cringe. "The only way we'll win this game is to establish the running game in the second half."

In the locker room, he told us the same thing.

"We have to be able to run the ball," he said. "In the second half, we'll establish the running game."

I sat there, shaking my head.

"WHAT?" I muttered. "They can't stop us. Doug and Gary are running free all over the place. Let's put the pedal to the metal and blow them out."

It was just typical Earle Bruce.

Sure enough, we tried to run the ball and couldn't do it consistently. One-two-three-punt. One-two-three-punt. It didn't take long for Penn State to get the momentum back. Once you lose momentum to a good team, it's very difficult to get it back.

We didn't score another point and lost 31-19.

I had passed for a personal-high of 302 yards, but for only 58 yards in the second half. I was so frustrated after the game, I just thought, "Screw it, I am going out for basketball."

With White Lightning on picture day in 1980.

I was glad football season was over. It was horrible losing to Michigan and then losing to Penn State the way we did to finish with a 9-3 record. We had gone from having no expectations two seasons earlier to within one play of winning the national championship to having the ultimate expectations and then losing three games.

Gambling started to creep into my life and I lost my edge during my junior year. I didn't lose it to the point I couldn't go out and play well. I just played angrily. I think much of that anger came from Dad, because he felt Earle should have promoted me more by opening up the offense.

Even during football road trips, I started to gamble more. A graduate assistant coach named Fred Pagac, a former tight end who played for Woody before I had arrived, was only too happy to take my money.

We would play gin or backgammon on the plane and nobody ever said anything about it. Fred, who wasn't being paid much as a graduate assistant, took no mercy on me. I always joked to him that I was the one who fed his family.

It was a bad year.

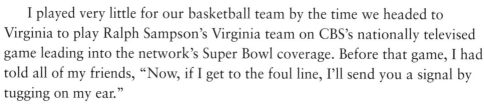

I played very little for our basketball team by the time we headed to Virginia to play Ralph Sampson's Virginia team on CBS's nationally televised game leading into the network's Super Bowl coverage. Before that game, I had told all of my friends, "Now, if I get to the foul line, I'll send you a signal by tugging on my ear."

Sure enough, we were getting blown out when I got into the game in the final minutes and got fouled. I stood there on the foul line, pulling on my right ear lobe like a real joker before shooting my free throws. Problem was, CBS had cut away from our game to go to the Super Bowl pre-game show. Nobody watching TV saw me tugging my ear, but the guys standing along the free-throw lane probably wondered what the hell I was doing.

We had a talented basketball team led by Herb Williams and Clark Kellogg, a team picked by most to be Big Ten champions, but we still finished with a disappointing 14-13 record that season.

The Virginia game would be my last experience with Ohio State basketball. I got very sick that week and the doctors thought I had mononucleosis, but it turned out that I was just very rundown and tired. My orders were to get some rest. I hadn't been playing much anyway, so I quit the team.

Without basketball, and having rarely attended classes, my gambling was about to be ratcheted up a few notches.

I was living in such a fishbowl. I loved hanging around my apartment out by the golf course to get away from it all. I had some freedom for the first time in my life with time on my hands. There was no football or basketball practice.

So, I started gambling more.

When Beulah Park, the winter horse track, was open, I was there. When Scioto was open during the summers, I was there. Then I made the next crucial step. I started betting sports regularly, starting with basketball, college and pro, through a buddy.

He was known as "The Q-Man," an Ohio State student I had met through Buckeye Boys' Camp a few years earlier. His last name began with Q, so everybody called him that. He liked to gamble like I did. He had the connections and I had the money. So he would take my bets and forward them to a bookie.

At first, it wasn't much, $50 on this game, $100 on another.

The Q-Man and I would win a little, lose a lot and he always paid the bookie with the money I gave him.

One Saturday, after we had been on a bit of a losing streak, we were growing frustrated, so I picked 32 college basketball games and told The Q-Man to put $200 on each game. Any real gambler will tell you that picking 32 games in one day is a sure sign of an amateur. Anyway, I hit 26 of the 32 correctly and was counting the money in my head when I called him.

"Guess how much we won today?" I asked.

"Guess what?" he said. "Since you'd been losing, I bet on the opposite teams you had picked. We actually *lost* 26 of 32."

The bad news got worse.

I now owed the bookie $4,000, money I didn't have. The worse news grew horrible when I realized the bookie knew my name. When we didn't pay him immediately, he called Dad.

Mom and Dad drove up to Columbus, walked into my apartment and Dad got right up in my face. Then he started hitting me.

"Why are you doing this to us?" he yelled.

I back-pedaled, trying to defend myself, while taking as much of the punishment as he could throw. I knew I deserved it.

"I am going to get this money for you," he said. "I'm taking it out of your mom's insurance money. You've gambled it all away. You've taken a piece of her body! You've taken this money *from her body!*"

Mom sat there crying. Then Dad starting crying. So was I.

Mom had lost a breast to cancer a few years earlier, and my parents had put the insurance money into the bank. That is the money they had used to pay off my $4,000 debt.

"What's it going to take to get you to stop this?" he yelled at me. "You're going to the track way too much. Now you're betting games. You've *got* to get a handle on this."

"I swear," I told them both. "I'll never do this again."

You'd think I would've walked out of there and slapped around The Q-Man. He'd always helped me out, doing odd jobs for me, taking some classes for me, but he never had any money to gamble with. I may have been angry with him for double-crossing me on the picks, but he still was my friend. He was just trying to change our luck and I forgave him for it.

The beating from Dad should've gotten through to me. I should've stopped gambling. But I was gambling the next week. And I continued gambling with The Q-Man like nothing had ever happened.

That's how sick I was, even as far back as my junior year at Ohio State. I just didn't realize it. And I had no clue that I would get much sicker.

That spring, I was minding my own business at the track when some guy named Wade approached me and whispered some words I never thought I'd hear. He wanted me to fix an Ohio State football game. He opened a bag filled with hundred-dollar bills.

"You could make a lot of these," he said. "You don't have to throw a game. Just take care of the spread."

"No thanks," I said as I turned and walked away.

I had some university officials track down the FBI agent who had spoken to the team earlier about the usual bad things to watch out for in public. The FBI agent called and I told him about Wade's offer.

Nothing ever came of it that I knew about, but I do want to make the point because I've been asked this question several times over the years—"Did you ever bet on a game you played in?"

NEVER.

I never, ever considered compromising the integrity of a game that I played in, college or pro.

I just wouldn't do it. I've done a lot of things I couldn't stomach, but that would've been the ultimate sin to me, because I respected the competition and the game too much, and I knew I could never cross that line.

And I never did.

Chapter nine

"BUT I COULD'VE DONE BETTER"

Celebrities and well-known athletes will tell you that there's a good and a bad side to fame. I experienced the bad during the summer and fall of 1981, my senior season, following some of my speeding escapades. As most people who lived in Columbus then knew, I had a serious lead foot. I was picked up for speeding all the time, probably fifteen to twenty times by the time my playing days were finished. I am not proud of that, but some of the cops pulled me over just to say, "Hi."

It usually went something like, "Man, Art, you got to slow down! Now take care of yourself. Good luck this week! Go Bucks!"

Then I would start the car and speed back down the highway. That's just how I learned to drive on the back roads of Fayette County. That's how all my friends drove. We just drove fast. From the age of 16 through 22, I had all kinds of cars, and even though I didn't know shit about cars or where to put the oil, I did know how to step on the gas pedal.

Dad had bought me a black and gold (Miami Trace's colors) Cougar after my junior year in high school. Then my grandpa bought me a scarlet-and-gray Thunderbird. It must have seemed like a lightning rod for the police … "There goes Schlichter!"

One of those speeding incidents resulted in the biggest scandal, splashed on the front pages of all the Columbus papers for weeks.

It was near the end of July, just before the start of my senior season when I arrived home from a long road trip as part of an NCAA Football promotion. Jim McMahon of BYU, Darrin Nelson of Stanford, Tommy Wilcox of Alabama and me, along with Alabama Coach Paul "Bear" Bryant and ABC's Keith

Jackson toured the country for a week.

It was fun, but exhausting because we traveled for much of it by bus because of the air-traffic controllers' strike.

I was in awe of the Bear. We would sit and talk and I could listen to his deep, gravelly voice all day.

"Do you remember me calling you on New Year's Day, 1978?" he asked.

How could I forget? Later, on that particular night, his Crimson Tide crushed Ohio State 35-6 in the Sugar Bowl in the only meeting between Bear and Woody. Still, I wasn't going to turn down Woody and the Buckeyes to head a thousand miles south to Alabama to play for the Bear, no matter how enthralling his voice was.

When I got home from that tour, Maria picked me up in my black Toronado. All I cared about was rushing off to Scioto Downs to bet on the final few races that night, so I took off down the freeway and reached at least 85 or 90 miles per hour.

I looked over and saw a car next to me and I thought, "Man, that car is going really fast, too."

Of course, it turned out to be a cop. I pulled over and as I got out of my car, I started, "Hey, I am really sorry... I am Art Schlichter and ..."

"I don't give a shit who you are! You were going 85 miles per hour! Now get back in your car and shut up!"

Then he got me back out of the car and had me up against it. I think what really pissed him off was that Toronado had a diesel engine and it really smoked. When he walked up to me, the smoke blew back into his face.

From that point, it was "Yes sir. Yes sir. You are right, sir."

I just stood there and took it. I wanted to get it over with so I could make it to Scioto and not miss any more races.

The next day, I called the police chief, whom I knew through my work for the Columbus Police Athletic League, and told him, "This ticket states I have to go to court, but you know that will be all over the papers, so can't I just pay the ticket?"

"Art, just send me the ticket and don't worry about it," he said. "You don't owe anything. Just sign an autographed football for the judge. He's a big Ohio State fan."

So that is what I did.

It was a speeding ticket, so I never thought anything more about it. It was not like I had run over some kids or anything like that. Well, I guess some newspaper reporter looked at the court docket for that day, and it read: "Art Schlichter, speeding, dismissed."

The story on the front page of the newspaper the next day reported that I had a speeding ticket fixed, even though that was never my intention. Eventually, I had to go down to court and there were TV cameras and media people everywhere, as if I had been arrested for murder. In the end, I paid a $100 fine and that was that.

Then came the fallout: The judge became the target of the press. He later resigned and I felt horrible about it.

I was dealing with that mess, my growing gambling problem, which I didn't think was a problem in the first place, and my frustrations with the offense as I tried to stay positive and focus on my senior season.

I thought we had a chance to have a decent team, but we had so many young kids on defense. We had lost Doug Donley, who was drafted by Dallas, so we had to find another receiver opposite Gary Williams.

Our offensive line was inexperienced. Jim DeLeone, our center, was about 5-foot-8 and 210 pounds. We always had great skilled people at Ohio State, but I think Earle had struggled recruiting big, strong offensive linemen when he first got the job.

Before the opening game against Duke, their quarterback Ben Bennett had been talking shit in the media, saying "Schlichter was overrated" and that he was the better quarterback.

We had no problems beating Bennett and Duke, 34-13, before beating Michigan State 27-13 in a game in which I turned my ankle. I had no clue then that injury would ultimately devastate my senior year.

Dr. Bob Murphy, Ohio State's longtime team physician, examined the ankle after the game and shook his head.

"We have to put it in a cast for four to six weeks," he told me.

"Doc, I am not doing that—that's my season," I said.

"It will get worse, Art," he said.

I had spent much of the off-season looking forward to our third game, at Stanford, led by their highly publicized junior quarterback John Elway. That game was billed as "Schlichter versus Elway." It was a game I had to play in and a game we had to win.

"I am not letting you put a cast on me," I told Doc Murphy. "I'll undergo treatment and be ready next week. We are playing Stanford and Elway ... I've been waiting two years for this game. How can we treat this to get me ready?"

Over the next few days, I ate anti-inflammatory pills like candy because that ankle hurt so much.

Earle had a rule that if you didn't practice by Thursday, you wouldn't play in the game on Saturday. My ankle still looked like a coconut by Wednesday, so on Thursday, I limped out to the field, took some snaps in the shotgun and then limped off of the field.

Officially, I had practiced.

I always believed in the old Wally Pipp deal. I didn't want to give anyone a chance to take my job, whether I had two good ankles, or just one.

During that flight Friday morning to the West Coast, my ankle blew up even bigger. Every time I glanced at it, I knew there was no way I should be playing on it, but there also was no way I wanted to miss this game.

Before Friday's walk-through practice at Stanford Stadium, I rode the golf cart to the field, limped to the grass, threw a couple of balls and got back on the golf cart.

I underwent treatment all night Friday. I knew I had to bite the bullet so to speak, so they shot me up with painkillers before the game. Suddenly, it was like I had a new foot. The trainers taped my ankle, put on my sock, taped over it, then put on my shoe and taped over it.

My foot looked like a block of ice and probably weighed 30 pounds.

Anyway, I played pretty well in the first half as we jumped to a 17-6 halftime lead. In the locker room, they stripped off all the tape, shot me up again, and then went through the taping process all over again.

I hit tight end Brad Dwelle for a touchdown pass that made it 24-6 early in the fourth quarter, before I discovered Elway's talent.

Elway, who also was playing on a gimpy ankle, started firing darts and two Stanford touchdowns later, we had a fight on our hands. Our defense stopped them in the final seconds as we held on to win 24-19.

By the end of the game, I looked like Festus from *Gunsmoke* running the option. I had passed for 240 yards and John had passed for 248, but neither one of us played anywhere near full strength.

I limped over to meet him after the game.

"Good game, how's your ankle?" I asked him.

"Pretty good," he said. "How's yours?"

"It hurts like hell," I told him. "Good luck the rest of the season!"

Once again, for the third straight season, we had started 3-0 and had high hopes.

Next up was Florida State, a real swash-buckling team that would play anybody anywhere. We were the second opponent in the middle of five consecutive road games for them that included Nebraska, Notre Dame, Pittsburgh and LSU.

They were an up-and-coming program coached by Bobby Bowden, but they didn't have the national name of an Ohio State back then.

That didn't matter to them as we fell behind and couldn't run a lick that day. They were bigger and quicker and beat us 36-27, although I set all of the Ohio State single-game passing records that day, completing 31-of-52 passes for 458 yards.

My ankle still throbbed when Earle called me into the office that next week.

"You played a great game," he told me. "I know you are playing hurt and I appreciate it."

We went over the passing game in great detail and I left there thinking we understood each other better.

Before the kickoff of our next game at Wisconsin, I had gone to midfield with the other captain, linebacker Glen Cobb, who was from my high school, for the coin toss before Earle delivered his pre-game speech.

Bill Myles and a few teammates told me about it later: Earle gave a rip-roaring speech using my situation—senior captain who was playing injured—to rally the troops.

"Let's win this one for Art!" he told the team. "He is playing hurt. He deserves better than what you are giving him. Let's play this one for him!"

I guess it wasn't inspiring enough, because we lost to Wisconsin 24-21 on a cold, wet day, to drop our record to 3-2. I hated Astroturf fields anyway, because when the field was wet, the ball would get wet and stay wet.

It was a constant concern for me because of my small hands and I always had difficulty throwing a wet football, as I did that day.

We came back to beat Illinois 34-27, Indiana 29-10 and Purdue 45-33.

I loved playing on Purdue's field because it was one of the few grass fields in the Big Ten at that time. I passed for 336 yards and four touchdowns, checked off and made all the right calls, amounting to almost a perfect game.

I had never, ever received a game ball in my four years as a starter at Ohio State and always had wanted one. So when Earle stood up in the locker room after the game, holding a football above his head, I knew this had to be it.

"This guy has done so much for this team," he said. "He really had a great game today, and he has never received a game ball and he really deserves this and I want him to have it ...

"...Cedric Anderson come on up here!"

Anderson blocked a Purdue punt and caught two TD passes, but it was a moment when I felt unappreciated by my head coach. It hurt. What did I have to do to get a game ball?

The next week, we traveled to Minnesota as a heavy favorite and jumped ahead of the Gophers 31-14 by mixing it up, throwing and running. Once again, we spent the second half sitting on the ball. One-two-three punt. One-two-three punt. And once again, an opponent got back in the game because of it.

Our defense really had its problems that season, especially trying to stop the pass. Minnesota rallied to within three points late in the game before their quarterback, Mike Hohensee, threw a desperation pass into the end zone. It bounced off the hands of one of our young defensive backs and into the hands of one of their receivers.

We now trailed 35-31 and were forced to throw. Four incompletions later, the game was over. I was so pissed off, I could not see straight after that game.

Our Rose Bowl hopes were over, too, and I realized we would never get another chance to play in Pasadena. As it turned out, with Michigan and Iowa losing, we would have gone to the Rose Bowl if we had beaten Minnesota, Northwestern and Michigan to finish the season.

But now we had three losses and everything we had hoped for was gone.

For the record, Earle finally gave me a game ball after the 70-6 win over Northwestern the following week. I knew it was just a token gesture, because we hardly passed that day and had won the game by *only* ten touchdowns. And I also knew that Fred Zechman had mentioned to Earle that week that I had never received a game ball.

All that was left to play for was the rivalry game with Michigan.

Michigan, ranked seventh, would win the Big Ten championship and head to the Rose Bowl with a win against us. We already had three losses, so nobody knew where, or if, we were headed to a bowl.

It snowed so hard that Friday night when we got off the airplane in Ann Arbor that we couldn't see the buses. I had never played in a blizzard before, but I envisioned trying to do it the next day. Me, with the smallest hands in the nation, trying to throw against the wind and snow—it wouldn't be a pretty picture.

Fortunately, it stopped snowing before the game, so it was just cold and wet. I got knocked down after that first pass and a huge rush of ice-cold water shot up my back and down the crack of my ass.

"Oh shit," I thought. "This isn't going to be comfortable, playing the entire game with a cold, wet butt."

Later, that water damn near froze to the inside of my leg. As it turned out, our young team battled hard that day and the elements hurt Michigan more than us, because they could not throw the ball at all.

I scored one touchdown to put us up 7-6, but they kicked a late field goal to go ahead by two points. We were buried deep in our own territory on the next series, facing a third-and-long.

My senior season was about to be flushed down the toilet. It would end with four losses, another loss to Michigan and no bowl trip ... all in all, a disaster, if we didn't do something fast on the next play.

The play that saved us was a simple route to running back Tim Spencer near our bench, but it was just enough to pick up the first down. Then Tim followed with a 12-yard run, before Gary Williams made a great catch. Once we crossed the 50-yard line and the clock ticked down, I thought I lost the game for us on a quarterback sneak.

All I needed was a yard, but after I picked up the yardage, I lost the football in the pile.

The officials must not have noticed, because they signaled first down.

A few plays later, we faced another crucial moment. It was third-and-goal at Michigan's six-yard line.

Again, the coaches called "Play Pass 21," the run-pass option that had won the UCLA game for us two years earlier.

But this time, as I rolled to the right, the intended receiver, tight end John Frank, was not open. I knew a field goal would win it for us, so I wasn't about to take any chances by throwing into coverage. I just tucked the football and juked to the inside. Vaughan Broadnax, our sophomore fullback, was in front of me. As I saw three Michigan defensive players head inside to cut me off, I cut outside, and Vaughan blocked all three of them. I got lucky and slipped into the end zone.

That play gave us a 14-9 win and a tri-Big Ten championship with Michigan and Iowa (which went to the Rose Bowl). It was a huge moment for us.

I grabbed the football out of the referee's hands following the final play of the game and happily headed into the locker room, the win over our rival taking some sting out of the disappointing season. Dad came into the tunnel and someone allowed him to step inside the locker room door.

I handed him the ball.

"This is for you," I said, tears in my eyes.

"I love you Arthur," he said, tears in his as well.

As I sat in the middle of the room talking to the media, Dad sat in the corner of the room watching me, hugging that football like it was his first-born baby.

After I finished with the media, I peeled off that soaking wet uniform and headed to the shower. As I stood there alone, the hot water running off my back, enjoying the solitude and the aftermath of such an important victory, an elderly figure walked in.

Through the steam, I could see that he was wearing a trench coat.

It was Woody Hayes.

Earle had invited Woody to the game as an honorary guest. It was the first time he had attended an Ohio State-Michigan game since coaching the game we had lost during my freshman season.

He extended his hand.

"Didn't I tell you that you would be the best quarterback ever to play at Ohio State?" he said. "Well, you are."

He shook my hand, I thanked him and he smiled and walked out.

I thought how ironic that moment was. Three years and three months earlier, I had to face him in his office following that opening loss to Penn State, the legendary coach standing there naked and me beaten and bruised emotionally and physically. He predicted then that I would be the best quarterback ever to play for the Buckeyes.

Now here it was all this time later, he appeared frail and had aged way beyond those three years without a team to coach. Now I stood in the shower naked as he congratulated me on my career.

To have him say those words to me and recognize me with that honor … that still is my favorite story of Woody Hayes.

It was a total letdown to go to the Liberty Bowl to play Navy. Memphis certainly was no Pasadena. It was cold and wet the entire week. I had played well in the previous three bowl games (47-of-76 for 804 yards), but we hadn't won any of them, so this time, I planned to play well again, win a bowl game and be named the bowl's MVP. That's all I had left to play for.

The fact is, I didn't play well at all (11-of-26, 159 yards, two touchdowns) in my final game, but we managed to hang on to beat Navy 31-28.

I played the game as if I just wanted to get my career over with. That's because I did. I was worn out mentally and physically. I was 22 years old and disappointed the way my college career had ended, especially enduring those six losses over the final two seasons.

I had been frustrated with the way Earle had treated me. It was as if he went out of his way to treat me equal or even worse than he treated other players. I thought it should have been the opposite.

So I peeled off my uniform for the final time and told one of the managers that I was headed back to the team hotel with my family.

"You cannot go back with your family, you have to ride the bus," he told me. "You will get into trouble."

"Trouble?" I asked. "What kind of trouble can I get into? I am done. I am a senior. I just played my last game. What are they going to do to me?"

A few days later, Bob Atha and I flew to the West Coast to prepare to head to Hawaii to play in the Hula Bowl. We discovered we had an extra day, so we flew over to Las Vegas.

It was the first time I had ever seen the place and I liked it right away.

I went through probably a few hundred dollars and the next day, we had to report to Los Angeles for the teams' flight over to Hawaii.

If I had my druthers, I would have rather stayed home. I knew the Hula Bowl invitation was a reward for a good career, an honor, and I shouldn't turn it down. As it turned out, it also gave me an opportunity to get a few things off of my chest.

I had bit my tongue the past two years, not mentioning a word to the press about how I disliked the offense and Earle's conservative philosophy. Our pass protection package forced me to take my drop with my back to the line of scrimmage, executing the play-action no matter what the down and distance was, and I really believed it was ridiculous.

If it was third-and-20, I dropped back just as I would on second-and-three—with my back to the line of scrimmage using play-action. I always believed that anytime a quarterback's back is to the line of scrimmage, he is at a disadvantage.

The games in which we sat on the ball after passing so successfully, too many games to mention, are what infuriated me the most. We would have won several more games, if we would have continued to throw the ball, instead of sitting on a lead.

Back then, coaches just stuck to their systems and forced the players, no matter how great they were, to adapt to it. Woody did it, Earle did it, Bear Bryant did it. Every coach. It was the old-school way.

Today, you see more coaches mold their systems to the talent they have at the time. Look at what Jim Tressel has done at Ohio State. In 2006 with Troy Smith, he threw the football all over the place. Other times, he has relied on a power running game.

Well, all of that frustration was about to bubble over, since Earle was the East team's head coach for the Hula Bowl.

As a contrast, BYU's Jim McMahon played for the West, and when we talked before the game, he went on and on about how much he loved his head coach, LaVell Edwards, who coached the West team that week.

I played the first quarter and then the third quarter as planned. LaVell Edwards was a smart coach—he played his second-best quarterback in the first quarter and saved McMahon for the final three quarters.

We fell behind, so I wanted to get back on the field in the fourth quarter to battle McMahon and try to pull the game out for us.

"No, you're done," Earle told me.

Okay, no more Mister Nice Guy. This was my chance.

I stood behind him on the sideline and unleashed two years' worth of frustration.

"YOU HAVE BEEN SCREWING ME FOR THE LAST TWO YEARS!" I screamed. "TWO YEARS!"

As I continued to scream at him, other players on the East team just spread out, getting as far away from me as they could. They vacated the area as if there had been a bomb threat, as I stood there venting like a madman at my head coach.

I just let it all go, all my frustration and anger unleashed in a flurry and I didn't care who was listening or watching. I think Dad's bitterness toward Earle had filtered into my brain and out of my mouth at that very moment.

Earle heard it all, but never responded. He then put me back in the game, but we still lost.

Anyway, I think my tirade really shocked him. It strained our relationship for a few years, but eventually, we made up.

I know now that I was wrong for standing there screaming at him. I felt very bad about it later once I calmed down. I had spent four years at Ohio State doing my best to handle myself with class. Then I ended my college career with such a classless act. For that, Coach, I apologize.

From Hawaii, I flew to San Diego to play in the Olympia Gold Bowl, a new all-star game in its inaugural year.

Unlike the Hula Bowl, there weren't many All-Americans scheduled to play in the game, so they had needed a big name to help promote the game. They had called Dad a few weeks earlier and offered me $5,000 to play.

"Five thousand?" I said. "I don't think so."

I was scheduled to receive an award from the Washington, D.C., Touchdown Club the night of the game, so there was no way I could play in it anyway.

"What if we pay him $10,000?" they asked Dad.

"No."

"Fifteen?"

"No."

Finally after about four telephone calls from the bowl officials, I told Dad, "Tell them if they pay me $20,000, fly me, you and Mom to Hawaii for the Hula Bowl, then back to San Diego for the game, and then have a private plane to get me to Washington in time to receive that award, I'll do it."

I never figured they would accept those terms. I had just found a way to turn them down.

Guess what?

They agreed to it all.

Philadelphia Eagles Coach Dick Vermeil coached my team for the game and I also spent time working with Sid Gillman. Those were two great football minds and I learned a lot in that one week.

I completed 9-of-10 passes in little more than a quarter of play, putting the East team ahead, before they replaced me with another quarterback as planned.

I headed to the locker room to change into street clothes, met Mom and Dad outside the stadium, hopped into a limo and was rushed to the airport to get on the private plane they had arranged for us. On the way to Washington, Dad and I changed into our tuxedos and Mom into a new dress.

As we approached D.C., we figured we had dressed nicely for our impending funerals.

This tiny airplane wobbled back and forth on the approach just like one of my passes I had thrown into a 40 mile per hour wind at Northwestern during my junior year. As we flew over the Potomac, it was snowing and blowing, the cockpit curtain was open and we could see the pilots struggling to gain control.

This happened to be only days after an Air Florida flight had crashed into the Potomac, killing 78 people. Through the snow, we could see recovery equipment below at the crash site.

It surely wasn't a sight that would boost our sagging confidence that we would land safely.

Somehow we did, hopped into another limo and arrived late at the Touchdown Club banquet. Mom and Dad found their seats, just as the announcer said, "Ladies and gentlemen, just off an airplane from California where he was named the Most Valuable Player of the Olympia Gold Bowl, Art Schlichter, quarterback, Ohio State...."

I walked out and the first person I saw was President Reagan. I walked over to him, shook his hand, and found my seat at the head table.

I had no idea I was named the MVP of the game, but my brother John had told Dad about it when he called before the banquet. He had watched the game on TV and the announcers had said the MVP of the game received a new car. We didn't know about that, either. Later, the bowl officials told Dad, "Look, we gave him $20,000. He doesn't get the car, too."

"But the MVP of the game gets a car," Dad told them.

In the end, I was paid $20,000, they flew me to Washington on time to receive my Touchdown Club Award, I met the president and on top of it all, I had new wheels to drive.

Not bad for one day.

It sure beat arguing with Earle.

As for my Ohio State career, it's like that other line in *The Natural*, when the girl tells Robert Redford's character in the hospital that he had a good career.

"Yeah," he said. *"But I could have done better."*

And that's how I feel about it.

Almost 30 years later, I still hold Ohio State's career passing (7,547 yards) and total offense (8,850 yards) records, all of the single-game passing records set during the loss to Florida State, we won 36 games, went to four bowls, beat Michigan twice, and yet, *I could have done better.*

The one-point loss in the Rose Bowl will always haunt me, as will not having beaten Michigan at Ohio Stadium.

I should have done a lot of things differently, such as going to school and

The basement of our farmhouse is where we displayed my trophies.

getting my degree. I understand now that my gambling distracted me, too. Maybe I was a great college player at times, but I could have been better.

Looking back, I am glad I didn't transfer. I loved Ohio State and I loved being a Buckeye.

I still do.

95

Chapter ten

WELCOME TO THE NFL

"*Art, this is Frank Kush.*"
"*How are you Coach?*"
"*We are going to draft you with the fourth pick. You don't have any problems playing for me, do you?*"
"*No sir, I would be honored to play for you.*"
"*Okay, congratulations! You are a Baltimore Colt!*"

It was April 27, 1982.

News helicopters had just landed on our lawn as Mom prepared tons of food for our family, friends, and the media, who milled around our house waiting for the story: Which NFL team would draft me?

So we ate, made small talk and waited for the telephone to ring.

It didn't take long for the head coach of the Colts to call, and with that concise conversation, short and sweet, I officially started my professional career.

That night, I drove up to Scioto Downs and celebrated as only I knew how to celebrate—at the racetrack, betting on the horses.

I really had no idea which team would take me in the weeks leading up to the draft. By virtue of its terrible record in 1981, New England had the first pick in the draft, Baltimore the second, Cleveland the third, the Los Angeles Rams the fourth, and Chicago the fifth. The Rams, Colts, and Bears all needed a quarterback, and given those choices, I hoped I was headed to L.A.

But the team that worked me out the most, leading up to the draft, was Baltimore. I had worked out for Colts quarterbacks coach Zeke Bratkowski at the French Field House at Ohio State a few weeks earlier and we got along very well. I played pitch and catch with Zeke, who was in his late 40s, and couldn't help but notice that he threw the tightest, most-perfect spiral I ever saw. I never saw a football come off the hand so sweet every time.

Getting the call from the NFL.

The rap on me coming out of college was that I didn't throw a tight spiral all the time. The fact is, I didn't. I had small hands and the ball didn't always come off of my hand the way I would have liked.

Still, no matter what I told Frank Kush on draft day, nobody wanted to play for him, me included. He had come to the Colts from Arizona State and everyone had heard the horror stories about what a tyrant he was. I had heard that he was a Marine drill-sergeant disguised in coaching clothes.

Then the day before the draft, Baltimore made a shocking trade, dealing popular quarterback Bert Jones to the Rams for the fourth pick. Now the Rams had their quarterback and there was no way I was headed to the West Coast, while the Colts suddenly had the second and the fourth picks.

The picture was clear. It was almost certain that I would become a Colt.

After New England took defensive tackle Ken Sims from Texas, the Colts picked a linebacker, Johnnie Cooks from Mississippi State. The Browns then drafted USC's Chip Banks, the linebacker who tackled me on the goal line ultimately costing us the Rose Bowl more than two years earlier.

That was when Kush called our house.

That night at Scioto, I admit I had thoughts of becoming a millionaire, but the NFL's salary structure wasn't like it is today.

I had hired Tom Reich as my agent. Tom was a nice guy, but he was a baseball agent who had represented many of the Reds. He just wanted to get his foot in the NFL door, so I became his first football client.

There wasn't much to negotiations back then for NFL rookies and we agreed in June to a deal that paid me a $350,000 bonus up front, and salaries of $140,000 in 1982, $175,000 in '83, $220,000 in '84 and a team option for $240,000 in '85. (Compare that to Darren McFadden, the fourth pick of the 2008 draft, who received a six-year, $60 million contract with the Raiders.)

Tom and I flew to Baltimore and walked into the Colts' offices to sign the contract.

"Wait down here, while I go up there and tie up all the loose ends," he told me.

I wandered over to the weight room where I struck up a conversation with a muscle-bound kid who appeared to be about my age.

"What do you do around here?" I asked him.

"I'm Jim Irsay," he said. "I'm studying to be the owner of the team."

"That's cool," I responded.

I thought, "Studying to be the owner? How do you do that? I didn't know there were any courses for that."

Summer camp began and there were three quarterbacks. What puzzled me was why the Colts had drafted another quarterback, Arizona State's Mike Pagel, in the fourth round. If they had confidence in me, why take Pagel?

Besides Pagel and me, Greg Landry was the third quarterback in camp. Landry was 35 years old and entering his 14th year in the league, having played 11 years in Detroit. The players called him "Pops" and he had the worst knees of any man I had ever seen.

As we started our first long required run on that first day of camp, "Pops" told me, "Just hang back here with me. You'll be okay."

So there I was, jogging in the back of the pack with Landry, talking football, when I heard a scream: "SCHLICHTER! WHAT THE FUCK ARE YOU DOING? AREN'T YOU IN ANY BETTER SHAPE THAN THAT?"

It was Kush, and he wasn't using that nice, warm tone like he did the first time I spoke to him on the telephone.

The Colts soon cut Landry and brought in former Nebraska quarterback Dave Humm from Oakland. The Hummer and I got along fine, even though he was a smoker and a drinker and I wasn't, but you couldn't help but like him. We were different in a lot of ways—I would be out gambling all night while he would be out drinking all night.

He would burst into the locker room in the morning and get right up close to my face and scream: "HEY! I FEEL GOOD TODAY!"

I would sit there, sad and depressed, chewing on my pen, trying to remember the plays while gambling figures bounced around inside my head.

"Man!" the Hummer would ask me. "What is *wrong* with you?"

I wouldn't have had the time or patience to explain it all in detail, if I had to truthfully answer that question.

The truth was, I didn't even want to be in camp, or in Baltimore. I was so messed up at the time, having broken up with my girlfriend, Maria, that summer. Dad didn't want me to take her with me to Baltimore and I told her that she wouldn't be coming with me. It all went south from there. She was very hurt, and we started to drift apart. I really should've taken her with me.

In the end, she dumped me and it sent me into a state of mini-depression, which I carried with me to Baltimore like a gym bag.

By the time I arrived that July, I was gambling more and more and working out less and less. I was lonely, away from home, and uncomfortable.

The Colts' camp was held at Goucher College, which didn't have a football team so we had to practice on soccer fields. The whole place was a real dump, not fit for an NFL team. The dorms were old, the locker room was cramped ... just a miserable place.

I knew heading into camp that the Colts were getting a shell of the player they thought they had drafted and I guess I didn't really care enough to do anything about it. They had drafted me to start right away and taken Pagel to be a promising backup.

Still, I didn't realize just how out of shape I was until camp started that July. The first thing we did was run a timed 40-yard dash, but there was a trick to it. I ran a 4.7, which isn't bad for a quarterback, but then they told us we had to run ten more 40s, all within four-tenths of our first timed run. We had about 25 seconds inbetween each 40.

If I had known that, I would have run a 5.2 to begin with.

It took me a long time to get those ten 40s within four-tenths of 4.7. Then they wanted the quarterbacks to bench-press 240 pounds. When they stuck all of that weight on the bar, my arms were shaking like leaves in the wind.

"Get ... this ... thing ... off ... of ... me!" I said, straining with every word.

I couldn't do one rep.

An hour later, we had to run a mile and a half in 10 minutes or less.

"Stick with me," the Hummer said. "I'll get you there in time."

Dave wasn't a fast guy, but he had endurance. We started and I stuck right with him for about 400 yards. Slowly, he started to drift ahead and out of my sight. I was sucking air, because I hadn't run all summer. I trudged along, seeing the finish line approaching slowly as an assistant coach called out the time ...

9:51, 52, 53 …. I kept chugging … 55, 56, 57…

There were TV cameras filming the entire thing. As I fell across the finish line face-first at 9:59, a cameraman followed me to the ground, filming my agony.

Then we had to go out and practice that afternoon. I couldn't even move, let alone drop back and throw a football.

It probably was clear to the coaches within a day or two that Pagel was the better quarterback. Mike threw the ball much better than I did. He had a hell of an arm and was in better shape. He also understood the offense better, because he had played under Kush in college.

Everything was so different to me: The pass protection, the drops, the routes. It was all stuff we had never done at Ohio State. When you have a basic offense, as we did, you see basic defenses. When you run a complicated offense, you see complicated defenses.

I didn't pay much attention during meetings, either. It was a thick, extensive playbook and my A.D.D. (I would be officially diagnosed much later) was kicking in. Often during meetings, I thought about gambling.

Zeke was patient with me, but he couldn't figure out what was wrong with me. I had this big wind-up and couldn't throw accurately. I had been hurt so much during my senior year at Ohio State that I had developed some bad habits, especially with my footwork. The NFL football was slicker than a college football and I had trouble gripping it. My mechanics were horrible and I lost all of my confidence. When you lose your confidence as an NFL quarterback, you're done.

It was the perfect storm.

Everybody inside that team had to be asking, "Man, what is wrong with Art? They drafted *this guy* with the fourth pick and gave him all that money? You have to be kidding?"

It was never spoken to me, but I could see it in their eyes.

The guy who treated me the worst was veteran receiver Roger Carr, but he was brutal on everybody. At times, he wouldn't even get in the receivers line when I was throwing.

He was quoted in the newspaper: "After playing with Bert Jones, I don't want to play with these rookies."

At Ohio State, we had the normal two-a-day practices, but with the Colts, we practiced *three* times each day in camp. It was a living hell, a miserable existence. The nights were hot and the days hotter.

Kush had a team rule forbidding players from removing their helmets, even during stretching. One day while I reached for my toes, a river of sweat poured down my face into my mouth. I started to hallucinate and was about to faint. I looked over to the sidelines and thought I saw Mom and Dad standing there.

I remember praying to God to make it through that first camp.

By the end of it, it was clear that Pagel deserved to start ahead of me. He ended camp as the starter, I was second-team and the Hummer was third. I really have no idea why I was still number two. I deserved to be number three. The Hummer was in his 30s and couldn't get out of his shadow, but he was clearly a better NFL quarterback than I was and he knew the game better, too.

At that time, we knew a strike was looming. The NFL Players Association's rep on our team was Nesby Glascoe, a veteran defensive back. As rookies, we really had no reason to strike, because our salary structure was set. It was the veterans who pushed for it, wanting higher salaries and a better pension plan. The minimum salary at the time was only $38,000.

Before that first game, against New England, Kush cut most of the veterans anyway. That '82 Colts team was made up largely of rookies and free agents, with a few veterans sprinkled in.

Pagel started our first two games, a 24-13 loss to the Patriots and a 24-20 loss at Miami, as I held the clipboard.

The Monday after we returned home from Miami, on September 20, we had to report to an elementary school away from the Colts' property to hear Nesby's update on the labor issues. (We weren't allowed to meet on team premises.) Nesby put it to a team vote. It was unanimous. Every Colts player had voted to strike.

I know that not everyone wanted to strike, but everyone on that team wanted to get the hell away from Frank Kush. When the strike was approved by the NFLPA, we left the locker room slapping high-fives, because we knew we were leaving Frank behind us for a while.

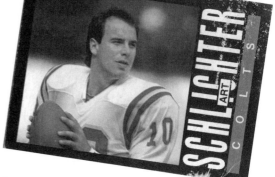

I picked up my paycheck and then the telephone to call The Q-Man and another buddy back in Columbus.

"Go to the airport tomorrow morning, I'll have two

plane tickets waiting for you," I told them. "Fly out here, grab a taxi from the airport and meet me at Laurel Park."

I took about $5,000 from that paycheck of $13,000 and stuck it in my pocket. Now I had cash in my pocket, time on my hands with no football to practice or play, no meetings to attend, and no Frank Kush screaming at me.

You could imagine how I felt.

Laurel Park was a thoroughbred track just outside Baltimore and by my second month in town, I knew many of the horse trainers there. That next day, my buddies arrived at the track and I handed them a few hundred bucks to bet with.

I excused myself and went to visit a trainer I knew.

"Listen, my horse is going to win today," the trainer told me. "Come down to the paddock before the eighth race and we'll get a picture of you in the winner's circle with him."

I looked at the board to see that his horse, the number two horse, had five-to-one odds. I told him I would be there, then I asked the horse's owner, "Who do you like with him?" wanting to gain some inside information of which horses were good bets to finish second and third.

"Well, I really like the five and the one," he said.

I looked at the board: The five horse was six-to-five and the one was five-to-one. I bet $2,000 on his horse to win at five-to-one. I also bet a few $400 and $200 exactas, using all three horses.

By now, my buddies had lost most of their money, although The Q-Man was convinced the five horse would win the race, so he put some money on him. We headed off to the grandstand to watch the race and they still had no idea what I had bet. By the time the horses galloped down the stretch, the five and two horses were neck-and-neck for the lead.

As they crossed the wire, we still couldn't tell who won the race.

I was sweating it out, knowing I had a huge payday if that two horse crossed first.

"I know the five won!" The Q-Man shouted. "I just know it!"

Several excruciating moments passed before they popped a "2-5-1" finish on the scoreboard. Then the number five suddenly started blinking, which meant there was an inquiry into the race for a bumping incident in the turn. Then they took down the five, moved the number one up to second, meaning I had won virtually every bet I made.

"Here, go cash these tickets for me," I told The Q-Man.

He took them without looking at them, still bitching about his horse losing, and headed off to the window.

All of a sudden, I heard him screaming.

"Yes!!! Look at all the money we won!"

"Shhhh … ," I told him. "Do you know where we are? We're in Baltimore! You'll get us killed!"

I had won $26,000 on the race and now had $30,000 in cash on me. I was wearing cowboy boots, so I shoved $15,000 in each boot and we walked out of there.

It was late in the afternoon.

"Come on," I told my buddies. "We're going to Philadelphia for the evening races."

We rushed out of the track parking lot, but got stuck in rush-hour traffic on the freeway, so The Q-Man pulled the car off to the side of the road and started passing cars on the shoulder. Sure enough, there was a police car sitting ahead. The officer pulled us over, had us out of the car and all I could think about was all that money in my boots.

If he searched us, he surely would figure we were drug dealers and we would spend the night in jail.

Instead, he handed us a few traffic tickets and let us go on our way. We hopped back in the car and sped off to Philadelphia, where I lost a couple of thousand that night, but I didn't really care at that point.

We left there and drove to Atlantic City, arriving at about two in the morning.

In three days there, I blew through all of that money. Then I took a credit card and got a few thousand more and lost that, too. At four in the morning on the third day, I told the guys, "Come on, we're going home."

And we started back to Baltimore.

We were dead busted, broke enough that we had to dig through the car seats for loose change to pay the tolls along the turnpike.

I wasn't working out at all, figuring the strike would wipe out the entire season.

And with plenty of time on my hands, my gambling problem grew worse.

I had been using a bookie back in Ohio until that point, a guy who my high school buddy had set me up with. Now I knew it was time to find someone local to take my bets.

I had discovered the best rib joint in town, The Corner Stable in Timonium, a Baltimore suburb. Eating at the bar one night, I asked, "Know of anyone who will take a bet?"

"Yeah, I got a buddy who works at a meat-packing plant," this guy told me. "He can hook you up."

I didn't know much about my new bookies, other than their names "Sid" and "Sammy." I started placing bets with Sammy under the code name "Fred."

The next few months, I bounced between Baltimore, Columbus, and Washington Court House, gambling on a daily basis. I played some pick-up basketball, but didn't focus much on staying in shape.

I came back to campus the week of the Ohio State-Stanford game in September, a rematch of the game a year earlier in which Elway and I hobbled around on gimpy ankles. This time, Elway was healthy. He rallied Stanford for a game-winning drive in the final minutes for a 23-20 win at Ohio Stadium, starting Ohio State's first three-game losing streak since 1966.

Meanwhile, I was going through one myself, betting and losing parlays on college football and then basketball.

My friends would tell you that I was better than anyone at picking the games straight-up. The problem was, I was addicted to parlays, meaning I had to win every game I played to cash the bet. I could hit two of three or four of five almost every night, but getting them all right is a very difficult thing to do. So, I lost.

In the years that followed, my love for parlays would prove to be my ruination.

Sure enough, I had Stanford in a parlay, but still lost it. That first weekend following the strike, I lost $15,000 and thought, "Holy God, what am I doing?"

We weren't receiving paychecks, but I knew I still had more than $300,000 of my signing bonus in the bank, so I didn't give it much thought. I chased that $15,000 into $30,000 the next week, then $60,000 the next week. Then I borrowed money from the banks in Ohio, where bank managers knew me.

I would walk in, open a line of credit for $30,000, and walk out.

It got to the point where I was betting $60,000 a night at times, trying to catch up. One night, I bet on 11 college and pro basketball games and told Bill Hanners I would meet him at the Miami Trace basketball game. I had two-team teasers, three-team parlays, all kinds of bets that night. To get the scores, I called a score line number in New York, which of course I knew by heart.

After checking on the scores that night, I was counting my money in my head: I had won $250,000. It was the greatest night of my life.

"Uh, Art, I don't know how to bring this up," Bill stammered, as we stood in the bathroom during the basketball game. "The guy called earlier and said, 'Hey, we can't get in touch with 'Fred,' so you need to tell him that he can't lay all that action on us.'

"I told them, 'Just cut everything in half,'" Bill said.

"In half?" I screamed. "I JUST WON $250,000!"

"Well," Bill said, "Now you just won $125,000."

I called the bookie the next morning.

"When can I get paid?" I asked.

"Oh no," he told me. "You can't just stop now and collect. You have to keep betting until Tuesday. Tuesday is payday."

"You've got to be shitting me," I said. "I want to get paid!"

I gave in, like a dummy. By Tuesday, it was all gone and I owed the bookie $50,000.

That next week, I was sitting around the house in Washington Court House when Nesby called.

"Art, we have to report back," he told me.

"Report back?" I asked.

"Yep, the strike has ended," he said.

I didn't like that news. I was hoping the whole season would wash out. I was probably the only disappointed NFL player that day. I was so screwed up mentally, I didn't want to see Frank Kush or a football again that season.

The Colts' morale was low before, but it was nothing compared to what it would be by season's end. When we reported back, Kush had us practicing two-a-days again. We were just busting our asses, perhaps as punishment for walking out in the first place.

The Colts were the NFL's running joke that strike-shortened season.

We returned to take a 37-0 whipping from the Jets in our first game back and then lost a squeaker, 20-17 to the Bengals, before a 13-10 loss to the Vikings. Somehow, we tied the Packers 20-20 in our best showing of the season.

In the next game, a 44-28 loss at San Diego, I happened to be standing behind our defensive coordinator, Bud Carson, when two of our defensive backs got confused and dropped to the same side, leaving Chargers receiver John Jefferson uncovered. Dan Fouts took the snap, stood up, and threw an easy touchdown pass to Jefferson as Bud exploded, "I AM DONE WITH THIS SHIT!"

I wasn't playing, so my job was to chart the plays on a clipboard. I had been betting other NFL games, but never a Colts' game, and was jotting betting notes on the team's clipboard. I know I was scoreboard watching quite a bit on Sundays during our games. When the coaches looked at the clipboard later, one of them asked, "What the hell is this?"

They couldn't decipher what I had written, so they took that job away from me.

This was before cell phones, so I had to use the locker room phone to place my bets, to check in with the bookie, or to check scores. I was on that phone so much that one day my teammates placed all of my equipment in that phone booth. The Hummer got a big kick out of that joke.

One time, the 212-score line even let me down.

I was lying in bed one night, having all these parlays tied up with one NBA game, the Denver Nuggets against somebody. Before ESPN's ticker ever existed, the score line was my lifeline. I called it, heard that the Nuggets had won, had covered my bet, and my parlay.

I went to bed thinking I had just pocketed $60,000.

The next morning, I called the bookie and asked, "What's my total?"

"A negative $20,000," he told me.

"What?" I asked. "Are you out of your fucking mind? I am up $60,000."

"Art," he said. "You had better check your scores."

I hung up and called the score line again.

The recording informed me of the bad news, "… and in a correction from last night, the Denver Nuggets lost …."

It seemed as if I couldn't catch a break, even from a taped recording. I just continued betting on losers, which the Colts certainly were.

We were so bad that before the final game of the season against Miami, we brought in some guard from Georgia, who was obviously not NFL material. I got into the game as we were getting whipped by the Dolphins, looked into his eyes in the huddle, and could tell he was petrified.

You've heard about the proverbial "look-out" block? I experienced the real thing thanks to this guy.

I took the snap, rolled to my right and just as I set myself to throw, I heard,

"LOOK OUT!"

I hadn't put on any rib pads that day, because I didn't believe I would get into the game. Well, whichever Dolphin hit me, caught me in the ribs and I knew right away a few of them were broken.

"I am so sorry! I am so sorry!" this guard said to me.

He continued his apology as we huddled for the next play.

"Don't worry about it," I told him. "It all will be over very soon."

After the game, a 34-7 loss, I was in some serious pain. The team doctor handed me some pills. "Take two of these," he instructed.

The Hummer looked at me and shook his head.

"You and I are going out tonight!" he told me.

"Dave, I don't even care anymore," I muttered.

That night, January 2, 1983, I headed to a bar with the Hummer and drank half of a beer, the most beer I had consumed in my life. I topped that off with a few shots of something else Dave shoved at me and that was it. I ended up staggering drunk for the first time in my life.

I came rolling into the locker room the next day with my head still spinning. I picked up my paycheck, cleaned out my locker, and headed to Atlantic City. I wouldn't come back for three days.

Getting drunk for the first time in my life and then losing more money in Atlantic City was the imperfect nightcap to my disastrous rookie season. We had finished 0-8-1, the only winless team in the NFL. I didn't play much at all, completing only 17-of-37 passes for 197 yards. I didn't throw a touchdown pass but was intercepted twice.

Worse yet, I left Ohio for Baltimore as someone who liked to place a few bets and returned as a full-fledged compulsive gambler on the chase. I continued to chase my losses, figuring the next bet would be the winner, the bet that would get me even.

I returned home a few days later and continued to bet with—and lose money to—the Baltimore bookies.

I didn't have any idea then, but I was on my way to losing almost one million dollars within a year since the day I was drafted. The way I figured it later, I had gone through my $350,000 bonus, would borrow another $600,000, as well as some loose change here and there.

One million dollars!

And you thought the Colts had a bad year.

But my problems were about to get worse, much worse.

Chapter eleven

MY PROBLEMS BECOME PUBLIC

It was just a matter of time before everyone, especially Dad, would discover how much money I had gambled away during my rookie season.

By February, seven months after I had signed my first NFL contract, my entire signing bonus was gone and the debts were piling up. The strike had wiped out seven weeks of my salary. And what paychecks I had cashed were wasted on the horses, basketball, and football games.

I called Dad and asked him to fly into Baltimore. I was 22 years old, didn't have a clue what I was doing on the football field for the first time in my life, was out of money, and almost out of hope.

"Where's your bonus money?" he asked.

"I lost it," I told him. "Lost it all."

We sat there and cried and cried that day, just as we had after he took a few swipes at me a couple of years earlier when he bailed me out. But this time, my debt was way beyond $4,000. And I didn't owe the money to some harmless college bookie, either.

Now I was in the hole to Sid and Sammy in Baltimore, two guys I really knew nothing about. They had never paid a dollar to me, even when I won and was ahead, like that night the previous fall when I should have won $250,000 and they refused to pay. I am sure their strategy was to coax me to continue to bet until I owed them, and it worked.

It always worked.

I had no idea if they were connected to the mafia or not, but I knew one thing: They started threatening me. Something bad would happen, they told me, if I didn't pay them and pay them soon.

"Arthur," Dad said. "I love you, but you have a problem. A serious problem. You have to get help."

We called Tom Reich, my agent who negotiated the contract with the Colts.

"I'll check on some things and call you back tomorrow," Tom told us.

To this day, I have never heard from Tom.

Nobody really knew what to do for an addicted gambler back then. I certainly don't remember it being thought of as a disease. It was regarded as a bad habit just like smoking or biting your fingernails. If you are betting, and losing, just stop betting, most reasonable people figured.

I knew better. I knew that I couldn't, no matter how hard I had tried.

My accountant, Bill Chang, lived in San Diego and had found some expert on addiction who also lived there. Bill claimed he was someone who could help me. So I flew to California in the spring, hoping this man had some magic potion to erase my gambling demons.

The night before I was to meet with him, Bill and I went out to dinner. The restaurant had a lounge where I bumped into Joe Theismann, who just happened to call the Liberty Bowl game, my final Ohio State game, on television a little more than a year earlier.

We chatted a while, as Joe continued to stare at this strikingly cute girl.

"I asked her to dance, but she turned me down," he told me.

I couldn't stop staring at her, either, so finally I approached her.

"What's your name?" I asked.

"Gidget," she answered.

After some small talk, we took a walk together. She had mentioned that she was 21, her father was a famous doctor, and she was flying out of town the next day.

"Can I have your number?" I asked.

"My dad's name is in the book," she said.

I guess she wanted to see how badly I wanted to track her down, but I looked up her father's name and dialed the number the next morning.

"Is Gidget there?" I asked the kid who answered the telephone.

"No, she went to Beach Blanket Bingo," he said.

"What?" I asked.

I never put that together until later. Anyway, she came to the phone.

"Gidget?" I asked.

"Who is this?"

"It's Art, we met last night."

"Well, my name isn't Gidget, it's Kim," she confessed. "I didn't know who you were, so I gave you a fake name."

I ended up dating her for the next two and a half years.

But first, I had to meet the man my accountant claimed would take away my urge to gamble.

His name was Thaddeus Kostrubala. He was about 50 years old, a medical doctor, and real eccentric. Little did I know when I flew to San Diego but his method of treatment involved *running*. I wasn't a big runner to begin with, but after being around this guy for a few days, I absolutely hated it.

One day, we took off for what I thought would be a morning jog. After an hour, I was dead-beat tired, but he wanted to continue.

"What you need is some weight to carry," he told me. "That will burn off all of your aggression."

Sure enough, he found a football and filled it with lead. It must have weighed 40 pounds.

"I want you to carry this as we run," he told me.

"You've got to be kidding me," I said.

He wasn't. We took off running again as I carried what must have been the heaviest pigskin on earth. It was hurting me, so I put it on one shoulder, then the other shoulder, as we continued to run. Pretty soon, we were so far out in the middle of nowhere, outside of San Diego, I couldn't see any civilization.

Finally, I snapped.

"I'm sick of this shit," I said, tossing that lead football to the ground. "Why don't you run back to the car and come pick me up? I'm not running anymore!"

"Art, pick up the football!" he demanded. "We are only at the halfway point."

I picked up the football.

"I'm not carrying it anymore," I told him.

"Give it to me," he said.

I tossed that football full of lead and just as he caught it, he wrenched his knee. I mean, he blew his knee out right then and there.

I felt so bad for what I had done.

As we headed back, me walking, him limping badly, he leaned on my one shoulder while I carried that lead football in the other arm. It was almost worse than the run out there. Picture me walking this man with a torn-up knee, holding that football, through the desert in the middle of nowhere in

California. It would have been comical if I hadn't been so exhausted.

I packed up and flew home, leaving California thinking the guy was some strange witch doctor. Needless to say, Thaddeus Kostrubala's unconventional methods didn't cure me of gambling.

I continued betting with the Baltimore bookies once I returned to Ohio, running my debt even higher. My signing bonus was long gone, but now I tapped into just about every bank in central or southwest Ohio.

The bookies would fly into Columbus once each week and either I or Bill Hanners would meet them and hand over a bag containing whatever money I lost. First it was $10,000, the next week it was $20,000, then $30,000 the next.

Finally, it was $60,000.

Before paying it, I tried to buy time. I told Sid I didn't have the money.

"Get it," Sid told me.

"I'll try," I told him.

Sid, who was about 6-foot-4 and very burly, made me a threatening promise.

"If you are one dollar short, I will break your throwing arm," he said.

I paid the $60,000 to him March 1, 1983.

The next week, against all common sense, I continued to place bets with the Baltimore guys. Finally, when it sunk in that they wouldn't pay me even when I had won, I just started taking shots at them, including six consecutive nights when I bet 30 three-team parlays per night for $2,000 each.

Naturally, as my debt grew worse, surpassing $360,000, the threats grew worse. Pretty soon, they were threatening to tell the Colts and the NFL about my gambling.

I was searching for money to pay them when a friend referred me to a Columbus businessman who had helped out former Ohio State athletes in the past. His name was Gil Kirk and he lived in the former governor's mansion and owned a lot of land in Upper Arlington.

Finally, with the threats from Sid mounting like my overdue bills, I called him.

"Mister Kirk, I need some money," I told him. "My Dad's farm is going down and I want to help him."

"How much do you need, Art?" he asked.

"I could use $300,000 or even $400,000," I said.

"Wow, what kind of trouble is he in?" he asked.

I made up some story about Dad having trouble, but would not let Gil talk to him, so I'm sure he was suspicious right away. I drove up to Gil's mansion in Columbus one day and continued to tell some tale about how Dad needed the money.

"Art, tell me what really is going on here," he demanded. "I will help you, I will stick by you, just tell me the truth."

I broke down like a baby and explained the whole sad story to him.

Gil called Chuck Freiburger, a lawyer in Columbus, to get some legal advice.

By mid-March, I could not hold the Baltimore guys off any longer. They were demanding their money or else. That night, I was supposed to meet Sid at the Columbus airport and pay him, just as I had done plenty of times in the past.

Chuck said he would go with me, tell him that he was my attorney and try to buy some time for me.

Sid exited his flight, spotted me, and walked over to us.

"This is my lawyer," I told him.

"What are you doing?" he asked me. "You are supposed to have the money."

"You will get your money," Chuck said. "We will get this thing settled out. We just need time to get it all together. It's a lot of money."

Chuck gave Sid his telephone numbers and said he would take care of my debt.

"Okay, I will tell you what," he said, shoving his finger in Chuck's chest. "YOU are now responsible for it. YOU are the one responsible. I will go through YOU!"

We walked out of the airport and I was feeling pretty good that he was headed back to Baltimore and we hadn't paid him a dime, when Chuck turned to me.

"Did you hear what he just told me?" he asked. "He said I am responsible now. Art, who are these guys? Are they mobbed up?"

When Chuck reported back to Gil, they knew they had to do one thing fast: Call the FBI.

They called Tom Decker, the FBI agent whom I had talked to a few years earlier when the guy at the racetrack approached me about fixing an Ohio State game.

If these guys were connected, as Gil and Chuck figured, Tom would find out.

Meanwhile, Sid continued to call Chuck at the office, demanding payment, and then he found his home number.

"You have to get this fucking money! NOW!" he demanded.

"They are calling the house now," Chuck told us. "I have a family and my kids are there. We can't go on with this much longer."

With the help of Tom Decker, Chuck had passed the bookies off to an undercover FBI agent, Stephen Glaser, who posed as my accountant trying to figure ways to come up with the money. Agent Glaser was one tough son of a bitch. When the Baltimore guys started threatening him, that's when the FBI finally decided to ask them to fly into Columbus, supposedly to be paid.

I was in San Diego at the time, recovering from my run into the desert.

"Art, you need to come home," Tom said. "These guys are flying in, we plan to arrest them, and we need you to identify them. We're just tired of dealing with these punks. They are threatening our guy now."

Tom explained what the FBI had discovered. Sid was a guy named Harold Brooks, 26, who worked at Golden Home Meat Service. Sammy was Samuel R. Alascia, 30, of Catonsville, Maryland. They weren't connected to the mob at all. They were just small-time punks who found a sucker to drain. They would take the money I paid them and head to Atlantic City and blow it on booze, hotel rooms, girls, and gambling.

"They have been living it up on your money," Tom told me.

On April 1, 1983, the Baltimore guys flew to Columbus, along with two other men they had hired. The FBI had positioned undercover agents on the airplane, sitting all around them.

I knew that day the entire mess would become public.

The four men from Baltimore walked off the airplane and I recognized Sid. I had never seen the others. My "accountant," who held a briefcase which was supposed to be filled with bills totaling $65,000, the first of three installments, said, "Listen, I don't want to give you this money and have these other guys jump me. Where are all your guys?"

Sid pointed them out.

"Don't pull any funny business on us," Sid told him.

"Turn around," the "accountant" said. "THIS IS THE FBI. YOU ARE UNDER ARREST!"

I could tell by the looks on their faces that they were flabbergasted. It was April Fool's Day after all.

The FBI guy walked me out of there and that was that.

It turned out that Sid had paid the others only $50 each to fly with them to act as muscle. They worked cheap, because they had no idea the huge amount that Sid was supposed to collect. Sammy had stayed behind in Baltimore, but was picked up by the FBI simultaneously with the airport arrest of the three others.

In two days, the FBI's sting made national news.

Along with it, my gambling problem went from something only my closest friends and family were aware of, to the whole world suddenly believing that Art Schlichter, Ohio State's All-American quarterback only a year earlier, was a degenerate, low-life gambler.

On April 9, 1983, this was the *Columbus Citizen-Journal's* banner headline: SCHLICHTER FEARS FOR CAREER, LIFE. The story detailed the sting, my gambling problems, and stated that I was now in hiding somewhere in Ohio.

The next week, *Sports Illustrated* published a five-page story in excruciating detail of the sting, the bust, and my gambling, which spurred it all.

The story quoted Frank Kush: "A lot of these kids go through the system—college recruiting and the rest of it—living in a fantasy world. People think by the time they reach pro ball that they're men. They're not. It's just an extension of what they knew in high school and college—a fantasy world. The whole time they're coming up through the system, they think they can get away with anything. Then something happens and it's a shock to them."

Thinking about those words today, he probably was right.

The jokes were flying and the media was circling around me like moths to a porch light, as my life, career, and image were being served up as one sad punch line.

The running joke around Washington Court House at the time:

"Do you know who has the best-paying job in town? ...

"The guy who starts Art Schlichter's car."

With my addiction in the open, former teammates and even some coaches couldn't resist taking potshots at me.

I was watching ESPN once and heard Pagel say that I had stiffed him out of a $1,500 telephone bill during our rookie season and that I had called 38 states when we roomed together at Goucher College.

That's not true.

We had a high phone bill and I gave him money for it, but I called only Ohio and probably New York to get the scores.

I think he just wanted to tell a story, because we had competed for the job and never got along that well to begin with.

Not all the Colts took shots at me, however. The Hummer, one of the nicest guys I ever played with, called the house and talked to Dad. I guess he wanted to apologize for all the light-hearted locker-room comments he had made to me during my rookie season.

"Tell Art that I'm sorry," he said. "I didn't know he was sick. I just thought he was lazy, confused, or irresponsible."

Not everyone was that understanding.

One time I visited the football coaches' office at Ohio State when the recruiting coordinator, Bob McNea, said to me, "You know the word out there is that you threw the Rose Bowl by not pitching the ball on that option play at the one-yard line."

"You know Bob," I started, my voice rising, "that is the biggest piece of bullshit I ever heard. I played hurt when I was here. I always played hard, and I always played to win. I wanted to win more than anybody. So if anybody ever says that to my face …"

I was never a fighter, but I believed I might have taken a swipe at anyone who ever suggested such crap. As I said, I would never even think of throwing a game. Never thought about it. Never happened.

I laughed over the years when people asked me if I ever had any connection with organized crime. If they would have checked my track record, they would see that I was the most disorganized criminal ever.

Not everyone believed it, however.

I remember one night I told an old girlfriend back home about my problems. I never heard from her again. I guess some people were scared of being near me.

As the newspaper stories mentioned, I was hiding out—either at Gil Kirk's house or Chuck Freiburger's house. They became great friends to me and I will always appreciate them for all they did. Wherever I went over those next few months, I wore a hat or a hood to cover my identity.

I couldn't hide forever, so dealing with my problem became the next task.

Dad, Gil, and Chuck sent me to see Dr. Robert L. Custer, a psychiatrist who specialized in gambling addiction, in Washington, D.C.

From that first meeting, we struck up a friendship. He was probably the nicest, sweetest man I ever knew.

"Art, let me ask you some questions and I want an honest answer to each one," he explained.

There were 60 questions on this paper. I answered yes to 59 of them, and I think I hedged on the other one, just so I wouldn't have a perfect score.

Dr. Custer looked over my answers and gave me his instant diagnosis.

"Art, I want to tell you something very important," he said. "This is not your fault. You are sick. Very sick. You are a compulsive gambler. You need help. I can help you."

I started crying.

"Thank you," I said. "Thank you for telling me I am sick. I just thought I was dumb, stupid, or just had terrible luck."

It didn't take long for the NFL to contact me to discover the depth of my addiction, when, and on what games I had placed bets and for how much money. Commissioner Pete Rozelle wanted to know every dirty detail, so he sent Warren Welsh, the NFL's director of security, to Columbus. I had hired John J. Chester, an attorney who once worked for President Nixon during the Watergate scandal, to represent me.

Welsh grilled me one day in John's office, asking several questions, but these were the two most important, as far as the NFL was concerned:

"Did you bet on NFL games?"

"Yes."

"Did you bet on your own games?"

"No."

The NFL also asked me take a lie-detector test. I agreed and passed it. They were satisfied that I had never bet on Colts' games, which was the truth.

Rozelle then summoned me to a meeting at the NFL office on Park Avenue in New York on May 10.

I was accompanied by my lawyer, Dr. Custer, Gil, Chuck and of all people, Thaddeus Kostrubala, the running doctor from the desert. He limped into the meeting on crutches, having gone through reconstructive surgery on his torn-up knee.

Rozelle looked at him and must have thought, "Who the hell is this guy?"

I wanted to chuckle if the meeting wouldn't have been so serious, so crucial to my future.

"What are you doing now to get better?" Rozelle asked me.

I told him about Gamblers Anonymous and a treatment center in Amityville, New York, which I was scheduled to check into.

I think Rozelle and his assistants really wanted to learn about the illness, how it works and what it takes to be cured, if that was possible. They realized that I didn't throw games or anything like that. Heck, I hadn't played much during my rookie season anyway, but I wouldn't have crossed that line even if I had been the Colts' starting quarterback.

One newspaper report at that time quoted one of the Baltimore bookies stating that the only reason I never bet on a Colts' game was because we were such a "lousy" team. Not true. If that report were true, knowing we were so lousy, I could have bet *against* the Colts.

But I never would have done that, either.

And Rozelle realized that.

On the other side during that meeting, my lawyer begged for mercy for me because we realized a suspension was coming. The rest of my legal team also said something on my behalf and we walked out. It was short and sweet. We had waited longer in the waiting room to see the commissioner than we had spent in the meeting.

My impression of Rozelle was that he was a real good guy, laid-back and very business-like and I believe he relied on his lawyers' advice to make decisions.

I checked into South Oaks Hospital in Amityville, an addiction treatment center, within a week. They admitted me under the name "Fred S." and placed me in detox with all these other people addicted to drugs and alcohol.

Within days, one of the workers there informed me that a reporter from *Sports Illustrated* was outside, snooping around, but he never found me and had driven away.

On May 20, ten days following my meeting with Commissioner Rozelle, my parents and John Chester called the center. They had summoned me to the office and placed a speaker phone on the desk.

"Art," John said. "They suspended you for life."

"For *life*?" I asked. "I told them the truth and came clean … how can they suspend me for life?"

(It turned out the suspension was "indefinitely" and if I did all the right things, it would probably last for no longer than one season. Rozelle released a statement when announcing the suspension: "Art now fully appreciates the damage his action caused to the team and to the entire NFL as well as to himself and his family. He fully understands the consequences of further conduct detrimental to the integrity of the National Football League and the public confidence in it.")

After I exploded when I heard the severity of the suspension, I stood up. I wanted to get to my room as fast as I could and pack my things.

"Well, I'm coming home!" I said. "I'm tired of all this stuff."

"No, no, you need to stay right where you are," Dad said.

They convinced me that I had to stay the entire 30 days.

My name was now linked with Alex Karras and Paul Hornung, the only two players the NFL ever suspended for gambling. It wasn't a group in which I wanted to be included, but it was what it was. I made my bed and I had to lie in it.

In a day or so, I decided to put the 30 days to good use. They had a little gym there, so I worked out daily, doing sit-ups and push-ups and even running. I lost 30 pounds in those 30 days.

I also attended Gamblers Anonymous meetings. One day, as I slouched into my chair in the back of the room listening to all these sad stories, a man named "Howie M." told his story.

"You know, I am the sickest, most compulsive gambler there is. My wife is ready to leave me. I never would have come here tonight, but I read in the newspaper about this sick bastard football player named Art Schlichter. The newspaper said he is getting help and getting treatment. Well, I thought, 'If *he* can get help, *I* can get help.'"

A few days later, I was walking down the hallway at the South Oaks treatment center and here came Howie M. walking toward me.

I stopped him.

"Hey man, did you check in here?" I asked him.

"Yeah, I did," he said.

"I was at the GA meeting the other night and heard you talk," I said. "My name is Art."

"Art?" he asked.

"Art Schlichter."

"GET THE FUCK OUT OF HERE!" he said, his eyes wide as saucers.

"Yeah, it's me."

Well, Big Howie and I became the best of friends. He was about my age and his family owned several supermarkets, but he was as addicted as I was.

He told me about the time he won $110,000 and gave it to his wife to use it as a down-payment on a house.

"Honey, whatever you do, do not give that money back to me," he told her. "I mean it! DO NOT give that money back to me under any circumstances. Promise me!"

She promised. Well, Big Howie went out and lost $140,000 the next week and I think he was threatened by his bookie. He went back to his wife for the money.

"I'm not giving it back to you," she said. "You made me promise."

She wouldn't budge.

He said he waited until she got into the shower, then turned on a hair dryer and held it above her.

"Give me the money, or I will drop this hair dryer into the shower!" he demanded.

She gave him the money.

"You know," he told me later, "I was a real sick bastard. I probably would have killed her if she didn't agree to give me the money."

You know how sick he was? He took $200,000 to Las Vegas one time and walked through the doors of Caesar's Palace and shouted, "Big Howie's here! I am going to own this fucking place when I leave here!"

Six hours later, he was busted.

Caesar's gave him $100 and an airplane ticket to get home.

He then lost the $100.

Finally, they drove him to the airport and put him on the airplane just to get rid of him.

Big Howie's story shows what a severe gambling addiction can do to a guy.

I knew first-hand better than anyone.

I continued with GA meetings once I returned to Columbus that summer.

The next morning following my first meeting, I opened up the newspaper to the headline: "GA MEMBER CLAIMS SCHLICHTER STILL GAMBLING!"

That was my final GA meeting in Ohio for several years.

"I lost all my anonymity, even in a GA meeting, which is supposed to be sacred and secret," I told my parents. "I can't trust anybody."

The fact is, I was still gambling.

One night Bill Hanners and I drove out to Scioto Downs, my old stomping grounds. This time, unlike the good ol' days, I could not afford to be seen there, so I sat in a car while Bill ran my bets in for me. I almost got nipped that night because Dom Tiberi, a good guy who was a reporter for the local CBS station, showed up with his cameraman.

"We hear Schlichter's here gambling," he told Bill.

"I haven't seen him," Bill replied.

Sitting in a car, in the parking lot outside the track, placing bets through a runner, only proves how sick I was. I was sick. Very sick. Addicted. A normal person would think, "I will just stop. Enough is enough."

But I couldn't.

Under suspension and without a paycheck, I had fallen into huge debt. I had to sell the condo I had purchased in Baltimore.

There were things I had to earn back before money—my image and respect.

I was getting pummeled in the media, so I did a few national interviews. David Hartman interviewed me on ABC's *Good Morning America*—"It was the worst time I ever went through, and maybe what I will ever go through," I told him. I went on the *Phil Donahue Show* as well.

Phil always took calls for his guests over his intercom. This one guy called in and asked, "I have a real gambling problem. I pick winner after winner after winner, but I cannot stop gambling. Art, help me, what can I do?"

"Can you give me your number?" I asked.

Phil didn't think it was too funny, but it got a good laugh from his audience.

I had not been out in public for months when Gil and I decided to go to Hank Williams Jr.'s concert in Columbus. I sported a hat and glasses for a disguise. It didn't work. Everyone recognized me.

As Hank sang his song, "The American Dream," which normally included the line, "the pitcher got a million dollars and the quarterback got two," he ad-libbed, *"the pitcher got a million dollars and Art Schlichter got screwed by the NFL!"*

The fans went crazy, but for the record, I never believed the NFL screwed me by suspending me. I think Hank had consumed a little liquid nourishment before that concert.

Ironically, Hank, a huge football fan, and I would become friends.

Before one of his concerts a few years later at Market Square Arena in Indianapolis, his agent invited me to Hank's bus.

"Hank," he said, opening the bus door. "Let me introduce you to Art Schlichter."

Hank hopped out of that bus, wearing those cowboy boots and a big-ass cowboy hat that made him look seven-feet tall.

"My God, I am a big fan of yours, Art," he told me. "But I got to tell you something, you cost me a lot of money on that Clemson game!"

He was referring to the Gator Bowl five years earlier, when I threw the final interception that led to Woody's firing. Turned out that Hank liked to throw down a bet or two as easily as he tossed down Jack Daniels.

That night in that bus, Hank removed his hat and showed me the scars from where he fell off that mountain in Montana.

"Numb from here on up," he said, pointing to his nose. "My eyes are so sensitive to the sun and bright lights that I always have to wear sunglasses."

We sat inside that bus shooting the bull about football and music until he had to head over to the arena.

Speaking of Woody, during my suspension I stopped at the ROTC building on Ohio State's campus to see him. His office was located inside the building, largely because he sometimes taught a military history course, during the last nine years of his life.

"You have to put this behind you!" he told me. "You can't let this beat you. You can't let it happen again!"

He asked about my parents and what was happening in my personal life. Woody was always a guy I just wanted to hug when I said good-bye, but he wasn't the type of guy who I felt like I could hug. He wasn't touchy-feely or soft.

I shook his hand—he always had the firmest handshake of any man I had ever met—thanked him and told him I would be back again someday.

I told myself that the next time I returned to his office, I would be a starting quarterback in the NFL with my gambling issues in my rear-view mirror.

In August, the Baltimore bookies pleaded guilty and received only a few months in jail, suspended sentences for real prison time, probation, and fines. I never heard from them or saw them again. I have no idea what happened to Sid and Sammy.

During my suspension, I had taken over the basement at my parents' house in Fayette County, driving Mom crazy. I would get out of bed at 11, throw my clothes all over the floor and create a real mess for her to clean up.

Mom would walk downstairs, survey the damage and yell at me.

"My God, Arthur, didn't you learn anything at that treatment center?" she asked.

"Mom, I went there to learn how not to gamble, not how to make my bed," I told her.

I was dead broke at the time, so I relied on Mom and Dad to support me for the most part. I passed the time by lifting weights, running, watching a lot of football, and mostly, staying out of the public eye.

The fact was, I was still sneaking a bet now and then, just not as often or as flagrantly. With my friends' help, I bet on quite a few horses at Scioto while slumped in the back seat of a car. Pretty sick, when I think about it all these years later.

Dad and I spent the year talking football and planning how I would get back into shape to win the Colts' starting quarterback job heading into the 1984 season, if I was reinstated by Pete Rozelle, that is.

It was like old times, as he and I mapped out my future and how successful I would become on the playing field. This time, unlike my earlier high school days, I don't think that my optimism and confidence matched his.

The Colts had drafted John Elway with the top pick in the 1983 draft, but they couldn't sign him. I don't blame them for taking him. They didn't know whether I would be reinstated or not, and I showed so little that first year. I couldn't imagine they were counting on me to come back and win the job. I was the first one to admit that I had looked like a complete bust as a rookie.

I was glad when Elway was traded to Denver, because it meant I still had a chance to come back and make the team.

On December 18, the Colts beat the Houston Oilers to finish my suspended season with a 7-9 record, a huge improvement from our winless team a year earlier. I saw only two or three of their games that season, because networks didn't carry Colts' games in the Midwest.

Pagel had started 15 of the 16 games, passing for 2,343 yards. He had thrown 12 touchdown passes, but 17 interceptions, and I believed then that if I got into the best shape of my life and somehow regained my confidence, I could beat him out for the starting job the following summer.

I couldn't wait to get back to Baltimore to redeem myself.

I never imagined the Colts wouldn't be there.

Chapter twelve

HELLO INDIANAPOLIS

"Mom, guess what I did today?"
"Oh my God, what did you do now, Arthur?"
"I got saved!"

A man by the name of William "Sonny" Walters, who had coached my seventh-grade and eighth-grade football and basketball teams, was a devout Christian who had been a great mentor for dozens of young kids in our county.

I grew very close to him during the year I was suspended. Sonny had given me a cassette tape of Gospel music called "More Than Wonderful" by a singer named Sandi Patty. I listened to that tape at least once each day, until it became scratchy. I instantly fell in love with the way she sang the lyrics to the song.

That song had moved me to think about God and why we were put here on this earth. I knew something was missing from my life, too. I had been suspended from football, had a gambling addiction and things weren't going well.

One day Sonny told me about a Christian crusade at Washington Court House High School.

My parents had always taken us to church when we were kids, but I never really grabbed the concept of God. I went to church because my parents had taken me, as if it were some chore like cleaning out the pigpens or feeding the cattle. I went to see my friends. I had prayed daily as I became a teen-ager, but I didn't put much thought into religion or why I was praying, as most kids don't.

That day at the crusade, when I was asked if I wanted to be saved, I jumped at the chance.

I went into a back room at the school with Sonny and confessed that I was a sinner, that I indeed believed that Jesus died on the cross for my sins and I now wanted to turn my life over to God.

It was October 16, 1983.

That is the day I was re-born. I rushed home to tell Mom the good news. Once I explained everything, she was happy for me, but Dad never said anything about it.

A little more than five months later, on March 29, 1984, I turned on the television and couldn't believe what I was seeing. Fifteen Mayflower 18-wheelers were moving the Colts out of Baltimore on a cold, snowy night.

They were packed and headed for Indianapolis, where team owner Bob Irsay had struck a deal to move his team into a new indoor stadium, the Hoosier Dome.

While the fans of Baltimore felt anger and betrayal, I was one ecstatic, happy son of a gun. Now I could drive three hours down the road from Fayette County to my new NFL home.

I also knew how Irsay may have felt, wanting a new stadium, because Baltimore's old Memorial Stadium was absolutely horrible, the worst stadium I ever played in.

I had never spent much time in Indianapolis, but I was from the Midwest, and I knew Indiana fans would welcome the Colts with open arms.

When the move was announced I was playing wide receiver for Kirk's Raiders ... in the United States Flag and Touch Football League. My buddies Chuck Freiburger and Gil Kirk had played in the league for years and Chuck was the established quarterback of the team. In fact, Chuck was inducted into the inaugural class of the USFTL National Hall of Fame.

I spent that spring playing touch football and the summer playing pick-up basketball, getting myself into the best shape since I'd been in high school. I also ran quite a bit and threw often, wanting to be ready if Pete Rozelle decided to lift my suspension.

On June 22, the commissioner did just that, announcing what I had eagerly awaited: I had been reinstated by the NFL.

That day, Chuck, Gil, and I held a press conference at the Athletic Club in Columbus. I told the media: "I'm certain I'm over the worst of it. My inner feelings tell me that. I am aware that I have a problem and I am aware that I have to work on it day by day. I will be in therapy for a long time. I don't think I'll ever be cured. Being a pathological gambler I'll always have to deal with the sickness and be aware of it and fight it, but I think that each day it continues to get easier to fight it."

That sounds about what I would say today. My feelings haven't changed over the years. The only thing I would add is that the consequences get greater and greater the longer you're involved in something so destructive. It never gets better. It really never gets easier.

As soon as the press conference finished, Gil, Chuck, and I headed upstairs to play some basketball—Gil and I teamed up to play Chuck and another guy. Chuck was intense when he played anything. I drove for a shot, he undercut me, and I landed on the side of my left foot and sprained my ankle, letting out a scream.

"Chuck!" Gil shouted. "I told you not to get so physical! Look what you've done!"

I never blamed Chuck, since he was a competitor just like I was.

That night, we went out to celebrate my reinstatement with a nice supper, then to a nightclub. I was out on the dance floor on that ankle like nothing had happened. After all, I had sprained my ankles about 2,000 times before.

But when I woke up the next day, my ankle was swollen about twice its size and as blue as a Smurf.

I had a job again, a purpose, something to look forward to, but now I had an ankle to rehab as I tried to maintain my peak shape. I spent the next two months running in a swimming pool and received treatment on that ankle daily.

By the time I arrived in Anderson, Indiana, the new location of the Colts' training camp, I felt great about the team's new city and my new start.

For starters, I was in great shape, for a change.

But I got off to a rocky start in camp and couldn't find my rhythm in practice during those first few days. That is when Kush pulled me aside.

"Hey listen, you have to relax," he said. "I know you're rusty, but you're going to be here, so don't worry about getting cut or any of those things. Just work hard."

That did make me feel better and I appreciated what he told me, so I worked ever harder.

One day after practice, I was standing near the field when a woman approached me.

"Are you Art?" she asked.

"Yes, I am."

"Art, my name is Sandi Patty," she said.

I was floored. I knew all about Sandi, her music and her career—she was one of the country's most renowned Gospel singers along with Amy Grant—but I had no idea she was a big football fan.

It turned out that she lived in Anderson, and Sonny had given her a call, asking her to go meet me.

What are the chances that I would become such a big fan of hers at the same time that Bob Irsay had decided to move the Colts to Indianapolis, and to establish a training camp in her hometown?

I told her how much I loved her music and how much her lyrics had helped me through a difficult time.

From that day, Sandi and I became very good friends.

The Colts helped me see a psychiatrist then and the NFL watched me like a hawk, but I know now that I still wasn't receiving the type of help I needed to recover. I still had the bug. My problem was that I had the bug in the 1980s when treatment for gambling addiction wasn't as effective as it is today.

No matter how hard I worked, though, I still didn't have any confidence throwing the football. When you lose your confidence in that league, it's all over for you. I tried to regain it, but I couldn't.

The Hummer was gone and now was a backup with the Los Angeles Raiders. Mark Herrmann, the former Purdue quarterback, had backed up Pagel in Baltimore during my suspended season, and entered the camp as the second-team quarterback, behind Pagel, and ahead of me.

To begin the '84 pre-season schedule, we traveled to Miami to play the Dolphins in the Orange Bowl. Trailing 31-0 at the half, in which I did not play, Kush came in to the locker room and delivered one of the best lines I ever heard from a coach: "Alright you rinky-dink sons of bitches, let's go out there and get our asses kicked for another half."

Priceless.

Before I ran onto the field to start the second half, my first action in more than 20 months, I was as nervous as I ever had been on a football field.

Frank grabbed me, "Okay, take your time. Don't try to do too much."

I rolled out of the pocket, ran to my left, looked downfield, figuring I was screwed because nobody was open. I reversed my field, ran all the way around to the right, saw an open receiver and threw the ball 40 yards downfield. One of the Blackwood brothers, Glenn or Lyle, ran it down and intercepted it.

As I walked back to the sideline, Frank smiled at me.

"I guess I got that over with," I said, letting out a chuckle.

Then Frank laughed, too.

Since it was my first time wearing a football uniform since my gambling issues became public, it also was the first time I heard the catcalls from the fans.

And I heard it all that night:

"SCHLICHTER, WHAT'S THE SPREAD?"

"SCHLICHTER, WANNA BET?"

"SCHLICHTER, LET'S GO TO VEGAS!"

I never reacted to fans in my life, figuring they paid the price of a ticket, so they had the right to yell what they wanted to yell, so I sat there, acting as if I was deaf.

Vernon Maxwell, a second-year linebacker from Arizona State who won the Defensive Rookie of the Year Award during my suspended year, was sitting next to me, listening to the taunts.

Finally, he turned around and came to my defense. Not articulately, but I appreciated it all the same.

"FUCK YOU!" he shouted.

Then he flipped them off for emphasis.

The next pre-season game was the highlight of my NFL career.

The city of Indianapolis was fired up to have an NFL team, so the Hoosier Dome was packed for the first-ever game. It was a playoff atmosphere in that big bubble, even for a pre-season game.

I was a midwestern boy, so the fans loved me, at least at the beginning. There were "Start Art" signs everywhere and the fans booed Pagel that night against the New York Giants.

I ran around back in the pocket, made three or four great plays, threw a couple of nice passes to running back Frank Middleton and also scored on a scramble as we won the game. The Hoosier Dome went crazy that night.

After the game, they pulled me out of the locker room to do a live radio interview over the Colts' network, which also was broadcast inside the stadium. As I talked, fans screamed, "Art, we love you!" and "Welcome back, Art," before chanting "Start Art! Start Art! Start Art!"

It felt great to play well, to win a game, and to hear the fans' approval again.

Still, I knew it was Pagel's job from Day One, or at least it was between him and Herrmann. They wanted to bring me along slowly and I was never in contention to be the starter at the beginning of the season.

I also figured that no matter what Kush told me, all of our jobs were on the line. That's just the way it is on a bad team, and again, we were a *bad* team. The coaches were under a lot of scrutiny, too.

We played another pre-season game at Denver in a few weeks and I got to see Elway again. It started raining so hard right before the game, a real monsoon. I had never seen it rain that hard in my entire life. The field turned into a quagmire.

It was Pagel's game to start and he slid all over the place, but on the other side, Elway was throwing BB darts into the wind as the Broncos moved right down the field. I couldn't even grip the football that night and he was throwing passes on a dime like it was a hot, sunny day with no wind. That's the night I realized John Elway was something special.

Through our first 10 games that season, we had a 4-6 record and I hadn't played much, although I did come off the bench to complete two of three passes in a violent rainstorm to help beat the Jets 9-5 at the Meadowlands.

Then the Colts traded Herrmann to San Diego and Kush started me the next week against New England. I completed 16-of-32 passes for 188 yards but we got trounced 50-17.

I played a lot during the final four games that season, all losses, but didn't do anything significant other than run for my life. I still didn't have any confidence. When I released the ball, I was throwing

Getting sacked, a frequent experience for me in the NFL.

with the hope it would get to the right place. My mechanics had eroded for the most part.

It showed in my statistics, too. In that 4-12 season, I completed 62-of-140 passes for 702 yards and only three touchdowns. I was intercepted seven times.

Before the 15th game of the season, at home against Miami, Kush made me the starter again. Gil, Mom, and Dad drove to Indianapolis for the game and

I was excited to be starting an NFL game with my friends and family in the crowd.

I drove the offense down the field on the first series, reaching Miami's 30-yard line before attempting a little dump pass which linebacker Bob Brudzinski, another Ohio State guy, tipped and then intercepted.

Frank approached me as I walked to the sideline and said, "We are going to put Mike in for a little bit."

"What?" I said, wondering if he was serious. "You're replacing me after ONE series?"

When I realized he was dead serious, I exploded.

"FUCK YOU FRANK!" I screamed. "You've got to be kidding me! You are humiliating me after just one series!"

I stood there and called him just about every name in the book.

"That'll cost you $500," Kush responded.

"You think I give a shit about $500?" I asked. "Make it $1,000, you son of a bitch!"

It was the first time since the Hula Bowl I ever raised my voice to a coach. I continued screaming at him as I stood behind the bench, until a few assistant coaches came over to calm me down.

A few minutes passed before Frank walked back to see me.

"You can forget about the fine, I know you are upset," he said.

"Fuck you!" I screamed again, walking away.

The next week, he resigned with one game remaining in the season.

On the day of his resignation, I really felt terrible that I had gone off like that and screamed at him. I walked into his office to apologize as he was placing all of his belongings in boxes.

"Hey Frank, I really didn't mean what I said the other day," I told him. "I appreciate what you did for me this year. You hung with me and cared for me. I wanted to thank you for it."

I had tears in my eyes, and I could tell he was starting to well up and was about to cry as well.

"Art, I know what you have been going through with this addiction," he said. "I don't understand it, but I do know it's hard for you. I will help you anyway I can. I wish you luck."

We shook hands and I walked out.

The Colts named Hal Hunter the head coach that day and he immediately named Pagel the starter for the final game, at New England.

Figuring I wouldn't play, I didn't look at the scouting report that week or prepare at all. It was freezing and snowing in Indianapolis that week and while trying to run the scout team, I couldn't complete a single pass. I just wanted the season to end.

On Saturday morning at 6:30, my telephone rang.

"Art, you asleep?" the voice asked.

It was Zeke Bratkowski, the Colts' quarterbacks coach.

Hoping to find someone open downfield.

"I just wanted to make sure you had brushed up on the scouting report and that you know what we are trying to do tomorrow," he said. "You need to dig into that scouting report and the game plan when you come in today, because you are starting."

I held the telephone off of my ear and whispered, "WHAT?"

"You have got to be kidding me," I thought after hanging up with Zeke.

It turned out that Bob Irsay had overturned Hal Hunter's decision to start Pagel.

It was cold and windy that Sunday at New England, not my type of day to throw the football with my small hands. Yet, I was playing decently and had passed for 188 yards and a touchdown, as we hung close to the Patriots. Trailing 16-10, we drove down the field and had a chance to win the game, but my final pass was intercepted.

My next pass, however, delivered that night at a restaurant outside of Indianapolis, would be completed.

Chapter thirteen

MARRIAGE AND FATHERHOOD

As the 1984 season came to a close, my relationship with the girl from California, Kim (Gidget), that had been on and off for the past two and a half years, was about to be off again.

Long-distance romances often don't work out well. This one was no exception.

A couple of my buddies, Dave and Billy Shepherd, who were prominent businessmen in Indianapolis, told me their brother Steve's wife had a best friend who was perfect for me.

"We've got somebody we can fix you up with," they told me. "She goes to Ball State and we think you'll really like her."

She was waitressing weekends at a small place in Carmel, Indiana, so I walked into the place to see what she looked like.

That was the first time I saw Michelle Marie "Mitzi" Shinaver.

She was a good-looking girl, so I gave the Shepherds the go-ahead. They made a date for all of us to go out to eat dinner that Sunday night after we arrived home from our road game at New England.

During the game, Patriots linebacker Andre Tippett hit me underneath my facemask, opening up a huge gash across my chin. I had been hit on the chin plenty of times before, but this time, it had opened up like a sliced grapefruit.

I walked into T.G.I. Friday's for our blind date looking like Abe Lincoln, sporting this huge, ugly patch on my chin. There were about six of us at the table, but Mitzi and I really hit it off. Then we went out dancing and I could tell right away that she had her act together.

She was very attractive, sweet, somewhat innocent and knew absolutely nothing about sports, which was just fine with me. She came from a good family and I could tell she always did the right things. She worked hard in school, majoring in business at Ball State in Muncie, Indiana.

I wasn't searching for "the one," as they say, but I wanted a good girl to be steady with at the time. I guess everybody wants someone to settle down and have kids with, and I was no different.

Little by little, we started seeing more of each other and I fell in love with her.

I played basketball on a team made of Colts players that off-season as we barnstormed the state of Indiana, competing in celebrity games. Mitzi came along with me and we had a blast.

She graduated from Ball State in the spring of '85, and by the summer, we had grown very close.

Of course, gambling still was a large part of my life.

I had been playing golf with some guys in Indianapolis, and losing money, since I wasn't a great golfer. I owed this guy $2,000 and wrote him a check.

"Once the season starts, and I've received a paycheck, you can cash that check," I told him.

I never thought another thing about it.

The Colts had named Rod Dowhower, who had been the offensive coordinator of the St. Louis Cardinals and had worked with quarterback Neil Lomax in a complex, wide-open offense, as the new head coach. During my first meeting with him, he told me, "Be ready. The competition will be wide open and the best guy will play."

I liked that idea.

I had worked with him in the off-season inside the Hoosier Dome and he really helped me. He knew a lot about the quarterback position and how to improve my footwork and mechanics. He was the first coach who ever charted every pass thrown during practices.

During that summer camp, it was nip and tuck between Pagel and me. I held my own and was feeling pretty good heading into the pre-season schedule.

In our third pre-season game at Denver, I threw a pass and crashed my thumb into a Bronco player's helmet on my follow-through. I knew it was broken but continued to play. By the middle of the third quarter, the ball was just rolling off my hand. I couldn't grip it at all.

I didn't practice at all the next week, which was Pagel's turn to start anyway. I knew my thumb would be an issue, but I was close to being named the starter and I didn't want the Colts to X-ray it.

Pagel didn't play very well in that game, so Dowhower named me the starter for the season-opener, at Pittsburgh. I think the Colts' coaches and ownership took the approach: "Hey, this is our number one draft choice, so this is it. He will either make it or break it this season."

Against the Steelers, I completed 12-of-25 passes for 107 yards, but we were getting killed in the second half when one of their linebackers, Mike Merriweather, hit me low and my knee just ripped apart. It was so swollen after that game, a 45-3 loss, I couldn't get my pants off.

I limped around for the next three weeks and watched Pagel start all three games.

On Thursday before our game with Buffalo, Dowhower called me into the office.

"Art," he said. "We hear you have been gambling again."

"I haven't been gambling on any ballgames," I told him.

"Well, on Monday, you have to fly to New York to take a lie-detector test for the NFL," he said.

That Sunday, we were leading Buffalo 49-17 at home and I heard fans screaming to put me into the game. Dowhower never made the move, so I figured there was a problem.

He called me in again the next day.

"Here's your plane ticket to New York, Art," he said. "I am releasing you today."

"What's this about?" I asked.

It turned out that the guy I had lost money to playing golf had called the Colts, wanting to know when his check would be good. That led to a series of events that had the Colts and NFL communicating, each believing I was gambling on football games.

I told Dowhower about the golf game.

"Sorry, Art," he said. "I am still releasing you."

I walked out of his office and never even stopped to clean out my locker. I just left everything—books, shoes, clothes, and equipment. I was humiliated.

It was October 7, 1985, three years, five months and 11 days after I took that draft-day telephone call from Frank Kush, and suddenly, I was no longer a Colt.

That also was the day when I realized Mitzi Shinaver was the one.

Her feelings for me never wavered after my release. She told me she would stick with me no matter what, or where we had to move.

She never cared that I played in the NFL or had been a star quarterback at Ohio State. And now, she didn't care that I was an ex-NFL quarterback without a job. She loved me for me.

I followed through and took that lie-detector test, but never heard anything about the results, so I figured I had passed. Otherwise, the league would have announced another suspension.

I still hadn't given up on making a career as an NFL quarterback, if only to redeem myself.

The next June, the Bills signed me as a free agent, to battle Frank Reich, Brian McClure and Bruce Mathison for the starting job during camp. As summer camp progressed, I believed I would win the starting job.

On the Thursday before the third pre-season game, as the team gathered on the field, Bills owner Ralph Wilson and his entourage walked over to address us.

"I have bad news and good news," he told us. "The bad news is that the United States Football League won its lawsuit against the NFL. The good news is that the damages are only one dollar. That means the USFL is folding."

No matter what Wilson told the team, it was terrible news for me. The Bills held the rights to Jim Kelly, who had played for the USFL's Houston Gamblers.

We flew to Houston to play the Oilers a day later. I started and remember throwing a beautiful 50-yard pass to Andre Reed, down the sideline, but he dropped it. We had the ball about 10 plays the entire first half. On the final play of the half, I threw an interception that was returned for a touchdown.

It was my final pass.

The next day, August 18, 1986, the Bills cut me and signed Kelly.

I returned to Columbus and sold insurance for a while, but absolutely hated it. I also sold vans for a Ford dealership, but the owner wouldn't place price stickers on the windows and we were just burying people with bad deals, and I didn't like it. I picked up my paycheck just before Christmas and walked out for good.

That next August, I had one more chance to play in the NFL when the Bengals wanted to sign me as a backup to Boomer Esiason. We had a deal all worked out but the league would not approve it because I had been arrested for illegal gambling a few months earlier.

I had been gambling on sports with The Q-Man again, this time in Indianapolis, through some golfing buddies. One of them was a bookmaker and the other was the moneyman who backed him.

The Q-Man and I had been winning week after week. Well, the moneyman grew suspicious, thinking the bookie was in cahoots with us. We had no idea, but he began taping our calls with the bookie to make sure we had been betting above board.

One night, the bookie and his buddy had too much to drink in an Indianapolis bar. They were shooting off their mouths about gambling while a guy sitting next to them overheard every word.

"So, you're bookies?" he asked. "I've been searching for someone to take some bets for me."

They hooked this guy up and took his bets. It turned out he was an undercover cop. When the police later raided the bookie to shut down the operation, my name and voice were all over the tapes they found. They arrested me and I later pled guilty and received probation.

Ultimately, that arrest prevented me from having one final shot at the NFL.

I was crushed. That was a horrible time because I felt I was ready to play and I knew my chances were dwindling.

It would turn out to be my final flirtation with any NFL team.

My final NFL career statistics: Thirteen games played, 91-of-202 for 1,006 yards, three touchdown passes, 11 interceptions, 161 rushing yards, one touchdown.

It's hard to tell how good I could have been if I had my act together. I know I was distracted the entire time, from the time I was drafted in the spring of 1982 until the NFL nixed my final chance in the summer of 1987.

I probably could have been really good, but it's not a guarantee. I had a good, strong arm, not an Elway-esque arm by any means. Then again, how many of those are there? He had the most incredible arm I had ever seen. Warren Moon was right up there, too.

And even though I saw guys in the NFL who had weaker arms than my arm, play a long, long time, I don't begrudge Elway, or Marino, or any of those guys who were about my age for any of their success. I didn't like McMahon much, just because he came off so cocky when I was around him, but I realize many of those other guys were better than me.

Those quarterbacks who received all of those accolades over the years and made all of that money … I could never say they didn't deserve it. *I* didn't deserve it. What happened to prevent me from being there with them is entirely *my* fault. I could have had a productive career, no question. I could have played eight or 10 or even 12 years.

Looking back to all the accolades and great things that were said about me after my sophomore year at Ohio State probably didn't help me. I had a couple of years left in college and I had to live up to those words and it placed a lot of pressure on me. We all know how I escaped that pressure. If they had said, "He needs to strengthen his arm, work on his footwork, do this or do that to someday become an NFL quarterback," that might have helped me.

In college, I needed more of the drive that I had in high school when I was trying to prove something to the people who booed me. In college I had those people telling me how great I was.

To be a great quarterback in the NFL, you need total focus, confidence in your ability, great mechanics, and a drive to succeed.

I learned it's impossible to possess any of those ingredients when you're fighting an addiction.

Mitzi and I became serious even though it was a three-hour drive to see each other. She had moved to Columbus for a brief time while my agent searched for another team that would sign me. But one day we broke up.

The Q-Man was at the center of it, mentioning some past indiscretion that happened before I had met her. She believed what he told her, packed up, and moved out of our apartment.

She moved back to Indianapolis, signed a lease on an apartment, and got a job, all in one day. By the time I arrived to try to talk her into taking me back, she was obligated to stay.

"Look Mitzi," I told her. "I don't want it to end this way. Let's get back together."

I wasn't cheating on her, and she believed me, unless you count the gambling.

Gambling was my only mistress.

After six months she took a job in Nashville and we continued to see each other long-distance.

We had reached the point where it was time to make a commitment or go our separate ways, so I sent her some roses and a poem. At the end of the poem, something silly that began "Roses are red …, " I asked her to marry me. It was on her birthday, February 20, 1988.

She said yes.

I knew she wanted to have kids. So did I, even though I was hell-bent on destroying my life by gambling. Mitzi, on the other hand, always believed in the common good and in doing things the right away.

Gil had been calling some Canadian Football League teams to see if there was any interest. Soon, the Ottawa Rough Riders offered me a deal in March and I accepted. The contract called for a $30,000 signing bonus and $120,000 salary, all in Canadian dollars.

The Rough Riders hadn't had a winning season in about 10 years and wanted a name player.

I went to camp but wasn't sure I would even make the team, so Mitzi didn't come up with me right away. I had a great pre-season camp, so she drove up with her sister and we found a place to live. I loved Canada, but I didn't love playing in Canada.

I started off fast, completing all nine of my passes in our first exhibition game and the fans figured they were getting the next coming of Johnny Unitas. Newspaper stories were describing me as the savior who would lead the Rough Riders to their first winning season in a decade.

I started the first couple of games, but that team was bad, very bad.

Funny thing about the CFL was that we played a game on a Tuesday night, then on a Saturday night, then a Wednesday night—three games in eight days.

I took a mean shot to my ribs on a Saturday game and couldn't breathe. That Monday, they X-rayed me and I still had trouble breathing as we caught a flight to Calgary for a Wednesday night game. I just thought they were badly bruised, but it felt like the worst injury I'd ever experienced.

It turned out that my ribs were broken, so they placed me on injured reserve in Calgary. Following my 30-day stay on the injury list, they waived me.

We packed up and headed back to Columbus.

Sadly, it takes me a while to remember the day we were married. I think it was … it was January 7, 1989, and it was very cold. We had a big wedding, with more than 200 people, in Carmel, and my brother John was my best man. Sandi Patty sang for us that day. Mitzi and I cried through the entire ceremony.

I had been sick with the flu the day before the wedding and struggling emotionally with my addiction worsening. Dad paid for our honeymoon in Jamaica as a wedding gift.

I entered the marriage struggling emotionally, trying to hide my addiction from Mitzi and yet, she knew most of it. The fact that I can't quickly recall the date of our wedding, yet I can remember the scores of games I bet on years earlier, is telling.

Getting away to Jamaica was good for both of us, because we were in a place where I could not gamble.

I rented a jet-ski one day and we headed out to sea. When Mitzi fell off the back of the thing, she couldn't get back on it. She must have tried for 15 minutes to climb back on that jet-ski but couldn't.

"Wait a minute," I told her. "I'll jump in and then push you up."

So I did, pushing her up on the jet-ski. Then I couldn't get on. We must have splashed and flopped around the jet-ski for half an hour, trying to get on that thing at the same time. It was comical.

On the airplane ride home, the laughing stopped.

I turned to Mitzi.

"Honey, I have to tell you something. I'm $10,000 in debt from writing checks I can't cover," I said.

Neither one of us had much money, just the gifts and cash we had received from our wedding. When we returned home, she returned them all for cash and handed me the money we had received. I think it amounted to $9,000.

Then she wrote thank-you notes to everybody.

That's when she realized she had married a gambler.

By the summer, Mitzi was several months pregnant and I was getting into deeper trouble than just accumulating debt. I had passed a bad check at a convenience store in Columbus and was arrested July 4.

Dr. Custer told me, "Look, you have to get treatment. There is a treatment center in Las Vegas and you need to check into it."

Las Vegas?

I was a compulsive gambler, sick as they come, and they wanted me to go to Las Vegas for treatment?

So I took off to Vegas one night that October.

I had about $600 with me when I landed. I gambled all night at the Gold Coast Casino, lost almost all of that money, then reported to Charter Hospital the next morning.

I met a wonderful psychiatrist there, Dr. Rob Hunter, who specialized in problem gambling. After two weeks, he told me, "Art, you are sick and need help. This would be a good place for you to live. We have an excellent GA here. If you can stay away from gambling in this city, you can stay away from gambling anywhere."

If anybody in authority told me I had to move to Las Vegas, I wouldn't argue. I put Dr. Hunter on the phone with Mitzi and told him to repeat what he told me.

She agreed. We would move to Vegas, if that was what it would take to get me cured.

I returned home to Columbus and one day my buddy Chuck Grubbs called, mentioning something about heading to Beulah Park to try to win a twin-trifecta. I grabbed some money and headed to Burger King, our meeting place near the track.

Since my troubles became public in 1983, I went to great lengths to conceal my appearance at the racetrack, never driving my car there. I even had the windows on Chuck's car tinted dark so I could sit in the back seat and watch the races without any race fans spotting me.

I would drive my car to the Burger King and meet Chuck and we would drive his car to the track.

One rainy day, about a year earlier, Chuck, Bill Hanners, and I narrowly avoided a real tragedy.

As I watched a race from the backseat of his car, the horse I told Chuck to bet on for me came cruising ahead of the pack across the finish line. The problem was, Chuck didn't place my bet for me as I had instructed him. He had bet on another horse, costing me a lot of money.

We started to argue about it and as I swore at him, he snapped at me. "I don't need to take this abuse from you," he said. "We're leaving."

We left the track as I fumed from the backseat. I became so angry that I started beating the back of Chuck's head as he drove, as Bill tried to calm me down from the passenger seat.

Just as we pulled into the Burger King, Chuck's right foot, wet from the rain, slipped off of the brake and onto the gas pedal, sending the car shooting through the door of the restaurant. Glass flew everywhere as Chuck's car plowed right into one of the countertops.

Remarkably, nobody was sitting there eating a burger at the time.

I scurried out of the backseat and headed to my car, yelling, "I wasn't here! I wasn't here!"

Chuck and Bill knew not to tell the police, who would be arriving soon, that I had been with them and that we were coming from the track.

There was a picture in the newspaper of the car resting inside the Burger King and it never became public that I was there or that my beating of Chuck had caused the crash. As it turned out, the police didn't give Chuck a ticket since it had occurred on private property and his insurance even paid Burger King for all the damage.

Thank God we didn't kill anybody and as the years passed, Chuck and Bill and I laugh about that day even though I never got over not winning that bet.

This time, though, Chuck and I hit the twin-trifecta that paid us $25,000. Instead of paying off some debts and bills, he and I packed up Mitzi's tiny Toyota Supra and drove 100 miles per hour toward Vegas.

Since Mitzi was pregnant, she had planned to fly out in a couple of weeks.

I was supposed to rent an apartment, buy some furniture, and arrange for the electric and telephone to be turned on before she arrived.

Instead, Chuck and I headed right to the casinos and gambled for 48 hours straight. We lost almost every penny. I saved just enough to get the apartment and have the electric turned on, but not enough to buy any furniture.

That's how we started our life in Las Vegas.

I landed a job as a salesman for a beer distributorship. One of my duties was to call on all the casinos, dealing with the food and beverage managers to discover who needed deliveries and so forth. I would walk into a casino at 6:30 in the morning, gamble all day, report back to work at the end of the day, and bullshit my way through some report to make it look like I had worked the entire day.

Mitzi knew I was gambling, but I think she just hoped I would grow out of it.

Soon, I was working as a used car salesman.

One day in early February, 1990, Mitzi called me at the used car lot and said, "Art, I think I am having the baby."

I rushed home, drove her to the hospital and stayed that night, sleeping on the floor. The doctors finally told us, "No, you're not having the baby for a long time," so I drove her home and I went to work. A few hours later, she called me again. "On my God, Art. I am having the baby this time!"

We checked into the hospital again, I slept on the floor again, before the doctors told us, "No, you're not having the baby yet."

This time, they admitted her.

I wasn't looking forward to sleeping on the hard floor for the third straight night, so I told Mitzi I was headed out to grab a bite to eat with one of my buddies. "Red Ronnie," as everyone called him because of his distinguishable hair color, was a sick gambler just like me.

"We'll get something to eat and be right back," I told Mitzi.

Red Ronnie had a food coupon at the Las Vegas Hilton. I walked into the casino and bet a wad of money on the LSU-Notre Dame basketball game. Laphonso Ellis was playing for Notre Dame then and Shaq was the center for LSU.

We ate and returned to Mitzi's hospital room.

"It will be only a few hours now," the nurse told me.

Mitzi was trying to hold off on getting the epidural as long as possible. She was counting her contractions, dealing with the pain, and demanding, "Art, look at me. Just look at me! ART, LOOK AT ME!" as she counted.

Well, there happened to be a television in the room and I had it turned to the LSU-Notre Dame game.

I would look at her, try to help her count, and as soon as her eyes looked another direction, I would steal glances at the television, trying to find the score of the game.

"ART, DAMMIT, LOOK AT ME!" she screamed in pain.

Finally, they gave her the epidural and our daughter was delivered soon after.

When Mitzi had been three or four months pregnant, I had seen a United Way commercial that the NFL had sponsored—they were common back then—with Jets quarterback Kenny O'Brien. In the commercial, Kenny said, "Let me introduce you to my wife Stacey and my daughter Taylor ..."

"Taylor," I thought. " ... I really like that name."

"Okay, you can have Taylor," Mitzi told me. "But I get to pick the middle name. It's Renee."

Taylor Renee Schlichter was born February 4, 1990.

With Mitzi and Taylor, in 1991

I lost the basketball bet, but gained a daughter. All in all, it was one of the greatest days of my life.

I was now a father, but even that status didn't stop me from gambling.

Times were hard financially in the next few months, so Mitzi accepted a job working as a telemarketer for Kelly Knievel, one of Evel Knievel's sons.

Out of the blue one day, I got a call from a man named Gary Vitto.

"Art, this is Gary Vitto, I am the general manager of the Detroit Drive of the Arena Football League," he told me. "Perry Moss is our head coach and we're looking for a quarterback. Do you have any interest?"

I didn't know a thing about the Arena Football League.

"Well, I live in Las Vegas and I have a pretty decent job here," I told him, which was a flat-out lie.

"Why don't you fly in and visit with us and if all goes well, we'll make you an offer?" he said.

I told Mitzi, "What do I have to lose?"

"Go see what they have to offer," she told me. "It has to be better than what we're making now."

The team sent a limo to the Detroit airport for me and treated me like a rock star.

"Listen Art, our practices start in three weeks and we want to win," Gary told me during our first meeting. "We'll take care of you if you sign with us."

I learned that most of the players in the league were making $400 or $500 per week, so I figured they would offer me that or perhaps a little more. They took me to a hotel and Gary sat across from me, prepared to offer me a contract.

"Let me write down what I think we can pay you for one season," he said, scribbling on a note before handing it to me.

I figured his note would read "$10,000" or "$15,000" at the most. As I said, I have bad eyes, so I was checking closely to determine if his scribbled figure was $7,000 or $70,000.

It was $70,000!

"Well, that is a nice offer Gary, but I got a nice job in Vegas, I have a newborn baby and my wife and I have been trying to get settled somewhere," I said. "We really like Vegas."

"To tell you the truth, if you really want a nice place to settle down," he said, "why don't you move here and work full-time for the team? We'll pay you even more and you can work in promoting the team during the off-season."

I paused for just a moment.

"Okay, but I need some money up front," I told him. "And I want a commitment that if we win, and get into the playoffs, I receive some bonuses."

I flew back to Las Vegas with a $15,000 signing bonus check, a contract for an $80,000 salary and bonus clauses of $5,000 for playing in the first round of the playoffs and $10,000 for reaching the second round.

I never arrived home with that entire bonus.

After cashing the check, I hit a few casinos, lost a few thousand, then went home to Mitzi. I handed her about $8,000 of the bonus and she was thrilled to death, but I didn't dare tell her about the rest that I had just gambled away.

I worked hard to get myself into shape over the next three weeks. Then I flew to Detroit to resurrect my football career.

Chapter fourteen

LIFE IN THE ARENA

B y the time I arrived in Detroit in the spring of 1990, I knew little about the city other than a lot of Michigan fans lived there. I knew even less about the Arena Football League.

I learned to love both.

Mike Ilitch, the founder of Little Caesar's Pizza who also owned the NHL's Detroit Red Wings, owned the Arena team and ran it as a first-class business.

I am sure the Arena franchise was just a toy for him. Even though he continued operating the team year after year in red ink, he loved the game and the pure entertainment it provided fans.

He wanted to win championships, no matter how much money he was losing.

And that was fine with me.

The Drive had won the first three league championships and Mr. Ilitch and Gary Vitto were looking for a fourth when I arrived.

The Arena Football League had been founded only three years earlier and many followers of the league believed it was ready to explode in popularity, although in 1990, there were only six franchises: Detroit, Denver, Pittsburgh, Dallas, Tampa Bay, and Albany.

I didn't learn the intricacies of the game—played on a 50-yard field with eight players per side—by watching film or studying the playbook. I learned through on-the-job training.

During our first game, I didn't know half the rules. I dropped back and saw two linebackers coming at me unblocked and thought, "What the hell? How am I supposed to stand back here and complete passes if our offensive line is so terrible?"

I was sacked three plays in a row. The opposing team, the Pittsburgh Gladiators, were penalized three times in a row.

Then I heard our coach, Perry Moss, just giving the officials holy hell.

"What are they doing?" he screamed. "They can't do that. You can rush only one linebacker!"

Rush only one linebacker?

What kind of rule was that? When we went into overtime that night, the coaches had to pull me to the sidelines to explain the overtime rules. Over time I learned the game very well.

Whether the coaches would learn to love me was another matter.

Calling a play for the Detroit Drive, in 1990.

Moss was one of those old school coaches who cussed about every other word.

Perry would stand off to the side during practices and I would run the offense through our series of plays. I remember during one practice, I probably was in a bad mood, maybe from losing bets and dodging bookies. We were practicing without pads, just playing pitch and catch, trying to get our timing down.

I dropped back to throw a quick hook and a young defensive lineman jumped up and knocked down the pass. One of the unwritten rules for a defensive lineman: Don't knock down your quarterback's passes during a light, walk-through practice.

"Keep your hands down!" I said. "We're just working on our timing."

"Fuck you, Mister Big-Time Quarterback!" the rookie shot back.

It pissed me off, so I told Reggie Mathis, an offensive lineman, "I'll fix this kid. Reggie, just step to the side this time and let that big son of a bitch come right in here."

I took the snap and took two steps back, Reggie moved to the side. I fired the football right between his eyes, as his head snapped back hard.

When he regained his senses, he charged me.

Fortunately, my linemen stepped in to protect me, making sure I didn't get my ass whipped.

Perry exploded.

"WHAT THE FUCK ARE YOU DOING?" he screamed at me.

"Just teaching that son of a bitch to keep his hands down," I answered.

"Goddammit, you rinky-dink Johnny Unitas wannabe!" he screamed. "If you ever do that again, I will cut your ass!"

Every time I think of that story, I laugh. I couldn't stay mad at Perry because I grew to love him and I don't believe he ever would have cut me, either.

I quickly learned one way to succeed as an Arena quarterback—throw deep.

All of these other quarterbacks in Arena football spent their time dinking and dunking underneath, but I loved to line our receivers up and send them deep all the time. Throwing the deep ball always had been one of my best throws anyway. And I believe that's why we were so successful that first season.

Once I learned the game, I called all of our plays. Opposing defenses couldn't stop us. I had some good receivers to throw to, like George LaFrance, Gary Mullen, and Dwayne Dixon, who later became a college assistant under Steve Spurrier at Florida and now coaches at Ohio University where my nephew Miles is a walk-on quarterback.

As we started racking up huge passing yards and winning games, *Sports Illustrated* sent a reporter to Detroit to write a story about me that first season.

"Everybody makes mistakes and we felt that Art's problems were all in his past," Gary Vitto was quoted as saying in the article. "And let's face it, he does have some name recognition."

The story also detailed how some fans on the road taunted me with gambling jokes. "The fans pay their money so they can yell whatever they want," I said. "Sometimes I get a good laugh myself."

I always had a good sense of humor and I certainly needed one playing in the Arena league. Those were the times, though, when I realized I was a long way from the NFL.

The team's equipment manager had used a long steel pole that slid through the locks of the team's equipment room. It was an extra security piece to prevent theft. The arena was located in downtown Detroit.

One day this big, tall, rookie defensive back—I cannot remember his name but he was from Southern University—got into a fight with Reggie Mathis in the locker room.

The rookie defensive back was stark naked, but that didn't stop him from grabbing this steel pole and chasing Reggie, who was wearing only his underwear. Reggie ran out of the locker room, moving quicker than I ever saw him move. He chased him out onto the field and then down under the stands at the other end of the field. Reggie knew if he could get under the stands next to all of the seat supports, there was no way the rookie would be able to swing that long, steel pole at him.

He didn't want to just take a swipe at Reggie, he really wanted to kill him.

I stood there watching the whole scene and thought to myself, "Only in the Arena Football League."

If that had happened in the NFL, about 10 reporters covering the team would have splashed it all over the front pages the next day.

I certainly didn't want Reggie to get hurt. Reggie, who was from Oklahoma and had played two years with the New Orleans Saints before falling into the Arena league, was one of my favorites.

There were a few other great guys on that team, such as Flint Fleming, a lineman who lived next to us, and Tate Randle, who came from Texas Tech and had played six years in the NFL. Tate, who had played three seasons with the Colts, coinciding with my time with the team, was the best defensive player in the league, and a large part of why we won the Arena Bowl championship by beating Dallas 51-27 during my first season. I was named the league's Most Valuable Player.

When my teams were winning, no matter what sport I ever played, it was always fun for me. But winning in the Arena league was even better. Whether it was my miserable experiences in the NFL and CFL, I don't know, but I can honestly say I had a blast, perhaps because I had not played on what I considered a successful team in 11 years, since my sophomore season at Ohio State.

Plus, it was fun playing for a great general manager like Gary Vitto, a guy I loved like a brother, Mister Ilitch who was a supportive owner, and Perry Moss who I greatly respected. We packed the house at Joe Louis Arena every game, although I think the Drive gave many of the tickets away. Their philosophy was to attract as many fans to the games no matter what it took. They made lots of money selling pizza and beer.

One of the perks of playing in the league was a two-week promotional trip during the spring of 1991 to Barcelona and Paris. I took Mitzi and we enjoyed each other more than probably anytime in all our years together. We walked on the beach in Barcelona and visited the Eiffel Tower in Paris, talked about our life, and about having more children.

It was a perfect setting for us to reconnect for one reason: I couldn't gamble overseas and I focused only on her.

Everything had come together to make it one of the most enjoyable times of my life.

I also loved living in Detroit and its lifestyle. We lived in a high-rise building on the river, looking across to Canada. Fortunately, this was before casinos had been built all around the downtown area. Naturally, I sniffed out the bookies and found the horse track. That's all I needed to get into trouble.

One Sunday night I told Mitzi I was headed out to meet a buddy of mine to watch some football and would be back in a few hours. Instead, I was headed to the DRC, the local racetrack, but first I had to get some cash.

I stopped by one of those quickie check-cashing stores, pulled out my checkbook and wrote a check for a few hundred dollars. The cashier was about to pay me when he noticed my account was on a blackballed list for bad checks.

"Let me go to the back a second, I'll clear this up for you and get you the money," he said.

I figured this could be a problem, but I couldn't walk out of there, because he had my driver's license. I peeked through the curtain and noticed that he was talking on the telephone. About five minutes later, I'll be damned if a police car didn't pull up.

"You're under arrest for writing a bad check!" the officer told me.

"Well, how do you know it's a bad check?" I asked him. "It's Sunday night."

He wasn't listening to any of my explanations. He just hauled me down to police headquarters and threw me in the holding tank. I knew I was in big trouble, with Mitzi home alone with Taylor and me due back in a few hours.

With my one phone call, I called Harold Fried, a high-powered attorney who had represented many professional athletes in Detroit.

"I am going to get into some real trouble if this gets out," I told him.

"Well, who is there right now?" he asked. "Is the police chief there or somebody high up I can talk to?"

It didn't take long for Harold to push the right buttons to get me released.

I arrived home at about 11 that night, told Mitzi I had been at a bar watching football with my buddy. I never told her about the bad check or the hours in jail.

The Drive increased my salary to $100,000 for the 1991 season, and we picked up right where we left off, throwing deep and winning games.

I think there were a few players in Arena football who could have played

Going deep during a game in 1991.

in the NFL, or *the league,* as players call it. But most of the guys were a step slow or a tad small and were just happy to be making $400 or $500 per game playing football rather than digging ditches during the summer.

At the time, I believed I could have succeeded in the NFL if I had been given another chance. I still believe that.

I was now 31 years old and more mature than I was when I was with the Colts. I had my confidence back and my skill level had increased to where it once was. I had worked on my mechanics and I was throwing the football better than ever. I really believed I was good enough to play another six or seven years in the NFL.

If only I could have stopped gambling and stayed out of trouble when it mattered.

But I knew there was no way the NFL would let me back in the league, especially after what happened four years earlier when the Bengals wanted to sign me. I was considered damaged goods and not worth the trouble.

By the end of the 1991 season, we had a 10-1 record, but lost the Arena Bowl championship game 48-42 to Tampa Bay.

You would think Gary Vitto would have wanted me to remain in Detroit and play as long I could, but I never learned my lesson from dealing with the Baltimore bookies. I owed some guys in Detroit from my gambling debts and that's a tough place to be a gambler who owes money. Gary had bailed me out two or three times, paying my debts. He gambled a little himself, so he understood my trap.

Following that season, the league announced Cincinnati had received an expansion franchise.

It was a natural move, for Detroit, Cincinnati, and for me, so the Drive traded me for the betterment of the league. Every team owner wanted the other teams, especially the expansion teams, to flourish and they knew I could attract fans for Cincinnati. The league itself was growing in popularity, as it increased to 12 teams for the 1992 season.

I signed a deal worth about $100,000 for my first season to play for the Cincinnati Rockers and Mitzi, Taylor and I left Detroit and headed back to Ohio.

I really wasn't sure how Cincinnati would take to the game until the first night we played. Ironically, the Rockers hosted my old team, the Drive, and Riverfront Coliseum was packed with fans. In fact, the Reds played at home that night and I think we had more fans at our game than they did at theirs.

We beat the Drive and I had a great game, throwing for a lot of yards and touchdowns. It was a great start.

Soon, Rockers tickets became the hottest tickets in town that summer. We averaged 13,682 fans per game.

We had a receiver named Ira Hillary, who had played four years in the NFL, including three with the Bengals, and he would catch just about anything I threw near him. We won seven of 10 games that season, but lost to Tampa Bay 41-36 in the first round of the playoffs. It would be the final organized football game I ever played.

The Rockers were owned by Cincinnati restaurant-owner Ted Gregory and his sons. It turned out that Gregory also had close ties to Turfway Park, the horse track just outside Cincinnati on the Kentucky side of the Ohio River.

It didn't take long for me to write some bad checks at the track, so the Rockers arranged to dock my weekly paycheck and reimburse Turfway. Some of my paycheck went directly to Mitzi and some of it went to Turfway through some special arrangement by the general manager, Keith Sprunk.

One afternoon near the end of the season, I turned myself in at Cincinnati police headquarters on a bad-check warrant, got booked and finger-printed, was released from jail, went to a pep rally, then passed for three touchdowns as we beat Cleveland the next day.

Not your usual pre-game routine by any means.

Cincinnati is where I got my start in radio, too.

I had teamed with a veteran broadcaster, J.C. McCoy, for "The Rockers' Report" on WSAI-AM, an all-sports radio station. J.C. also had a regular sports-talk show.

When the '92 season ended in August, station general manager Jim Woods called me.

"Art, J.C. is headed for a two-week vacation. Why don't you sit in for him until he gets back?" he asked.

"Sounds good to me," I said.

That first day, we just got bombarded with telephone calls from listeners wanting to talk sports with me. I really didn't know what I was doing. I just took the calls and talked about what I knew. There isn't a topic I know better than sports.

After a few hours, Jim came springing into the studio during a commercial.

"You're a natural!" he told me. "I want you full-time. Will you do it?"

"What time slot?" I asked.

"Drive time, three to six," he said.

"But that's J.C.'s slot," I told him.

"Not anymore," he said. "Now it's yours!"

J.C. arrived back from vacation and was given a later time slot and I was given a great contract.

By the time I talked to the Rockers about coming back for the 1993 season, their tone had changed. I think they had grown tired of my gambling antics and my bad checks. They had heard the stories of how much I owed to whom, so they offered me only $25,000 to re-sign.

"We would like you to take a pay cut," they told me. "We are worried about your public image."

"Well, I am not going to play for that," I said.

One day on the air, I made it official.

"Hey, I love it here on radio, so I won't play with the Rockers next season," I told my listeners. "I am retiring from football."

And that was that.

Those three years playing in the Arena league were a real shot in the arm for me. I loved playing football again and I had a great deal of success, which naturally made it more fun.

I know now that my career ended too soon.

When Detroit came to town to open the '93 season, I attended the game with Mitzi and Gary Vitto, who had grown close to her and Taylor. Sitting there that night, watching the Rockers and Drive compete, I felt bitterness about how I believed I had been forced out.

I think the Rockers later regretted it, too, especially since there were about 3,000 fans in the arena that night. They had a losing team that season on and off the field. Attendance dropped like a rock. The team lost more than a million dollars before folding operations.

It was a sad ending, for the Rockers and for me. If I had taken care of myself, and whipped my gambling habit, I know I could have played seven or eight more years in the Arena league, made a lot more money and enjoyed completing hundreds more deep passes.

But I was addicted and stupid.

I needed money so badly I sold my two Big Ten championship rings, my Rose Bowl ring, my bowl watches and trophies to a restaurant owner, Willie De Luca, who along with his father owned a popular restaurant in Cincinnati called Sorrento's Pizza.

"Don't ever sell them," I told Willie. "One day I'll buy them back from you."

Willie had put my things on display in his restaurant, and may have sold a few of them, but Sorrento's burned to the ground in 2005 in a fire that killed his father, Enrico. The mementos from my football career were lost.

And Willie died of a heart attack the following year.

Mitzi and I experienced our own heartbreak during our time in Cincinnati. It was January 17, 1992, and what happened is still very hard to talk about.

We lost a child.

Mitzi was seven and a half months pregnant with our second child when, during an ultrasound, the doctor could not detect a heartbeat. They rushed her to the hospital.

They quickly induced labor and hurried her to the delivery room, hoping for the best. As the doctor lifted the baby from her, I could see he was not moving.

Our baby was stillborn.

It was a boy.

"Art, what can you see?" Mitzi asked. "Can you see his face?"

I lied to her and told her he was not fully formed, but I saw my son's face and he was beautiful. I never told her that, because I knew that would only make it worse for her. She had been through enough.

We named him Shane Arthur Schlichter. It was the same day my Grandma Weatherly died.

I think we both blocked out the pain for a while and didn't know how to deal with it. It was such a traumatic experience for both of us, but we didn't know how to help each other through the pain. I blamed myself for his death because I realized my gambling problems had placed so much stress on Mitzi during her pregnancy.

The pain and stress of losing a child sent me into a gambling tailspin once again. Since leaving Detroit, I had been sending money to some buddies in Vegas to bet sports events for me. To numb the pain of losing my son, I starting betting more money, more often.

That next year, Mitzi became pregnant again.

Later, the doctors thought they saw something irregular in some tests.

"That could mean Down Syndrome," they told us.

They recommended more tests to be sure.

"No thanks," we said. "We'll love this baby whether it has Down's or not." We both felt that way.

Mitzi was scared to death throughout that entire pregnancy, worrying almost daily if this baby would be born healthy.

Naturally, I gambled heavily at the time and people at the radio station knew it. I even had conned some listeners who called in out of some money, so once I started mixing my job and my addiction, it was bound to end badly.

The station itself was having problems and was in the process of being purchased by another radio conglomerate. I had a choice: I could stay in Cincinnati, spin my wheels and face the music without football, or we could find a new place to live.

I also had a sneaky suspicion that my two buddies I was using to place my bets in Vegas, two guys I had met years ago at the racetrack in Cincinnati, were "booking" me. In other words, I would overnight money to them, but they were not placing my bets, figuring I would lose anyway and they could pocket the money.

You never want to believe your real friends would do that, but they were also sick gamblers like me. "Red Ronnie" and I had had our differences over the years, but I always have considered him one of my best friends over the past 20 years.

One day, before he had moved to Vegas, he had a tip on a twin-trifecta race at Lebanon Race Track, so I went around Cincinnati writing checks to gather enough money to make a big score. Sure enough, I won the first leg of the trifecta. When the second leg came, I had bet on a certain horse that *had* to win for us to collect about $60,000.

Well, that horse broke stride at the start of the race.

"WHAT THE HELL?" I screamed.

Ronnie acted as if it was no big deal, easy come easy go, because it wasn't his money. Then he made some smart-ass remark to me and I snapped and threw him up against the fence. He didn't talk to me for about two weeks after that.

When he moved to Las Vegas soon after that incident, he became my source for placing bets at the casinos.

On a Monday night the week of Thanksgiving, 1993, I got lucky and hit an unbelievable parlay that would have paid $20,000 on a $1,000 sports bet. I stayed up to 2 a.m. listening to the final game, sweating out every minute of it, until the parlay was secured.

It was 11 p.m. in Vegas, but Ronnie was not answering his phone.

I didn't want Mitzi to hear me, so I walked outside wearing nothing but my underwear, tennis shoes, and a coat, swearing into his telephone answering machine.

"You dirty son of a bitch," I said. "I want my money."

He called me back and said he didn't have the winning ticket.

I was paranoid I was getting screwed and that night only heightened my paranoia. I wanted the ability to walk into a casino and place the bets myself.

I called the owner of an all-sports radio station in Vegas to see if he had an opening. We had a nice conversation, he asked for some of my tapes and within 24 hours after receiving them, he called me back and offered a job.

The offer was a good one. The station would pay for our move, pay me $7,000 per month and 50 percent of whatever advertising I could sell for my time slot.

Talking Mitzi into even thinking about moving back to Vegas would be easy on only one account—she had loved her obstetrician, Dr. Jamison, during her pregnancy with Taylor four years earlier.

We flew to Vegas and visited Dr. Jamison on New Year's Eve day. Mitzi was five months pregnant and I know she wanted that doctor to see her through to delivery.

"Come out here to live and I will take care of you," Dr. Jamison told her.

I know that set her mind at ease.

That night, we saw Barbra Streisand in concert and had a great time. I knew Mitzi was not too happy about the thought of moving back there, but at the same time, she was thinking of her baby.

"If we move here, Art, this is your last chance," she told me. "I really mean it this time. I can't continue to live like this. If you screw up again, I am gone."

I promised her I would go back into treatment once we reached Las Vegas, but I figured then she would move with me, make sure the baby was born healthy, and if I had not straightened out, I would lose her.

Still, I didn't want to think about that. I was excited about the prospect of moving back to Vegas, the prospect of being able to bet legally without interference. No bookies, no go-betweens who would rip me off. No problem.

Within a year, I predicted to one of my friends, I will either make a million dollars or be headed to prison.

Chapter fifteen

BAD BEATS,
BAD CHECKS,
BAD LUCK

"*LADIES AND GENTLEMEN ... THE TRAIN, THE HOUSE ... HELL, HE BET THE HOUSE .... ARRRRTTTTT SCHLICHTER!*"

That is exactly how I was introduced each afternoon on KVEG, a 50,000-watt radio station in Las Vegas, where I hosted a show talking about what I knew best—sports, gambling, and sports gambling.

I loved doing radio, talking to guests, and taking calls. And I was good at it. I knew sports as well as anyone, had that gift of gab, and could offer an educated opinion on just about any player, any team, or any sport.

My show lasted four hours, but I could have talked sports for four days straight.

There's only one thing I could do longer without rest and with much more passion, but with much less thought—gamble.

Which, of course, led us right back to Vegas, arriving during the week of January, 1994, days before Super Bowl XXVIII between Dallas and Buffalo.

We had come full circle in only four years.

To recap our path since Mitzi and I began dating and subsequently married, we had lived in Indianapolis, Columbus, Buffalo, Columbus, Washington Court House, Ottawa, Columbus, Las Vegas, Detroit, Cincinnati and now we were back in Las Vegas.

All during a 10-year period.

Okay, we moved a lot. But addicted people always believe in change. A change of scenery. A change of location. A change of jobs, cities, spouses, etcetera.

An addicted gambler might think, "I'll move to Texas, since there are no casinos there," or "I'll move to the middle of nowhere because none of the people who are a bad influence on me will be there."

I was no different.

I was running away from trouble, leaving debts and bad checks behind me in almost all of those cities. Once I reached Vegas again, I really felt that I was on a crash course with either riches through a hot streak, or prison.

I was about to begin a year in which nothing, not a job or my family, would come before my thirst to gamble. I've faced this thirst my entire life, but in 1994, I was downright parched.

Take a weekend in February, as an example.

It was a Thursday and I had bet a few parlays on Major League Baseball exhibition games and college basketball games. After keeping a close eye on the scores as they trickled in, I realized that I had $5,000 in winning tickets to cash. I was eager to head to the casinos, collect that money, and bet on the late games that night.

But first I had a four-hour show to do. The station used an old transformer that blew up from time to time, knocking us off the air.

During a commercial that night, I asked my producer, a shaggy-haired guy, "Can you blow us off the air right now, so I can go cash my parlays?"

"No, I can't do that, we'll get fired!" he said.

"Listen, I just won $5,000, so knock us off the air, and I'll give you $500 of it," I said.

"Do you swear to God that you will give me that money?" he asked.

"I swear to God!" I responded.

He instantly started pushing buttons. Bing. Bang. BOOM! ... until the thing blew up. The producer then called the owner of the station, telling him the transformer had gone out on us again.

"Well, there's nothing you can do about it," the owner told him. "Shut her down and go home."

Go home? Right.

That began a four-day gambling binge that was wild even by my standards.

My producer and I rushed over to Treasure Island, where I cashed my tickets and slipped him the $500, as promised. By Saturday night, I had turned that measly $4,500 into $120,000 mostly by playing blackjack at $1,000 per hand, with a little craps, too, at Caesar's Palace.

Over the next three days, I would head home to the condo we rented on

Pecos and Tropicana to spend the days with Mitzi and Taylor, grab a shower, and as soon as they went to bed, head for the Strip again.

When Monday morning rolled around, I called the radio station and learned I was due to report back to be on the air at three in the afternoon. They had fixed the transformer.

I walked out of the MGM Grand to pick up my car, which I thought I valet-parked there the night before, but I couldn't find my valet ticket in my pockets. But I had a bigger problem. *I didn't have a dollar left to tip the valet guy.*

I had blown through $120,000 in two days of non-stop gambling.

"Hey man, I'm sorry but I can't find my ticket," I told the valet. "And I don't have any money to tip you."

"No problem, Art," the guy said. "Hop in this car and I'll drive you around until you find it."

Fortunately, most of the valet parkers knew me, either from my football career, my radio show, or simply because I was a good tipper. When we couldn't find my car in the garage, he drove me to the radio station. When we reached the station's parking lot, there was my car. Now I remembered—my producer had driven me to the Strip that Thursday night.

I arrived at 3:08 p.m. and began to fall asleep on the microphone since I'd barely slept in three days, as my producer counted down the seconds until I went on the air: "Art ... 30 seconds ... 20 seconds ... 10 ...."

When my producer concluded his intro, I lifted my head off of the microphone and slid into my introduction to the next four hours: "WELCOME TO SPORTS LINE! WE ARE TALKING SPORTS ALL DAY ... THIS IS ART SCHLICHTER AND WE'LL TALK RUNNING REBELS BASKETBALL, SPRING TRAINING BASEBALL ..." just as if I had spent the weekend on the couch, resting, reading, or watching television.

It was a typical Las Vegas weekend in the fast-paced, take-no-prisoners, messed-up life of Arthur Ernest Schlichter.

My gambling philosophy had followed one of our high school basketball philosophies: "Fire and fall back." It's what I did best, or worst—fire off a bet, then fall back to see if it worked out.

If it didn't, just fire again.

And even if it did work out well, I still fired again.

It wasn't in my constitution to walk away from the casinos that weekend when I was up $120,000, treat Mitzi to a nice dinner, buy some clothes, jewelry or even a new car.

An addicted gambler doesn't think that way, and I'm sure I was more addicted than your average gambler. I didn't care about nice dinners or jewelry or material things. I cared about the chase. I gambled more often and I gambled more money than anyone I knew or had heard of.

The answer is, an addicted gambler like me thinks he can turn the $120,000 into $500,000, then into $1 million.

Eventually, with that philosophy, you'll lose.

Eventually, I always lost.

When you're feeding the addiction, you don't think reasonably. You don't think ahead even to the next day. You think about this very moment on this very day.

That's pretty much how I thought, how I gambled and how I lost.

A few months later, the doctors had scheduled a C-section for Mitzi on May 19. It was so unlike Taylor's birth four years earlier when we checked in, checked out, and checked back into the hospital, not knowing when the big event would happen.

This time, it was almost like a business appointment. Our biggest concern, obviously, was whether the baby would be healthy. We crossed our fingers and I know I prayed often, asking God to give us a healthy baby.

When that little booger came out healthy, it brought Mitzi and I closer together. Our prayers had been answered.

Mitzi picked the name this time, Madison Brooke, and I took to calling her Maddy when she was real young. That's what I still call her.

Now we had two beautiful and healthy children, but I was probably at the worst point of my addiction. I did just about anything to get money to gamble. I even took money from Mitzi's purse. When you start stealing from your family and your friends, you know it's a matter of time before you're put in jail or you put a gun to your head.

I would walk into a supermarket and write a bad check. Or I would tell a friend to hold a check I had written, that it would be good in a couple of days, but it never was. I justified it by saying I would pay it all back.

A month following Maddy's birth, Mitzi's sister Christie came to live with us for a few weeks to help out with the kids.

Christie had her mail forwarded to the house, and during one of those binges when I needed money, I took a box of checks that were in her name and had arrived that day. She had an account in Colorado, but had closed it. I figured I could pass one of the checks at the casinos for cash, turn that money into big winnings, buy that check back and nobody would be the wiser.

Of course, as usual, I lost all of the money.

I tried to iron it out with the bank later, but the bank manager eventually called the FBI and reported me.

It didn't take long for the FBI to come knocking at our door. Mitzi answered it while I was at Caesar's Palace playing the horses with Red Ronnie, trying to raise the money to pay the bank. I knew they'd be coming down on me soon if I didn't come up with the money, but I never figured it would be so soon.

Mitzi called Red Ronnie's cell phone and he handed it to me. I could see a shocked look on his face.

"Art! You need to come home right away!" she said. "The FBI wants to talk to you!"

"Come on Mitz," I said. "Quit joking around."

"I am dead serious," she said. "They're standing here right now."

"Put one of those son of a bitches on the phone," I said.

She did.

"Listen," I told the agent. "You need to get out of my house right now! I'm asking you kindly to leave. This has nothing to do with my wife or her sister. I will meet you anywhere you want. Just get out of my house."

I met him in the parking lot at the Marie Callender's Restaurant on Sahara Avenue.

"Mister Schlichter," he said. "We can do this the hard way or the easy way. You tell me everything and I'll go easy on you, but you're still going to jail someday, I can guarantee you that."

"I'm going to jail no matter what I tell you?" I asked.

"Yes sir."

"Well then, once I get to jail, you can talk to my lawyer, but I'm not telling you anything now," I said.

I went out and hired a lawyer, Richard Cremins, because I realized the agent's words would ring true someday. I was building a mountain of trouble for myself by writing all these checks, and the FBI was following behind me, building its case.

I just couldn't stop.

I'm sure I figured that if I was headed to jail anyway, I might as well leave no stone unturned trying to win back the money I had lost. I always figured that winning would get me out of this mess.

Anyway, that episode with her sister's checks was the final straw for Mitzi. As she had promised seven months earlier, she followed through and told me that she would take the kids and head back to Indiana to live with her parents.

"I can't live this way any longer," she said. "I can't jeopardize our kids, our future, for all of the destructive things you do. I won't stand for it anymore. I am going home."

It took her a few weeks to get her things together. When that day came, I drove her, Taylor, and Maddy to the airport. I kissed the kids good-bye and stood there and watched that airplane pull away from the gate, all the goodness in my life pulling away with it. My heart was breaking as tears streamed down my face.

Once again, it was self-inflicted pain, one of the greatest of my life, and I knew it.

I left the airport and headed off to numb the pain. I probably was inside a casino by the time that airplane left the ground.

———————   ⬭   ———————

The summer of '94 had to be the worst gambling stretch I had ever experienced. I lost for 101 straight days, betting on Major League Baseball. I actually kept track of it. One hundred and one days of losing.

I take that back. There were two days I didn't bet—the Monday before the All-Star Game and the Wednesday following it. There is no baseball played on those days.

That summer, I may as well have flushed hundreds of thousands of dollars down the toilet.

To understand how I gambled and how I lost so much money in my lifetime, there are a few gambling terms to know.

A *bad beat* is slang for what gamblers label a bet that *should* have won, only to turn into a loss in the final minutes or seconds by a fluke or just by rotten luck.

Say I had bet on the Pistons to beat the Knicks and I had to give six points on the betting line. The Pacers have a 98-90 lead in the final seconds when a Knick player dribbles down court, fires up an otherwise meaningless three-point shot just before the final buzzer—and the shot happens to go in.

The Pistons still win the game, 98-93, but I lose my bet at the end of the game.

That's called a *bad beat*, and I literally had thousands of them over the years. I'm not exaggerating. *Thousands.*

A *parlay* is a bet involving at least two games. I liked playing them with three, four, and even six teams sometimes. Naturally, the more games involved in the parlay, the higher the odds.

For example, if I played a three-team parlay, meaning I bet on three teams, all three had to cover whatever their respective spreads were, in order for me to win my bet. By doing so, my bet would pay at six-to-one odds. If I wagered $100, I would win $600.

A four-teamer's odds are 10-1, a five-teamer is 20-1, a six-teamer, 40-1, and so forth.

Most professional gamblers, people who make a living betting sports, stay away from anything more than a two-team parlay, which pays 13-5 odds.

A *teaser* bet is when you can add a certain number of points to whatever team you want to bet on. However, the odds are much lower, thus stacked against whatever you wager for the bet.

It's like the old joke where the casino manager calls the big-money gambler and invites him to visit his establishment to make a sports bet.

"I'll send a car to pick you up," he says.

"Oh, you want to play parlays? Then I'll send a limo."

"You want to play teasers? Stay right where you are! I'll drive the limo over to pick you up!"

In other words, parlays and teasers are mostly loser bets.

Still, something about playing parlays—mostly the huge odds and huge payoffs—attracted me, hooked me, and wouldn't let me go. As much as I was addicted to betting sports, I was even more addicted to parlays. I loved the idea of being able to bet $1,000 and walk away with $20,000 or $40,000 in one day.

After estimating that I've gambled away more than $1.5 million in my lifetime, I've read through the years that FBI agents, gaming officials, or Las Vegas insiders questioned how I could be such a terrible gambler to lose that much money.

After all, I like to believe I was better than most at diagnosing the games, whether they were being played in the NFL, NBA, college football or basketball. I knew sports from the time I could dribble a basketball at the age of four. I knew how the games were played, what drove the competitors, and what matchups to look for before placing a bet.

The answer was in my love for parlays.

If I had bet a four-teamer, I would win three of the bets. If I bet a six-teamer, I would hit five. Great percentages if you are passing the football, but a loser if you are betting parlays.

A *money line* is a bet that eliminates the point spread. Whatever team you bet on, that team has to win the game, no matter what the spread is. Thus, the payoffs are adjusted accordingly.

Say that the Bengals are a five-point underdog to the Steelers, but I believe they're going to not only cover that point spread but win the game. I would bet on the Bengals on the money line and receive much more than the amount that I had bet.

For example, a plus *300* means I would have to bet $100 on the Bengals, and if they win the game, I would earn a $300 profit. If the money-line odds are minus *300*, which would accompany a team heavily favored, I would have to bet $300 on that team to win $100.

In baseball, I was a *run-line* bettor, usually always taking the favorite, meaning my team had to win by at least two runs. It's a sucker bet, but when you're doing it in a parlay, it's ten times a sucker bet.

I was betting these crazy, longshot parlays at $500 or $800 a pop, trying to win $12,000 or $15,000 with one ticket. It looks good when you're betting it, but they're nearly impossible to hit.

That is how I lost on baseball for 101 straight days.

Anyway, so many bad beats in the final game of what would have been winning parlays flood my memory, but there is one game in particular that combines all three—a parlay, a money line, and eventually a bad beat—I'll never, ever forget.

It was Friday night, September 16, 1994.

By now, I was desperate. I had been fired from my radio gig for stealing a stack of the owner's checks. My wife and kids had left me. I sat alone in my apartment with my dog Chelsea staring at me. I don't know which one of us looked more depressed.

Of course, I turned to my gambling mistress as I always did. I called my buddy Red Ronnie, who drove over to my apartment and picked me up.

I had one of my old checkbooks for which the account had been closed, so I wrote 20 checks for $100 each as we drove around to various bars and casinos, cashing each check. Bartenders and casino managers had no problem cashing $100 checks back then.

I had $2,000 cash in my pocket when we finished. We drove straight to the Golden Nugget and I gambled it up to $5,200. I paid Red Ronnie $500 for driving me around that night and I took the $4,700 into the Mirage. I lost $1,200 almost immediately playing blackjack.

By now, it was 4 a.m. and I started to check the college football odds for that day's upcoming games.

I played a three-team parlay, all underdogs on the money line, for $3,000, went home, and fell asleep.

When I woke up, I checked the scores and realized the first two teams in my parlay had won their games, so now I just needed LSU, which was an 11-point underdog, to upset Auburn and I would win the parlay and $34,000.

At that time, that $34,000 would get me out of a lot of messes, but LSU had to win the game first, not just cover the point spread.

Auburn entered the game riding a 13-game winning streak in Terry Bowden's second season and also was playing at home, but I just had a feeling that LSU would upset them.

Before the kickoff, I had called Red Ronnie to tell him about my bet.

With 10 minutes remaining in the game, LSU led 23-9 and I was just about counting the money.

The telephone rang. It was Red Ronnie.

"You're up 14 points," he said. "I'm coming to pick you up and we're going to cash that ticket and you can turn that $34,000 into $100,000 by the time we are finished tonight."

That's just how an addicted gambler, like me, like Red Ronnie, thinks. He's never satisfied with the win. He wants to gamble more.

"Okay, come get me," I told him.

As I walked back into the living room, LSU quarterback Jamie Howard threw late over the middle. Remember what Woody used to say about that? Auburn intercepted it and ran it back for a touchdown.

I walked over and kicked the swinging door in the kitchen, loosening it from the hinges. Chelsea heard that loud bang and ran and hid in the bedroom.

One minute later, Howard threw another interception and again, Auburn ran it back for another touchdown. Now the score was 23-23. I took my fists and actually starting punching myself in the head.

And although I wasn't laughing about it that night, I had advertised all of my furniture, knowing that our lease was up at the end of the month.

So as this game was turning in the wrong direction for me, people were knocking at the door, wanting to buy my furniture for $500. I sold everything but the television and a mattress.

LSU received the kickoff and put together a long drive. By now, my head was throbbing and my face was covered in welts from my own punches. LSU ate up much of the clock and moved to Auburn's one-yard line, but the drive stalled, so they kicked a field goal to take a 26-23 lead.

Auburn then threw three straight incompletions and punted with two and a half minutes remaining. By now, it looked as if LSU would win the game and I felt pretty foolish for punching myself in the first place.

LSU ran three times into the middle, eating up all of Auburn's timeouts. With two minutes remaining, LSU faced a third-and-four at its own 32-yard line. The obvious decision would be to run again to keep the clock moving, especially since Auburn had not done one thing offensively all night.

What did LSU Coach Curley Hallman do?

He called for a pass. Howard dropped back and threw late again. The ball was tipped, Auburn intercepted it and ran it back 42 yards for another touchdown!

Three interceptions, three touchdowns, all in nine minutes.

Now Auburn led 30-26 and I was feeling suicidal.

Howard drove LSU down to Auburn's 30-yard line in the final seconds, perhaps only to get my hopes up, and threw a fourth interception. As the Auburn defensive player returned it, LSU receiver Eddie Kennison knocked the ball loose and LSU recovered.

Howard had one last chance to win the game for LSU and $34,000 for me. With 30 seconds remaining, he threw into the end zone and ... that's right ... a fifth interception in one quarter!

Just then, there was a knock at my door, the one with the screen hanging by a thread.

"Come on!" Red Ronnie said. "We are going out!"

I had tears in my eyes as I told him what happened.

"Come on, man, don't screw with me," he said. "What was the real score?"

"Ron, I *am* serious," I explained. "LSU lost the game."

I was sitting on my mattress, the only piece of furniture I owned. I started to cry very hard. So did Red Ronnie.

"I've got to stop this," I said. "I can never bet again."

"Let me take you to the airport," he said. "You need to get out of Las Vegas. You need to go home."

I had $500 to my name, the money the people had just paid me for all of my furniture.

"To hell with it," I told him, holding up the $500. "Let's go turn this into some real money."

As devastated as I was, I turned to my "fire and fall back" philosophy. The only way to numb my pain now would be to bet again.

I quickly turned that $500 into $2,000 by playing blackjack, which is one of the few table games I ever played. I loved blackjack, but I never played poker, video poker, or slot machines. I never saw the attraction in those games.

Anyway, I took that money, headed to the sports book and examined the board for the late college games. All that was left was BYU versus Hawaii.

There's another term, *over/under*. It's the amount of total points odds makers predict will be scored by both teams. I saw the number was 60 for the BYU-Hawaii game, so I bet the $2,000 on the over. If both teams combined to score more than 60 points, I would have $4,000 in my pocket.

"Come on, I can't watch this game," I told Red Ronnie. "Let's go see a movie."

We saw *Forrest Gump* that night.

As I watched Forrest become a college football star at Alabama for Bear Bryant, then lose his wife at the end, my heart was ripping apart with each sad scene. Mitzi had just taken the kids and left me. It all was too close to home for me.

After the final credits rolled, I headed to a pay phone to dial the number I have dialed more than any other in my life—the New York score line. I must have listened to more than 70 scores, all given in chronological order as they became final that day, before the recording reached the BYU-Hawaii score:

"...With seven minutes remaining in the fourth quarter, BYU 6, Hawaii 3 ..."

I walked out of that movie theater as tears streamed down my face. My wife and kids were gone. So was my last dollar. So was almost every possession, except a mattress, a TV, and my dog—as was most of my hope.

There were times I talked to God about my gambling and this was one of those times.

"Don't You care about me?" I asked Him. "What am I doing? When is this going to change? Can you let me win, just once?"

I would think about all these huge casinos owned by conglomerates that had millions of dollars in the casino cages. If God was watching, wouldn't He want the little guy like me to win instead of these big casinos, which already have so much money?

Someone once asked me if I thought God was trying to send me a message by losing so much so often. Maybe He was trying to tell me to stop, to walk away, to quit for good. But I couldn't. I just *couldn't.*

Maybe I had reached the point where there was none of God's grace left for me.

I often thought that way, but my addiction overruled everything. I had to bet more to get the money back that I owed. The more I bet, the worse it got.

That year, with all of my checks floating around, I knew that if I didn't get the money through winning bets to reimburse everyone, I would go to prison eventually.

Or be dead.

One time, I owed an acquaintance of Red Ronnie's a few thousand from a bad check and he came looking for me. I was playing blackjack in the high-limit room at the Mirage when I noticed Ronnie outside, motioning to me.

I walked out onto the main floor of the casino.

"What's up?" I asked.

I could tell the other guy was agitated.

"Listen, I got a gun in my pocket," he told me. "If you don't pay me right now, I'm going to shoot you!"

"Okay," I said. "Do me a fucking favor, will you? Just shoot me! Let's get this over with! Come on! DO ME A FAVOR!"

I think I shocked the guy, because he walked away, and I returned to the high-limit table.

It was old hat to be threatened. The Baltimore guys were the first to do it, and over the years, I used to borrow money from loan sharks in the Midwest. They're not the type of people who forget a debt, and eventually I did pay them off to stop the threats.

But nobody ever threw a punch at me or pulled a gun on me.

The last two weeks of September were the craziest two weeks of gambling of my life.

After betting myself penniless the night we saw *Forrest Gump*, I started from scratch again, raising $200 here and $500 there, passing checks around town.

I really believe there was a subconscious part of me that knew I was eventually going to jail anyway, so I guess I didn't care what I was doing. Ultimately, I thought I didn't deserve such a good family, so I may have done illegal things to penalize myself, to kill the pain. Maybe psychologically, I even wanted to go to jail to punish myself.

My first big win during those two weeks came when I bet on a Broncos-Bills game on *Monday Night Football*. That weekend, I was gambling so much at Treasure Island, I asked for a comped room and they gave me one. I ran up a $500 phone bill in the room, calling everywhere, making arrangements to get more checks or to raise more money.

I won about $5,000 on the Broncos that night after taking the seven and a half points, then took that money to the Mirage and started playing blackjack, running it up to $45,000. As Ronnie would walk by and check on me from time to time—I never liked him watching me when I played—I would hand him $300 or $500.

During one break, I put $20,000 in one pocket for keeping and $25,000 in another for gambling.

"Ronnie, whatever I do, don't let me reach into this pocket," I pleaded with him. "I got to have that money."

A few hours later, I had gone through the $25,000 meant for gambling.

"Don't do it, Art," he said. "Don't reach into that pocket. Do not do it! You need that money!"

"Ron, I'm going to prison someday soon anyway," I told him. "What does it matter?"

I pulled out the $20,000 and by six in the morning it was gone, too.

As we walked out of the casino, I asked him, "You got 20 bucks so we can get something to eat?"

He shook his head. He, too, had lost all of the money I'd given him throughout the night.

We both walked out of there dead broke.

And hungry.

I repeated that scenario three times over those two weeks. I would raise money to gamble with, turn it into thousands, then blow it all.

The final time was the worst.

One night near the end of September, I had booked a red-eye flight for 10 o'clock to return to Indianapolis. My plan was to take Mitzi some money to care for the kids and try to reconcile and start all over again as one big happy family.

On that day, I had built my winnings up to $40,000 and I decided I would give half of it to Mitzi.

I had a few hours to kill before my flight, so I talked Red Ronnie into driving me to the Golden Nugget, where I proceeded to play blackjack at anywhere from $500 to $1,500 per hand.

In one hour, I'd lost $38,500.

Time after time, I was dealt hands of 16, 17, and 18, which real blackjack players know are usually high enough that you should not take a hit, but low enough that you'll lose four out of five times. Sure enough, the dealer drew to 19, 20, or 21 just about every time.

I motioned to Red Ronnie.

"Go get the car, I'll be outside soon," I said.

"Let's go now!" he said.

"No, I might as well see this to the end," I told him.

Usually, when I got into one of those moods, I didn't stop until it was all gone. Somehow, I stopped with $1,500 in chips. I don't know how I did it, but I walked out of the Nugget with that money.

I started walking down the street, crying. Then I started to throw punches at my face. I threw one haymaker after another, landing them all. I cold-cocked myself about five or six times, as hard as I had ever been hit in my life.

As I punched myself, Ronnie followed closely behind me in his car.

"Get in!" he demanded.

I had staggered myself. It was a case of releasing all of that anger on myself. I was a self-defeating person anyway, so I may as well be the one to unleash the punishment.

Finally, I stopped and climbed into his car, my face looking like I had just gone 10 rounds with Mike Tyson.

"My God, Art, you have blood all over your face!" Ronnie said, grabbing my arm. "Come on. You've got to get away from here. Let me drive you to the airport."

I agreed.

It was time for me to get the hell out of Las Vegas. I knew I would have to return someday to face the music, but I didn't care about that at the moment.

"I've got to get home," I told him. "Get me home."

I flew all night, landed in Indianapolis and checked into a Red Roof Inn at Interstate 465 and Keystone Road. I called Mitzi, who came to the hotel. I handed her the $1,500 as she started to cry.

Twelve hours earlier, I had $40,000 in one hundred dollar bills in my pocket, but she never knew that, and that made *me* want to cry.

I remained in Indianapolis, writing bad checks like a child eating gumdrops. Once I wrote one, I couldn't stop.

Now that I was 2,000 miles away from the tentacles of Vegas and the accompanying venom it spewed on my life, I thought my bad beats and the pain they inflicted on me would be a thing of the past.

Well, Joe Montana taught me a lesson about that.

On October 17, I was hanging out with some buddies at a bar in Lebanon, Ohio, a small town north of Cincinnati, watching *Monday Night Football*. I hung around the town plenty because I loved Lebanon Raceway, the local harness-racing track. That night, I had taken Elway and the Broncos once again, against Montana and the Chiefs. The bet was through a local bookie and would pay me about $15,000, but the Broncos had to win the game.

With only four minutes remaining, Kansas City kicked a field goal to take a 24-21 lead, but Elway still had some time on the clock and I had some hope. He drove Denver to midfield, completed a pass to tight end Shannon Sharpe, but he fumbled and the Chiefs recovered with only 2:45 remaining.

"SHIT!" I screamed. "I am outta here!"

I left my buddies and headed to my car, a pissed-off loser again. I turned on the radio as I drove home, to listen to the final painful moments of another gut-wrenching loss in a lifetime of gut-wrenching losses. By the time I had driven out of the parking lot, Chiefs running back Marcus Allen, who was the blocking back for Charles White in our heart-breaking Rose Bowl defeat 14 years earlier, fumbled the football back to Denver.

Five plays later, Elway scrambled into the end zone to give the Broncos the lead with only 1:29 remaining.

Thank you John! I started pounding on the steering wheel, screaming and celebrating right with him, relieved because I had a lawyer and other bills to pay for. I would give some money to Mitzi for the kids. I knew I was headed to prison soon anyway, but this money would allow me to get things in order and prepare for it.

Well, Montana didn't give a shit about me or my troubles. He drove the Chiefs down the field, completing seven-of-eight passes. Bam, bam, bam ... then a little out route to the right side of the end zone with eight seconds remaining. Eight seconds!

I banged my head against the steering wheel and had broken into a cold sweat.

Just as the game went final, the Chiefs winning 31-28 in a game that would be talked about for years, I passed the Lebanon Correctional Institution, a state prison, on State Route 63.

How fitting, I thought. Not only was I dead broke again, but I'll be inside a place just like that real soon. I rolled down the window, stuck my head out and mashed my foot onto the gas pedal. Barely able to see with the wind in my face, my car reached 80 miles per hour .... 90 .... 100. Why not get it all over right here and now? Just jerk the car to the right and hit a tree! Just do everybody who relied on me one final favor! I was ready.

I don't know why I didn't follow through. Whether God talked me out of it, or I was too scared, or I considered how my kids would react, how my mom would cry and cry, I don't really know.

Whatever the reason, I just couldn't do it.

Two weeks following Montana's miracle, my Las Vegas attorney called me. Fraud charges had been filed against me in Las Vegas for the checks I had taken from the owner of radio station, the act of stupidity that got me fired. I had taken nine checks, held them to the sunlight of a car window, and traced the owner's signature, pocketing $5,000. The lawyer had been negotiating with the FBI and prosecutors throughout the fall. There would be no grand jury indictment if I pleaded guilty.

"Art, you need to be back here November 10 for a hearing," he said. "I'll represent you there. You can make a plea, they will set a trial date, then you can go back to Indiana. They'll probably sentence you 60 to 90 days after that."

Now, the clock was ticking on my freedom.

My prediction of what would happen to me within one year after moving to Las Vegas had come true.

All things considered, I would have preferred I had become a millionaire.

Chapter sixteen

LOST AGAIN. THIS TIME IT'S MY FREEDOM

"*Mister Schlichter is a menace to the businesses of our society.*"
Those words ring in my ears today, because they officially kicked off the worst dozen years of my life.

I flew from Indianapolis to Las Vegas the morning of November 10, 1994, took a cab to the office of Richard Cremins, my attorney, and the ensuing events that day shocked my senses.

I had figured I would ultimately receive about 15 months, be required to report to a federal prison camp on a certain date since the crimes I had committed were considered "white-collar crimes." I also hoped that since I was a first-time offender, maybe I could get out of this mess altogether.

There was a big problem, however, and I had no clue it existed.

"I got some really bad news for you," Cremins told me. "Somebody from Indiana has called the prosecutor and told them that you have been writing bad checks back there. Is that true?"

"Yep," I answered.

"Well, they are going to pull you off of the streets today," he said. "They won't let you go. They are going to take you and put you in the system."

In the system? Today?

I knew the nightmare was about to begin.

It turned out that news of my pending case in Las Vegas had appeared in newspapers everywhere. In the days leading up to it, a man in Indiana whom I written a check to, but did not cover, had called the prosecutor in Las Vegas.

174

I walked into that courtroom a mental mess, although I still held out slim hope for a fourth-down legal Hail Mary.

Once the prosecutor told the judge everything, emphasizing that "menace to the businesses of our society" line, my fate was sealed.

"Mister Schlichter, I am detaining you," the judge said.

He ordered me to be held in the North Las Vegas County Jail until sentencing. They slapped handcuffs on me—the first time I had ever been handcuffed—and ushered me from the courtroom.

A wire-service photo of me exiting the courtroom, handcuffed in the front, and accompanying story of my crimes ran in most every newspaper around the country the following day.

I had no idea what to expect when they hauled me off to jail, but I soon discovered that my courtroom appearance had been all over television that day, because by the time I arrived at the jail, all of the inmates knew I was on my way. They walked me past the day area where about 30 inmates were watching television. They all looked at me, turned back to the TV and none of them said a word.

Then the corrections officers shut me in a cell and locked it, marking the beginning of a long stretch of hell.

I had no chance to call anyone, Mitzi or Mom and Dad, to tell them that I would not be coming back to Indiana.

That first night, I was extremely suicidal. I was staring at 18 to 24 months, but my sentencing was not scheduled for another 80 days or so. Thinking of that time ahead of missing my kids was as painful as anything I had ever imagined.

When you are locked up, you have nothing but plenty of time to think about all the mistakes you have made. Everything went rushing through my mind that night. What I did. How could I make it better? I had never taken a moment to think what it would be like to be away from my wife and children for a long stretch of time.

I laid on my bunk in this tiny cell that night, trying to fall asleep to erase all of the pain.

And the most painful part was thinking about my kids.

Before I had left, I had kissed Taylor good-bye and whispered, "Daddy will be back in a few days."

As the weeks passed with me locked up in Las Vegas, one day she asked Mitzi, "Mommy, how long is a few days?"

"Why?" Mitzi asked her.

"Because Daddy said he would be back in a few days, but I don't know what that means. A few days must be a long time, huh Mom? Where is he?"

When I heard that story later, my heart broke again.

The next day, I could make my first collect call and I talked to Mitzi and Taylor. I called them every three days or so. Those conversations always ended with tears running down my cheeks. Those first few weeks in jail, I was ready to die.

I must have weighed about 290 pounds when I went into the system, the most I had ever weighed. I started to starve myself and what food I did eat was all diet food.

As the days passed, I did sit-ups by holding my feet around the steel toilet. I did jumping jacks. I skipped rope in the rec area. I did pushups, any physical activity you could imagine. I may have been punishing myself or I may have decided that this was my wakeup call, and getting in shape was my first step toward turning myself around. I even walked in circles waiting for the phone to be freed up to make my collect calls.

I spent the nights looking out this tiny window and writing letters. From that window, I could see the Silver Nugget Casino. How ironic, I thought. That is another place where I had passed some bad checks.

When I finished my letters each night, I would lie there and cry until I fell asleep.

That was my existence for the first 80 days.

One night, I was lying on my bunk, when they opened my cell and in walked a guy about 6-foot-5, bald-headed, with a gray goatee hanging down about a foot off of his face. His body was covered with tattoos and he smelled really bad. In other words, he was the typical con you would see in the movies.

"Schlichter, you have a new bunkee," the corrections officer said.

"Oh my God," I thought. "I will not live through the night."

He had a lower bunk pass, because he had a bad back, so the first words I heard him speak were, "Get off my bunk."

No problem. I crawled on the top bunk.

He laid down, went to sleep and never said a word. I was awake all night, wondering if I would survive with this huge monster beneath me.

One day he asked me what my name was. When I told him, he was tickled pink. He was a football fan.

It turned out that this guy had robbed banks all over the West and was a heroin addict. He had been in Leavenworth, one of the worst prisons in the country, where he said he consistently bet on football games. When he got out, he violated his probation by using heroin again, and that is when they stuck him in with me.

They were holding him in Las Vegas, until he could be shipped back to Leavenworth.

Over the next few weeks, he taught me the system and "how to do time," as inmates call it.

There was a young gang member serving time who also made a big impact on me. His nickname was "Kilo" and he was part of the gang that had robbed Harrah's the previous April. He told me the entire story of the robbery one day.

Anyway, he found religion in jail and I prayed with him. As I learned later, it seemed that everybody, or almost everybody, found religion in prison. But then one day I saw him ripping somebody off, minutes after he had delivered the longest, most beautiful prayer.

That's the way it is in prison—it's crazy, it's contradictory and it doesn't always make sense.

On January 11, prosecutors in Indianapolis charged me with four more felonies. It seemed that people in Indiana came out of the woodwork once my troubles in Las Vegas became public, calling prosecutors to say that I had passed bad checks.

Just before my sentencing in Las Vegas, I met with Cremins. We reviewed all of my charges, all the specifics of the crimes the prosecutors claimed I had committed.

I looked at him and asked, "You must think I'm a piece of shit."

"You *are* a piece of shit for doing all of these things," he told me. "Guys like you are a dime a dozen."

I had studied the sentencing guidelines and figured that I deserved 15 months, not two years, since I was a first-time offender. He didn't agree with me.

"You did what you did, you are guilty and now you are going to serve your time," he said. "You deserve 24 months."

I called Dad and told him to get me a new lawyer.

I later learned lawyers in Las Vegas do not like outsiders who come into town and commit crimes relating to money or fraud. They look at it as if you are screwing the city of Las Vegas and specifically, the casinos, which is the city's lifeblood.

My sentencing was scheduled for January 27, and by then, Dad had hired a new lawyer to work my case.

That day in court, the prosecutor claimed that all of my bounced checks had amounted to $175,000.

An acquaintance, Arnie Wexler, an expert on gambling addiction, also would appear on my behalf. My hope was that he would convince the judge I was an addict, which I was, someone who committed these crimes but had no control over his actions because of the addiction.

That is what I believed with all my heart.

My new lawyer began to present my defense, but he stuttered and stammered and sweated bullets through his opening statements. It was obvious he was nervous and the prosecutor ripped him to shreds that day. I was thinking that this lawyer was worse than the first guy—and the first guy wanted me locked up and the key thrown away.

And he was on *my* team.

I figured I would be lucky to get out of this with anything less than two years.

Then Arnie Wexler stood up.

"What is your education?" the judge asked.

"Well, I got my GED," Arnie answered.

"No, I mean, what is your expertise in this field of addiction?" the judge asked.

"Well, I have been a compulsive gambler for 30 years," he said.

"No," the judge demanded. "What is your accreditation, your official qualifications?"

Arnie had none—and I had practically no real defense.

I couldn't blame Arnie, because he was just trying to help me, but it didn't matter if he had been a Rhodes Scholar, I was headed to prison.

By the time this courtroom circus concluded, I was happy I didn't get 24 *years*.

I walked out of that courtroom and headed back to jail, where they kept me for two more weeks. Then they put me on a prison bus for a four-hour ride to Los Angeles, shackled and chained at the wrists, waist and ankles. I would be jailed in L.A. until they could fly me to Indiana, where I would serve time in a federal prison in Terre Haute, Indiana.

I was housed in the Metropolitan Detention Center in downtown Los Angeles, coinciding with the O.J. Simpson double-murder trial. I could look out the window and see all of these news helicopters flying around.

Seven months earlier, I had watched O.J.'s Ford Bronco chase while on the air, talking sports in Vegas.

Fifteen years earlier, across town, O.J. sat with me on the Ohio State team bus, interviewing me for NBC's broadcast of the Rose Bowl. Now here we were, me in prison and him across the street on trial for double-murder.

From L.A., the feds flew me to a federal prison just outside Oklahoma City, in El Reno, Oklahoma, where I stayed for another two weeks. Inmates called this prison "The Bird Cage" because birds fly through the cell blocks. And it was cold, very cold.

From the time I left Las Vegas, it took me a month to get back to Indiana.

As the prison bus pulled up to the federal penitentiary in Terre Haute, I saw guns pointing at us from all directions and that 40-foot wall.

I could only wonder what awaited me inside.

Despite those ominous surroundings, I was happy to be closer to home.

I wouldn't stay in Terre Haute for long. After 30 days, they shipped me to the Marion County Jail in Indianapolis, where I stayed for about a month, and then they moved me to the Hamilton County Jail in Noblesville, Indiana, where I remained for seven months.

It wasn't a terrible place. The food was good and it was close enough that I could see my kids often.

In Noblesville, I met a con named Paul, who was a little bit older than me. He was very educated and thoughtful, a great guy for me to be around. He faced 10 years for dealing drugs.

I would walk around the track, moping and all depressed about the two years in prison I faced. One day, Paul gave me a lecture I needed.

"Man, what is wrong with you?" he asked. "You got this little bitty 24 months ahead of you and you are all depressed? Be a man! Suck it up and do your time! You got what you got, because you deserved it! You have a wife and kids, a family. So do your time, get out and change your life."

His words made sense to me and I took a different attitude about prison after our talk.

I re-paid Paul indirectly. My therapist visited me often and Paul would talk to her from time to time and they got along real well. After a while, he asked me if I cared if he wrote her a letter. It was fine with me. That evolved into them becoming good friends and pretty soon, she was visiting him in prison.

When he was eventually released, they married and last I heard, were still together happily.

Bob Costas visited me in prison, doing a story for NBC's *Dateline*. He didn't go easy on me, starting the interview by playing a tape of my voice saying just about every dirty word in the book. It was a tape of me screaming at bookies who wouldn't take my action, but I have no idea how Bob got ahold of it.

Anyway, I sat there sweating bullets as the tape rolled on national television.

Despite the nature of the interview, which detailed my problems and the addiction, I liked Bob. I thought he was a cool guy and he was just doing his job. We stayed in touch from the day of that interview through the next five or six years.

By the time the *Dateline* show aired, I was serving time in Cincinnati for a bad check charge there. There were about 50 guys in the cellblock with me and I had told a few of them that I would be on TV. But during the interview, I had named some names of bookies, which didn't sit too well with the other inmates. The one thing cons don't like is a snitch, and that interview gave them the impression that is what I was.

It was real uncomfortable.

On October 26, 1995, I pleaded guilty to the felony counts in Indianapolis. Then there were new charges filed for the same type of crimes in Cincinnati from my time there. I was sentenced to another 18 months.

The two sentences were to run concurrently, meaning they ran side-by-side, which was good news for me, and I even got 90 days knocked off for good behavior.

Finally, I was released from Terre Haute on my 36th birthday, April 25, 1996. I walked out after 532 days in the system.

Mitzi, who had visited me several times with the kids in Terre Haute, met me at the gate at 7 a.m. We hugged, kissed and cried like I was arriving back from purgatory.

I had to be at Indianapolis by 3 p.m. to check into a halfway house.

We went home to Mitzi's tiny apartment, where the girls were waiting. I walked in the door and hugged Taylor and Maddy and saw a little birthday cake on the table.

I cried like a baby and couldn't stop hugging them.

Mitzi wanted to give me another chance, mainly because of the kids, I am sure.

I think she figured I was an addict and could not control my actions. And she knew I loved the kids with all my heart. She wanted to see me get the help I needed and she believed I could turn my life around for the sake of the kids.

I couldn't.

I gambled almost immediately following my release. I hadn't received any serious treatment to that point, and I had to find money to support my family.

I had gotten a job at a company called Alexander EarthWorks and I took some of the owner's checks. He was a friend of mine and it was a ridiculously stupid thing to do, but I needed money. I filled out those checks, borrowed money from a friend named Rebecca, and gave her the post-dated checks as collateral. I told her the man whose name was on the checks was a business partner of mine.

Of course, I planned to take the money I had borrowed, make more of it by gambling, then pay her back and take back the checks. When I couldn't pay her back, she said, "Let's just go cash these checks."

"No, no, we can't do that," I said.

Rebecca, a lawyer, had mentioned to another lawyer-friend what I did and what I owed her, which was about $8,500.

"Well, he just committed a crime," the lawyer told her.

He made a few calls to the local prosecutors. Then one day in August, my state probation supervisor called me.

"I have some papers you need to come in and sign," he said.

"What papers?" I asked.

"Routine stuff," he answered.

I grew suspicious, figuring the state had been investigating me.

"Listen, I have to pick up my daughter at the baby-sitter today," I told him. "If you promise me I will be out of there in time to do that, I will come in to sign the papers."

He gave me his word, so I figured then he was telling me the truth.

As we talked in his office, a state police investigator walked in and I knew I was screwed. He arrested me, handcuffed me and took me to the Marion County Jail, by far one of the worst county jails in the country. It's nothing but a dirty dungeon with bars.

Nobody would be there to pick up Taylor. God, what have I done?

When the baby-sitter called Mitzi, she had no idea of what happened to me until she heard it on the radio: "Art Schlichter was taken into custody today for …"

I had violated my probation, and when you violate your probation, judges tend to hit you right between the eyes with a tough sentence.

On January 17, 1997, a judge in Indianapolis sentenced me to eight years in prison. Before I was sent away to begin serving the time, they tried to treat my addiction by sending me to Harbour Center, then a gambling treatment center in Baltimore, of all places.

I became very despondent after I arrived in Baltimore, knowing I faced a ton more prison time and Mitzi talked to me about wanting to finally push the divorce through so she could move on with her life.

"To hell with it," I thought. "Eight years! How can I do eight years?"

Not caring what happened to me at that point, I started gambling at the center almost immediately, largely because I hung around with another patient who may have been hooked even worse than me.

We were allowed to come and go from the center and I ate supper with this guy in a sports bar almost every night, as we studied what bets to place through his bookie. We would lose each night, then swear off gambling forever.

Always, at just about six in the morning the following day, he would bust into my room holding the newspaper, opening it to the betting lines.

"Alright, let's go again," he would say. "Who do you like tonight?"

It wasn't until he left the center that I started to make some progress. The treatment started to make sense to me. I stopped gambling and during the next six weeks, I had some hope.

Then one day as I sat in a meeting and glanced out the window, I noticed a man standing on the corner dressed in blue pants, blue coat and a hat. I knew the look. It was the look of an FBI agent. It turned out that the treatment center was surrounded by the feds. What the heck is going on, I wondered.

They had come for me.

They entered the building, grabbed me and told me I was headed back to prison right away for gambling.

Prison for gambling during treatment?

I knew you could be incarcerated for serious crimes and for doing illegal things to acquire money to gamble, but not for gambling itself. I learned later that one of the doctors had written in her report that I had gambled at the center. A judge read it and promptly notified the feds to violate my supervised release.

They yanked me out of that treatment center and transported me to the Baltimore County Jail. The doctor had said I shouldn't have been taken from the treatment center and that she was concerned that I may hurt myself.

Therefore, the judge decided to place me in the suicide-watch tank at the jail. They dressed me in a man-made diaper, I kid you not, and tennis shoes, without the strings, and placed me in a room that was about 50 degrees.

I laid there on a Styrofoam mattress, with no blankets, no clothes, nothing. An officer stood nearby and watched me the entire time. Other prisoners would walk by the window, point at me and laugh. It was humiliating.

When I appeared in court a day later, the public defender leaned over to whisper, "I have good news and bad news."

"Get it over with," I said. "Tell me both."

"The feds want to take you back to Indianapolis. You can fly back with them after a few more days in treatment. But the state wants you detained now. And if the state takes you, it will be on a bus and take about 30 days," he said. "Which do you want?"

"I'll go with the feds," I said.

The problem was, the judge didn't allow me to return to treatment. He ordered me back to the suicide-watch tank, where I remained for three more excruciating days.

Then I flew with the feds to New York to drop off some mobster on our way to Indianapolis and the Marion County Jail. I had more of the same awaiting me.

"Schlichter!" the jailer said there. "Pack up your shit, you are going to the suicide tank."

They figured that since I was in the suicide block in Baltimore, I spend more time in the suicide-watch tank in Marion County. I couldn't talk to anybody, although I did wear clothes this time.

Four days later, they moved me to the main cell block.

That summer, the Indianapolis forgery charges from the time I was arrested after being released from Terre Haute resulted in a 15-year sentence, since I had violated my state and federal probations.

The feds then sent me on a long journey through the system which would take me from the Marion County Jail back to Oklahoma for a month, to the Atlanta Federal Penitentiary for three weeks. While in Atlanta, I was locked down and could not go outside at all. The first day, we had to walk in single file down this long hallway and I was following orders.

"Do not get out of line!" the prison officer shouted at us.

Just then, a guy in front of me wanted to be with his buddy, who was behind me. He stopped in his tracks. I veered around him to continue walking in the line.

Just as I did that, the officer had turned around.

"Okay, Mister Tough Guy, Mister Football Fucker, I got something for you!" he yelled.

They placed me in the hole, which was a segregated portion of the prison. Some inmate down there had a little transistor radio and had slipped it to me one night. I laid there alone, listening to Braves' games and country music.

It was the first time I ever heard the song "Butterfly Kisses," by Bob Carlisle. If you ever heard the lyrics, you would understand why I cried harder that night than I had ever cried:

My two favorite visitors, Taylor and Maddy, 1998.

There's two things I know for sure:
She was sent here from heaven and she's daddy's little girl.
As I drop to my knees by her bed at night
She talks to Jesus and I close my eyes and
I thank god for all the joy in my life
Oh, but most of all
For butterfly kisses after bedtime prayer; sticking little
*   white flowers all up in her hair;*
"Walk beside the pony, Daddy, it's my first ride."
"I know the cake looks funny, Daddy, but I sure tried."
In all that I've done wrong I know I must have done
*   something right to deserve a hug every morning and*
*   butterfly kisses at night.*

That song was high on the charts at the time, and every time I heard it all I could think of were Taylor and Maddy—one daughter whose heart I had broken and another who knew me only through her visits to prison. I wondered what they were doing at that very moment. I wanted to see their faces, to kiss them, to hug them, but I was five-hundred miles—and yet it felt like light-years—away from them.

One of Mom's many visits to see me in prison.

One day, the officer came to me.

"Pack up Schlichter," he said. "You are leaving tomorrow."

They never told me where I was headed next in the system, but I figured it had to be back north somewhere. That next morning, at about 3 a.m., they woke me up, along with the other sixty inmates who were to be transferred, stripped us naked and made us stand there in this holding area. Finally, they dressed us in these travel khakis and stuck us back in the cell.

Then they pulled us out one-by-one, shackled us at the hands and ankles. We stood there shackled for another three hours, just waiting. Waiting to go where, I had no idea.

At about 7 a.m., they placed us on a prison bus and we headed north on I-75. When the corrections officers stopped at McDonald's to eat, they handed us some dry bologna sandwiches and water.

We headed through Chattanooga, where they dropped off some prisoners, and then on to Ashland, Kentucky, to a federal correctional institution, a low-security prison.

Ashland was a great facility for me. I played basketball and touch football in the yard. It turned out to be one of my favorite places to do time and it was close to home, although there was no air-conditioning there. It was about 100 degrees inside during the summer. I went outside one day and got sunburned so badly, you would have thought I had just come from Miami Beach.

Four years had passed since Mitzi left me the first time, following that fiasco with her sister's checking account while we were living in Vegas. She had taken me back when I had been released and I still hoped I would make it through the system, get released, and make our marriage work someday.

My hopes were soon crushed.

Now she had made up her mind. She was just tired of it all and wanted to go another direction and I really couldn't blame her. She wanted to break clean. Her family wanted her to break clean.

I was devastated the day I received the divorce papers Mitzi had mailed me

185

to review.

Not only had I held out hope to reconcile with her again when I was released, I wanted to be in my daughters' lives every day. They were only eight and four years old, but now I realized that would never happen and it broke my heart.

That day, I walked about 100 laps around the outdoor track at the prison, mumbling to myself, thinking about the time I spent with Mitzi, my kids and the divorce.

It was just another loss for me in a life full of losses, but a devastating loss all the same.

Our divorce became official June 19, 1998, ending our marriage nine years, six months and 12 days after it began.

Chapter seventeen

BORN TO RUN

Since 1994, I've spent endless hours dealing with lawyers, prosecutors, and judges. I closely studied sentencing guidelines, motions, writs, judges' rulings, and listened intently as lawyers explained the legal system, enough that perhaps I could have made a career in law myself.

If only I'd remained on the right side of it.

One thing I learned through it all is that the length of prison sentences, unless you are incarcerated for something serious like murder or rape, are not to be taken literally. Eight years doesn't always mean *eight* years. Especially, if you steer clear of trouble in prison, which I did for the most part.

By March of 1999, my security level—every inmate is assigned a security level relevant to the crime and the amount of prison time remaining—had dropped enough that they had moved me to a prison camp in Peru, Indiana.

In addition to good behavior, I had learned I could have time knocked off my sentence by earning a college degree.

I always had regretted not attending class much at Ohio State and wanted to make it right. I enrolled in a continuing education program through correspondence at Indiana University. I had tutors helping me in prison, but I did everything I was supposed to do, and earned an associate's and then a bachelor's degree.

The latter diploma knocked 18 months off of my sentence.

Therefore, in September, 1999, after 13 months inside during my second stretch of incarceration, I was released again, although I still faced probation and eight years of prison hanging over my head if I messed up on the outside.

I was a free man.

But I was not a changed man.

Without any consistent and effective treatment, I still gambled. I still lost. I still chased. I still committed the crimes that had put me away twice before. I still did all the stupid things that I'm ashamed of today.

I had been free for six months when Ohio State head coach John Cooper and Bill Myles, one of my favorite assistant coaches who now worked in the athletic department, called and asked me to speak to the football team about the dangers of gambling.

At the time, April 17, 2000, I am sure they figured I'd learned the error of my ways and had turned my life around since I'd been imprisoned twice and released twice.

Bill put together a nice highlight tape of my playing days and showed it to the team before I spoke. Then I told my story to the current players, a few of whom weren't even born when I played my final college game more than 18 years earlier.

Those players had no idea that I was about to start running for my freedom again as the feds built yet another case against me. I had just taken my father's American Express card and used it to obtain about $40,000 to gamble. Dad reported "an unauthorized use" of the card. That's why I knew that day at the Woody Hayes Athletic Center would be one of my final days on the outside again. The feds soon would be issuing an arrest warrant in my name.

After I left campus, I spent the night with Dad at his house in north Columbus. We sat down and had a heart-to-heart.

"Just lend me the money and I will pay off the credit card company and I can stay out of prison," I told Dad.

"I don't have it Art," he told me. "I'm in trouble myself. I don't have much money left."

He wouldn't tell me all of the details, but I knew it wasn't good. He had saved some money of his own. He had to have the money to help me, but when I pressed him on the issue, he wouldn't budge with any details.

"I just don't have it," he repeated.

I left there the next morning in a car he had leased for me, knowing it was a matter of time before I was behind bars again. I didn't have any money to pay the restitution to the credit card company. I was on a daily reporting program at the time and my probation officer told me the feds were investigating me again.

They were building a case to violate my state and federal probations.

My probation officer, a man named Eric, called me the following week at my apartment in Indianapolis.

"Art, the feds want you off the street," he said. "They want to violate your probation. You need to turn yourself in."

"Eric, I'll turn myself in but I need three or four days to get some things in order," I told him. "I wanted to make arrangements to fight my case."

"Okay," he said. "I'll file the paperwork on Friday and I'll give you the weekend. You come in on Monday morning."

Agreed, I told him.

The next day, he called back.

"I can't get you the time. They want you NOW!" he said. "Turn yourself in NOW!"

"Eric, that's not what you promised me," I said.

"It doesn't matter," he answered. "You have to turn yourself in. They want me to file the paperwork, so there'll be a warrant for your arrest if you don't come in."

"So be it," I said. "I'm not coming in right now."

I told Mitzi to pull the girls out of school. I needed to hug each one of them, because I was going away again. I hugged Taylor, who was 10 at the time and told her I loved her, but that I was headed back to jail.

"Oh Daddy! Why? Why? What did you do?" she screamed at me.

She cried and cried and cried that day, wanting to know why I did the things I did. I know that moment, along with all the others, probably did some damage to her and I'll never forgive myself for it. Maddy was six and didn't know what to think.

As I drove away from them, I just fell apart emotionally. That's when I seriously thought about killing myself. I may as well get it over with.

I called Dad.

"This is too much pain to go through," I told him. "I'm thinking of killing myself."

"Why talk about it?" he said. "Why don't you just go ahead and do it? Get it over with."

His words were not what I expected to hear.

A moment later, he had another suggestion.

"Why don't you just go somewhere for four or five years?" he asked. "Just leave. Go to another country. Maybe the laws will change and you won't be facing as much time later."

"Dad, I can't do that," I said. "I can't go that long without talking to the kids, or seeing them, even if I'm in prison."

"In there, you're no good to them anyway," he said.

I guess my kids are the reason I never ended it all. Mitzi had told me that at least if I was in jail, the kids would know I was safe. I had done enough damage to my children. How could I kill myself and have them live with that, too?

I knew I was just buying time on the outside. When the feds send out the dogs, they always come back with the carcass. I knew that I could be arrested at any time, so I drove back to Columbus to get money from friends there so I could keep running.

As I drove through campus, I thought, "Well, I may as well see what downtown Columbus looks like. I probably won't be back, for a long, long time."

I drove south on High Street, looked into my rear-view and saw a motorcycle cop with his lights flashing.

It's all over now, I thought.

I made a turn down a side street and stopped the car. I got out just as the cop shouted, "Get back in your car!"

I complied. Then I waited as he started walking toward me until he was about halfway from his motorcycle to my door. I hit the gas pedal and took off. I just panicked.

I turned down another street and somehow ended up in this circular parking lot. As I drove out, he was headed directly at me. It was just like playing chicken. He swerved to the side and I continued, almost hitting another car. I really didn't come close to hitting him, though. I knew enough not to do that.

I drove about 60 miles per hour through town, before I hopped onto I-70 heading east. I figured they'd be sending helicopters out to find me, so I exited the freeway and drove along a parallel road for about 30 miles. My mind really played tricks on me now, thinking there would be an all-out manhunt for me.

When I reached St. Clairsville, located on the very eastern edge of Ohio near the Pennsylvania border, I found a hotel on a hill and registered under a different name. I had some money in my pocket, but I called my buddy Chuck Grubbs for some help. He gave the hotel clerk his credit card number and I checked in.

That night, I called Dad, "Is there anything going on there?"

"No, what do you mean?" he asked.

"Nothing on the news about me?" I said.

"No."

Naturally, I took what money I had and went to Wheeling Downs across the West Virginia border the next day, hoping to win some more at the racetrack.

The next day, I called Dad again.

"Anything?" I asked again.

"You son of a bitch," he said.

"What?" I asked.

"You know what," he told me.

"Dad, what are you talking about?"

"What happened to you two days ago in Columbus?" he asked me.

"I had a visitor today. It was a motorcycle cop. When I answered the door, he asked, 'Are you John Max Schlichter? I am here to arrest you for reckless operation. You almost ran over me and killed me!'

"I told him, 'That sounds like my son.'"

By the time the officer left Dad's house, Dad had talked him out of filing any serious charges. He said they even shared a nice conversation and he wished him, and me, luck.

I stayed in St. Clairsville another night until I was broke. I called a guy in Louisville who had bought a few Final Four tickets from me. I had taken his money, but never sent the tickets.

"Look," I told him. "I have a check with me to cash. You can cash it, take the money I owe you, and give me the rest."

"Come on over," he said. "I can't come to you. I am staying in town for the Kentucky Derby tomorrow."

That's all I needed to hear. I drove all the way to Louisville that Friday, May 5, to meet him at Churchill Downs. It was the day of the Kentucky Oaks, the annual race the day before the Derby. As I stood next to the track, Peyton Manning walked by. That's a coincidence, I thought. A Colts quarterback and former Colts quarterback at the same place and at the same time.

I continued calling the guy and he continued to tell me he had been delayed. I grew suspicious. So I hid high in the grandstands and waited. I called him again.

"Where are you?" I asked.

"Right out by the fence," he said. "See that number one horse? I am right in front of him."

I looked down by the fence in front of the one horse, and sure enough, there stood the guy.

"I am wearing a blue shirt," he said.

I noticed the guy in the blue shirt had a huge bulge on his side, the obvious outline of a holstered gun. He was not the one talking on the phone. The man next to him was.

"Are you with anybody?" I asked.

"No, why?"

"You're a liar!" I yelled into the phone.

I ran out of the track, hopped into my car and headed for the exit to the parking lot. The problem was, all these cars were flooding into the lot for the Kentucky Oaks and I was headed against the traffic. Telling the guy to go screw himself was a dumb move, instead of buying time for my getaway.

What if they block the exits?

My mind was playing tricks on me again. I wasn't exactly Al Capone. The feds weren't going to block off the entrances and exits to Churchill Downs on the second-biggest racing day of the year, just to nab a small-time guy like me.

I headed to Grove City to stay with Chuck and slept on his couch for a few nights. We even gambled that Sunday night on a Major League Baseball game between Colorado and San Francisco. I bet on the Rockies on the run line, meaning I needed them to beat the Giants by at least two runs to win my bet. They won 10-9.

Typical.

When Chuck went to work the following day, I grabbed one of his credit cards and headed to the bank to get some cash with it. Then I decided it was time to get out of Ohio, so I planned to drive to Detroit to see Gary Vitto, the former general manager of the Arena league team who still was a good friend.

The next day, Chuck called me. He was pissed off, naturally.

"Art, I called the credit card company to stop you from using my card, but they told me I had to file a police report," he said. "I don't want to do this, but I have to."

"Just file it," I told him. "It won't make any difference at this point."

When I arrived in Detroit, Gary was glad to help me. He gave me a ticket to the Tigers game and told me to meet him at the ballpark.

"Tell you what, we'll put you up in a nice hotel downtown," he told me.

I remember Hideki Nomo pitched that day and the Tigers got bombed by Kansas City 6-0. While relaxing at the ballpark, the game took my mind off my troubles if only for nine innings. I stayed in Detroit for three nights, laying low and mostly eating off the room service menu.

Then Gary called me.

"Art, you have to get out of the city," he said. "The FBI called me and they know you're in Detroit."

Chuck had told the feds where he figured I was headed.

I rushed out of that hotel and drove to Toledo, found a secluded hotel, and started calling what friends I had left to send me some money. Now if I'd put the money to good use, that would be one thing, but of course, I headed to Raceway Park, the local horse track.

I spent four days there, betting on the horses every night, losing every night, wearing the same clothes, and feeling absolutely miserable. I knew some of the horse trainers at the track from my days playing in the Arena league in Detroit and this one particular guy, Mike Croucher, was a really nice guy.

On a Sunday night, I had just bet $100 on the final race. Mike and I stood by the betting windows shooting the bull when I turned to look at the horses at the starting gate and saw several security guards running full-speed.

"There he is!" I heard one of them yell.

I instantly took off running for the door, ahead of them, sprinting to the parking lot, trying to find my keys and my car at the same time. I remember it was the biggest parking lot of any racetrack I had ever seen and it seemed that I ran forever. I looked over my shoulder to see them scurrying about in the parking lot.

When I arrived at this eight-foot fence, I hit it running, and hopped over it in one leap, but I cut my hands as I cleared it. I kept running through one of the roughest neighborhoods in Toledo, looking over my shoulder with every other stride.

It was about 11 p.m., I had no money, no car, my hands were bleeding, and the feds were on my trail.

I sprinted up to one of the main roads and flagged down a mini-van. The driver was an older lady.

"Ma'am, my girlfriend and I got into a fight and she left me out here without a car," I told her. "Can you give me a ride to the nearest bus stop?"

As we drove, I saw two police cars whiz by as I slumped lower in my seat. We arrived at the bus terminal and I saw three policemen standing outside the entrance.

"You know ma'am, I got a better idea. Can you drive me over to a truck stop on the interstate?" I asked.

She drove me about 20 miles down the highway and dropped me off in front of a Denny's. I thanked her and walked inside to make a few telephone calls.

First, I called Dr. Valerie Lorenz, my therapist from Baltimore.

"I think this is it," I told her. "I think the feds are closing in on me. It's a matter of time."

I called Mitzi and told each of the kids I loved them. Then I called Mom and told her I loved her. Just as I started to walk out, I saw two cops walking in. I quickly darted for the bathroom. For the next 30 minutes, I sat in a stall, just waiting for them to come grab me and haul me out of there in handcuffs.

Finally, I couldn't take it anymore. I tiptoed out of the bathroom, peeked around the corner and saw them sitting at the counter, eating. I quickly walked out behind them and took off sprinting across the overpass ramp.

I found a trucker at the truck stop and approached him.

"Sir, I need to get back to Dayton, can you give me a ride?" I asked.

"I would love to," he said. "But I can't. We can get fired for picking up hitchhikers."

I pleaded with him.

"Sir, I will sit there quietly and not bother you at all. I won't tell anyone."

"I'm sorry, can't do it," he said.

I walked over to a 7-Eleven just as a driver pulled into the lot. I coaxed this guy to give me a ride to the next exit, about five miles down Interstate 75. I couldn't hitch a ride there, either. I had nowhere to go, but noticed a hotel a few hundred yards away. By now it was 3 a.m.

I walked into the lobby and started to tell a sob story to the hotel clerk … "I just broke up with my girlfriend and left my billfold in her car. I don't have a driver's license, any money, anywhere to go. Can you help me?"

Miraculously, she gave me a free room for the night. I told her to give me an 8 a.m. wakeup call. I walked into that room, lay down on the top of the bedspread in my sweat clothes, and fell asleep.

I called Raceway Park the first thing the next morning but was told Mike Croucher had not reported to work yet. He was late. Great, I thought. The FBI must have detained him for questioning. I tried again and he still wasn't there. On my third try, the man who answered the phone said, "Hey, he's pulling into the lot right now."

Mike took the phone and asked, "Who is this?"

"You know who it is," I said.

"Who is this?" he asked again.

I didn't want to say my name in case the feds were with him, but finally, he figured it out.

"MAN! WHAT THE HELL HAPPENED TO YOU LAST NIGHT? WHY DID YOU TAKE OFF RUNNING LIKE THAT?" he asked.

"The cops were running after me," I said.

"What are you talking about?" he asked. "They weren't running after you. They were running to break up a fight in the parking lot. Your car is still out here. We tried to get into it to find a way to get a hold of you."

"Are you kidding me?" I asked. "Tell me the truth. Is the FBI standing right next to you?"

"Art, I am telling you the truth," he said. "Where are you?"

I directed him to a gas station I could see through my hotel room window. That way, I would watch him pull into the parking lot and be able to see if any FBI agents were with him, or tailing him.

Sure enough, Mike came by himself, picked me up and took me back to get my car at the horse track.

"Mike, can you give me a few dollars?" I asked.

He handed me $500.

"Can you sign something for me?" he asked.

I had remembered Mitzi had made me take some of my Arena football equipment from her garage a few weeks earlier. I had stashed the stuff in the trunk and forgotten about it. I opened the trunk, pulled out my old Cincinnati Rockers helmet from the 1992 season, autographed it, and handed it to him.

I signed, "Thanks Mike! I'll see you when I get out of prison!"

Sadly, I haven't seen him since that day.

And I never did find out if that horse on which I had placed my last $100 won the race that night.

I started driving toward Cleveland, figuring I would call Perry Bayley, my horse-trainer friend I first met at Beulah Park in Columbus the day after the 1979 win over Michigan.

Running like I was running was not fun at all. It may sound exciting and adventurous, but I was not really free in my mind, because I knew that I was not going to be free. I wasn't going to Mexico or Canada, as my dad had suggested. I wasn't going to kill myself. I wasn't going to get out of this mess until I went to prison and served more time—unless the feds killed me first.

I checked into a hotel near Cleveland and called Perry's house in Ravenna, Ohio. He wasn't home, so I left a message with his wife. Thirty minutes later, he called back.

"Perry, I'm in big trouble," I told him. "I need help."

"Why don't you come out to the farm?" he said. "Nobody can find you out here and you can clear your head and decide what you want to do."

Over the next few days, I slept on his pullout couch at night and drove the truck around Perry's horse track during the day, helping him train his horses. His wife was in a wheelchair, but she was a very sweet woman. One of those nights we were watching television when the local news aired a story saying that I was on the run, and the FBI had started a manhunt with dozens of agents tracking me.

The report also said I had tried to acquire a handgun.

"Art, what are you going to do?" Perry's wife asked me.

Well, for starters, I wasn't going to shoot myself. I never tried to get a gun. I hated guns since the day one of my buddies was shot and killed in a hunting accident when he was 14 years old. I never touched a gun since that day.

Even though he was mad about me taking his credit card, Chuck Grubbs had asked me days earlier, "Is there anything I can do to help you?"

"Yeah," I answered. "Get me a gun, so I can shoot myself."

I was joking. It was typical of me to find some humor even in the most discouraging of circumstances, but when Chuck later told the FBI about my comment during their interrogation of him, they figured I was armed.

The next day, May 18, I rode with Perry as he drove down to Amish Country to pick up some hay. Before we left the farm, Perry told his son, "Let us know if anybody comes looking for him."

I had loaded about 100 bales of hay that afternoon and was sweating my ass off. Over lunch, Perry and I decided enough was enough. It was time for me to turn myself in.

"Let's go back to the house and have supper," Perry said. "Then I'll drive you to Indianapolis so you can turn yourself in. I'll bring your car back to Columbus and give it to your dad."

Perry called his son to tell him of our plans.

"You might not want to bring all of that hay back to the farm," he said. "Drop those bales off at another spot. We don't have room for the hay you picked up."

We knew what that meant. FBI agents were swarming Perry's farm.

"I'll drop you at this restaurant so you can eat and I'll go back and get rid of those guys," Perry told me. "Then I'll come back and get you."

I walked into the restaurant, grabbed some popcorn and a Diet Coke and sat down. An hour passed. Two hours passed. Finally, I called his cell phone.

"Art, they're all over us," he said. "They're here right now."

"Just tell them where I am and have them come pick me up," I told him.

I walked across the street to buy one of those long-distance cards, so I could call my lawyer. I walked back to the restaurant and dialed my lawyer's number on the pay phone in the breezeway. Just then, several FBI agents flooded into the place.

Every one of them had their shotguns drawn.

"Oh my God, they're here already," I told my lawyer. "I've got to go."

I hung up and walked over to this agent standing at the door holding a shotgun.

"I think you're looking for me," I said.

"Just who are you?" he asked.

"Art Schlichter," I answered.

"GET DOWN ON THE FLOOR, YOU M —- F—-!" he screamed.

He was pointing the gun in my face and shouting, "WHERE IS THE GUN?"

"I don't have a gun," I said.

A few more agents jumped on my back and pinned me down, roughing me up pretty good as they handcuffed me behind my back. I had walked over to an agent and turned myself in voluntarily, and they acted as if I was Charles Manson on the run.

They carted me off to the Ravenna jail and I slept like a baby that night, my first good night's sleep in weeks.

And I never saw Perry again.

Chapter eighteen

"DON'T WORRY ABOUT ME ARTHUR. I'LL SEE YOU LATER..."

It's never good news when the telephone rings at four in the morning.

When Mitzi and I were living in Detroit in the summer of 1991, the telephone had startled us from our sleep one day.

"Who the hell could this be?" I whispered to Mitzi.

Taylor was one year old and I hoped the phone didn't wake her up, too.

"Yeah?" I answered.

"Arthur," Mom said through her sobbing. "Your father wants a divorce! He says he loves another woman! I have nowhere to go ... "

Now I've been through some shocking things in my life, enough sadness, heartache, and disappointment to last three lifetimes, but hearing that your parents are divorcing ranks right up there on the misery meter.

Hearing that your mother is an anxious, emotional wreck because the only man who ever existed in her life no longer wants to be married to her, just broke my heart.

She had called me from the road somewhere near Toledo and was headed our way. An hour or so after I hung up the phone she was at our door. She walked in crying, as Mitzi and I hugged her.

My parents had been high school sweethearts, married since their senior year in high school in 1954. Having them together, raising us three kids, and then seeing them stay together even through my highly publicized problems, had been a foundation for me, but perhaps something I took for granted.

Now that bedrock was no longer there, either. I immediately called Dad to hear his side of the story.

"I don't want to be married anymore," he told me. "This time in my life is my time. I gave everything I had to you kids and to her for 37 years."

"Dad, will you try some marriage counseling?" I asked him.

"No," he said. "I've made up my mind."

So Mom picked up the pieces and started over. I was dealing with my gambling problems, the accompanying debt, and the chase, so I'm sure I wasn't as helpful to Mom as I could have been, but I felt horrible for her.

I still do to this day. Their divorce still bothers me.

The worst part of it all was that Dad got involved with one of Mom's better friends, a woman named Sue who was in the antique business with her, and she had plenty of money.

He wanted to remain in our house because he still was a farmer and he needed to be surrounded by all of the farming equipment to make a living. Anyone who knew my mom, knew how great a person she was …. He flaunted that relationship in front of her …. He was a gutless and a classless person.

I have zero respect for the other woman, who was ten years younger than Dad.

My brother and sister wanted to stay out of our parents' bickering, but I know Dad had a way of shaping the story to make it look like he had been the victim. I stuck with Mom. She didn't deserve to be treated the way he treated her.

Mom was very angry and bitter about it all and she still is. It's been almost 20 years, but I don't think she'll ever get over it.

This event was the start of my semi-estrangement from Dad.

A few years later, I once attempted to mend the so-called fence and visited him at the house. I walked in there and looked around and it was eerie. It was so strange without Mom living there. Dad once was my best friend, but all of a sudden it was like I didn't know him at all. He was a completely different person.

Maybe he felt repressed since they were married and had kids at such a young age. It was obvious he was going through some sort of mid-life crisis. He even had grown his hair long and wore an earring.

The whole thing made me want to gamble more. When I faced the disappointments in life, and this was a huge one, I ran to my mistress again …

my gambling mistress. Divorce is one of the biggest disappointments a child can face, no matter how old that child becomes.

The Schlichter family, as it once was in the 1970s.

About a year later, on New Year's Eve, Dad and Sue married in Columbus. It was her third marriage and Dad's second. I hadn't planned to attend the wedding but John talked me into it. He and Dawn both believed it was the right thing to do. It really was a tough decision for me.

Dad soon sold the farmhouse and he and his new wife bought a house on the Olentangy River, just north of Columbus.

Over the years, he visited me once in a while when I was in prison and we talked on the telephone some, but it was never the same between us. Some of the anger I had earlier in life, I blamed it on him. Only later through treatment, I learned he could be responsible for only some of it, but ultimately it was my doing that got me into trouble. After all, he wasn't with me 24 hours a day to tell me to gamble.

Soon after I was released from prison in September, 1999, I started buying and selling tickets through my sports connections, all kinds of tickets from football to basketball to whatever. Dad would front the money for me to buy them and I would sell them at a huge mark-up and then we'd split the profit.

Then he started having financial problems of his own. His cash flow grew low, so he turned to his American Express card to help pay for the tickets. We did it several times. I would pick up the tickets using his card, sell them, and then I would pay him back so he could pay off his card.

When he gave me his credit card to use to pick up the batch of Final Four tickets worth thousands of dollars, I took money off of it and used it to gamble. And once again, I lost.

He had given me permission to use his card, and even had faxed his signature to the ticket broker for the purchase. Then when he found out I used the card to get cash but had not purchased the Final Four tickets, he called American Express and reported that the charges were unauthorized.

That led to a big investigation, which naturally ended at my doorstep and led to that crazy month on the lam in the spring of 2000. The ensuing charges, and a few others added for good measure, violated my state and federal probations.

That resulted in the feds zeroing in on me at the Ravenna restaurant, and I ultimately ended up back in the Marion County Jail. I desperately needed to talk to Dad about his testimony, to encourage him to tell the truth so my charges would at least be reduced. The problem was that they monitored all of the inmates' calls. That's when I pleaded with my attorney, Linda Wagoner.

"Linda, you have to get a phone in here for me," I said. "I have to talk to Dad about this."

"You get me the phone and I'll bring it in," she said, knowing my innocence in the situation with Dad.

I had a friend drop off a phone to her, so she could slip it to me during one of our consultations. I then tucked it into my underwear and the guards never noticed it during my patdown as I walked out of the room.

"Dad, you got me put in prison!" I shouted. "You have to withdraw your statement. It was a lie."

"I can't," he said. "If I do, I'll lose my marriage."

"Dad, your wife is worth fifteen million dollars, so how are you going to lose your marriage over $40,000?"

"All of our money is gone," he told me.

"What?" I asked him.

"All of it?" I pressed him.

"All of it!"

When I questioned him further, he just snapped, "Arthur, trust me … it's all gone."

Linda ended up getting into hot water when she admitted to giving me a cell phone.

Dad visited me in jail a month later, January, 2001, as I awaited my sentencing. He had paid for my attorney to work the case, but I still faced five to 10 years.

"Dad," I demanded. "You have to tell them the truth. You have to tell them you gave me your card and signed for it."

When he learned of the severity of my pending sentence, he finally relented. He said he would tell the truth and get the heat off of me. He walked out of the jail and headed to the lawyer's office.

He returned later that night.

"I can't do it Arthur," he said. "The lawyer told me that the prosecutor said, 'If he changes his statement now, we will get him for lying to a federal prosecutor (for his original statements) and that's a five-year sentence.'

"Art, I can't do five years."

He broke down and cried in front of me.

"Okay, okay," I told him. "Let it go. I'll take whatever they give me. You just promise me one thing. You take care of my kids. You help Mitzi out however you can."

He made that promise to me and walked out of the jail.

It was the last time I would ever see him.

I still believe the prosecutors were trying to scare him and they never would have given him any prison time, but I didn't take the chance. I just accepted my time and let it go. He was still my dad, after all, and I was wrong in the first place, because I lied to him and had started the whole mess by gambling again.

I guess I believed I deserved the prison time because of my lies and gambling.

I pleaded guilty in federal court to 10 charges of credit card fraud on January 16 and was sentenced to five years in prison on April 5.

Again, after two brief stints of freedom, I faced hard time. I had no idea of how I would get through it.

By the summer of 2002, I had been serving my sentence in the Oklahoma City Detention Center, awaiting a transfer flight to the federal prison in Cumberland, Maryland, in a few days.

I called Dad September 2, hoping he could make my arrival in Maryland much easier.

"Can you send some money to my commissary in Cumberland?" I asked him. "I need to buy some things when I get there."

"I'll send it," he said.

I could tell something was wrong. He was real solemn and quiet and barely spoke.

"Dad," I asked. "Are you okay?"

"Arthur, I'm just tired," he said.

There was a long pause, complete silence.

Then he said, "Arthur, I love you."

He hung up.

That following day, I called my friend Elizabeth in Indianapolis. She was a woman about my mom's age and a huge Colts fan who I'd met years earlier. She became a great friend who would visit me from time to time and relay messages from me to my parents and from them to me.

"Honey, you need to call your brother as soon as possible," she told me.

I hadn't talked to John in months, so I asked, "Why?"

"You just need to call your brother right away."

"Is it Mom?" I asked.

"No."

"Is it Dad?"

"Yes."

"Is he dead?"

"I don't want to be the one to tell you," she said. "Just call your brother."

"Elizabeth," I pleaded, "just tell me."

"He's dead."

I dropped the phone.

I was devastated. I started to cry my eyes out. I immediately told the prison officials my dad had died and I wanted to go home for his funeral. They told me to file a petition, but because I was in transit and about to be shipped to another prison, I knew a petition wouldn't do any good. I knew I wouldn't be there for my father's funeral.

I spent that night in shock, lying on my bunk, crying into my pillow.

The next day, they placed me on a flight—shackled and chained just like Nicholas Cage in *Con Air*—to Maryland. It was the worst flight of my life.

Soon, I learned the details of Dad's death.

He had taken a bunch of sleeping pills and went into the deep end of his pool. He never could swim, but he had put on a foam belt so whoever found him wouldn't have to drag his body off the bottom of the pool. I remembered our conversation two years earlier when he advised me to stop talking about suicide, to just do it.

My dad did what I couldn't do.

He had left a suicide note for me, which I didn't receive until two years after his death:

"Arthur, I am sorry that I have been unable to help you. I feel I have failed you in every way. I tried to be a good father, but I guess I failed. You can get out of jail and straighten your life out. I know you can do this. Please do it for your girls. I have sent Linda the information on the federal charges. I hope that somehow that will help you. I love you, Dad."

I read it with tears in my eyes.

Dad's final act before taking his own life was to try to help me. That's one thing he always did best, I guess. No matter how it worked out in the end, or who got in the way, or what his motives were, he always *tried* to help me.

I loved him for it. I always loved him. I just wish he would have done a lot of things differently, but he had his demons just like I had mine. He lived through me and through my accomplishments when I was younger, and then when I went through all of my problems, it hit him hard.

My life had been a fairy tale to him for the first 22 years and then the rug was pulled out from under him. He always clung to the hope that I would get straightened out. The way my life turned out was a great loss and a great disappointment for him.

Later, after the divorce with Mom, he faced more problems of his own. I learned about his losses in the stock market and some troubles with the IRS. In the end, I really believe his financial problems pushed him over the edge.

Naturally, I missed not being able to see him one last time, to tell him goodbye and to tell him how much I loved him.

A few nights after his death, I had the most vivid dream of my life. In it, he came to me:

"Where are you?" I asked him.

"I can't tell you, but I can tell you this: I am okay. Don't worry about me, Arthur ... I will see you later."

It was so real, so vivid, and it made me happy in a way, because I believed what Dad told me in the dream. I slept like a baby that night. I woke up the next day and have never fretted about his death since. I believed his words that he's in a good place.

And that's how I've left it.

The divorce and then Dad's death had pretty much disintegrated our family.

He was cremated. I knew that's what he wanted because he told me a long, long time ago, "When I die, I want to be cremated. Don't waste time crying over me. I lived a good life. When I am gone, I am gone."

And now he was gone, dead at the age of 65.

It's been almost seven years since Dad died and not a day goes by when I don't think of him. I'll always have my memories of all the good things he did for me, the special times we shared together.

I can still picture the time he walked in the door after kicking that skunk, or the times that giant steer dragged him through the bean field, or the moment we shared when I handed him the game ball after I scored the winning touchdown against Michigan in 1981.

Through it all, good and bad, he was my Dad. And I'll always miss him.

As I was finishing this book, I received a call from a lady who worked for Dad. She mentioned something about a video.

"What video?" I asked.

"I'm sorry," she told me. "I thought you knew."

In addition to the note he left for me, she informed me, Dad also made a video for the prosecutors and lawyers. In it, he exonerated me for that illegal credit card use.

I have yet to watch it.

Chapter nineteen

A DOZEN YEARS WASTED

Dad's exoneration of me never reached the proper people. He had wanted his wife to send the note to me and to send the video to my lawyer. For whatever reason, neither was ever sent.

When I spoke to Linda, my attorney, to break the news of Dad's death, she was stunned.

"Oh my God, Art, he left me a message on Friday but I was out of the office," she told me.

His correspondence probably wouldn't have freed me anyway. The prosecutors had filed other charges against me, including the theft of Chuck Grubbs's credit card, its fraudulent use, and money laundering. Then they tacked on violations of my probation.

In addition to the five years they hit me with on April 5, 2001, they added six more years for violating probation from a forgery conviction four years earlier. On July 16, 2004, I pleaded guilty to fraud stemming from a ticket-selling scam in which I had taken money from 22 people who expected tickets to sports events—tickets they never received. The authorities tacked on another eight years.

That amounted to 19 years of sentences.

Fortunately for me, they were to run concurrently not consecutively, or I never would have survived prison until the age of 59.

And there would have been no escaping, as Timothy Robbins did to regain his freedom in *The Shawshank Redemption*. Robbins's character, a banker named Andy Dufresne, was held in *one* prison all those years. It may work that way in the movies, but not for me. I bounced around the state and federal penal systems like a rubber ball, since they first stuck me in the North Las Vegas County Jail on the afternoon of November 10, 1994.

If I remember all of my unpleasant addresses correctly over the next 12 years, they included county jails in Las Vegas; Indianapolis; Noblesville, Indiana; Rockville, Indiana; Baltimore; New Castle, Indiana; Cincinnati, Ohio; Ravenna, Ohio; Medina, Ohio; state prisons in Pendleton, Indiana; Tell City, Indiana; and New Castle, Indiana; diagnostic centers in Plainfield, Indiana; prison camps in Medaryville, Indiana, and Peru, Indiana; and federal penitentiaries in El Reno, Oklahoma; Terre Haute, Indiana; Cumberland, Maryland; Lewisberg, Pennsylvania; Atlanta; Chattanooga, Tennessee; Manchester, Kentucky; Ashland, Kentucky; and Elkton, Ohio.

I didn't just pass through some of these facilities one time. I spent four different stretches in the federal prisons in Terre Haute and three in El Reno, Oklahoma.

In eight different stretches, I spent a total of three and a half years of my life inside the Marion County Jail in Indianapolis. It's probably one of the most horrible, most depressing county jails in America. It was hard time. The food was slop, the showers were dirty, and the bunks were hard as a rock.

What did I miss while I was serving time in all of those jails and prisons? Well, it would be better to ask, what *didn't* I miss?

I missed good food. I missed the quiet. I missed sleeping with the lights off. In prison the lights are on 24 hours a day. They may be dimmed a little at night, but they're always on. I learned to live without the superficial things in life, like a great cheeseburger or lying in bed watching sports, as well as the not-so-superficial things, like sex, but I missed the ability to do what I wanted to do, when I wanted to do it. I missed my privacy. That's one reason I hate being around big crowds to this day.

Most of all, I missed my kids.

I could live without all the other stuff, just knowing that they were safe. I missed talking to them every day, watching their lives progress.

Anybody can shut themselves off from the world, but you can't shut yourself off from thinking about your kids, or wanting to talk to them, or wondering how they are doing. Moving forward and thinking positively is very difficult, because your emotional state is at its lowest.

The last six and a half years, my final stretch of three stints of incarceration, were the hardest for me.

Today, some people say to me, "I can't believe you spent 10 years in prison."

Hey, I can't, either.

I've seen a lot of terrible things in my life—my stillborn child, the unmistakable pain on the faces of my wife, kids and parents, the wrong end of a gun barrel held by an FBI agent, and the heart-breaking words of a suicide note written by my father.

I've also witnessed the horrors of America's prisons up close and personal. I have seen inmates burned for trivial transgressions, raped because they were weak, or beaten badly over a stolen postage stamp (stamps are cash in prison).

The Federal Correctional Institution in Cumberland, Maryland, is one prison I didn't think I would survive. It was the roughest, meanest place I ever served time. Even the corrections officers were as tough as nails. They had to be because of the inmates they dealt with on a daily basis.

The prison population was made up mostly of blacks who had been transferred from a maximum-security prison in Washington, D.C., or those who had grown up in Baltimore. There was a lot of violence in Cumberland because most of the inmates faced a lot of time. They had nothing to lose.

One morning at about seven o'clock, the fire alarms sounded. I grabbed my pants and my radio, my most-coveted possession in prison, and the hacks walked us out of the smoke-filled cellblock. I looked over to the cell where the fire had started, and heavy smoke drifted from it as they wheeled out an inmate who had been burned badly.

This poor bastard had snitched on somebody and his enemy had burned him out, torched him from the outside of his cell by throwing oil on his mattress and then tossing a lit match on it. He had no place to go to escape. He just fried and I never heard later if he lived.

During my first week in Cumberland, Mom had planned to drive there from Ohio to visit with me.

A group of white guys had asked me to join their flag-football team in the yard one day. Flag-football was a big deal at that prison. I rolled out to the yard that day and realized my entire team was made up of Aryan Brothers who had never won a game before, and we were playing an all-black team.

"Man, I haven't thrown a football in years," I told them.

"Just stand back there and throw. You don't have to move around much," one of them told me.

I looked around the perimeter of the yard and saw that it was surrounded by inmates.

"Damn," I thought, "a lot of people came out to see me play."

I even made a reference about the crowd to one of my teammates in the huddle.

"Art," the guy said, "they aren't here to see you. It's getting ready to go down in here."

Translation: The prison population was on the verge of a riot. The Baltimore blacks and the D.C. blacks were posturing, preparing for war.

"When it happens," my teammate told me, "just stay in your cell."

On that Friday, the prison was locked down, preventing anyone from visiting. Meanwhile, my mother sat in a nearby hotel room, waiting to visit me. She had to return to Ohio without seeing me.

I never once told Mom about my prison life, the horrible conditions and constant danger, because I really wanted to protect her from anymore pain. Mom has stuck with me through the thick of the worst times and was the person who visited me the most. My sister never visited me and my brother visited me once, when I was in Elkton, Ohio, and he was on his way to the Ohio State-Michigan game in 2003.

Anyway, the ensuing riot was all over the news and my poor mom had no idea if I was involved or not.

We were locked down in our cells for 12 days with no shower, no phone calls, nothing. The hacks would come get us out of our cells to interrogate us. After about two weeks, everything calmed down and an uneasy peace existed in that prison.

Most of the time, in most of the places I served time, I had people who protected me. I always made plenty of friends when I was free, so there was no reason not to make plenty of friends on the inside. I always got along with all the black guys I had ever played football with on the outside and I got along with black guys in prison, too. Most of them loved sports, so they liked me. And I could relate to them.

Whenever I entered a new prison, many inmates may have figured I was some big hotshot, but once they got to know me, I like to think that they liked me. In my 10 years behind bars, surprisingly, nobody ever tried to take a crack at me.

Once near the end of my time inside, there was a fellow inmate who wanted to kill me. My lawyer, Linda Wagoner, informed me that this guy had made several threats regarding me but I had never seen him, so I had no idea what he looked like or why he wanted to kill me. All I knew is that he had one arm.

It turned out he believed Linda had screwed him on a case, so he sent threatening letters to her, stating that he would get her back by killing me, since I was her client.

I spent many sleepless nights worrying about that guy. They ended up placing him in the hole for the threats, then transferred him out.

Another time in Elkton, an inmate owed me money from gambling. I went to him and demanded payment. He got scared, and had the Mexican gang place a shank in my locker, hoping the prison hacks would find it. They did, but they knew I wasn't the type of inmate to use a shank.

I also witnessed many inmates turned into "Popeye's punk," as they say in prison. In other words, they were forced to be an unwilling partner in, how should I say it?—domestic relations. That never happened to me, and I never got beat up, so I consider myself fortunate.

I learned all of the tricks of survival in prison. If I ever saw a candy bar or a bag of potato chips lying on my bunk, I never ate it. If you accepted a gift like that, it meant that you belonged to whoever placed it there.

There were times I noticed lookouts watching the door for other guys who were having sex, and then those guys inside the room would head to the visiting room to see their wives and kids. That's only a small part of the insanity of prison.

Amazingly, I made some very good friends in prison, guys I still talk to today.

There was a guy named Eddie, who served time at the Central Industrial Facility in Indiana with me from 1998 to 2000. He was in for battery and for acquiring steroids. We became the best of friends, meeting every day in the yard to play basketball, run, lift weights or just talk. I loved the guy and we always had each other's back inside.

He and I teamed up to play two-on-two basketball all the time. We made a great two-man team. He'd grab all the rebounds and I would do all the scoring. I called him "Burro" because of his physique. He was about 6-foot-3 and weighed 220 pounds, sleek and muscular, and he could have been a great athlete.

Eddie also had one thousand stories to tell, most of which were astounding, but too far-fetched to believe. He would talk at one hundred miles an hour.

When I was released in 2000, he had been released, too, and we spent some time together in Indianapolis. It didn't take long to realize every one of those stories he told me had been a complete lie.

Finally, as he started to tell another tall tale one day while we were driving down the road, I snapped.

"Eddie!" I yelled. "Just stop lying to me! All this crap you told me over the years isn't true!"

He started crying his eyes out. I mean, I never saw a grown man cry this hard.

"I just wanted you to like me," he said through his violent sobs. "I'm a nobody and you are somebody."

"Eddie, I'm going to be your friend no matter what," I told him. "I will always be your friend."

Another guy I became close with just happened to be the biggest Michigan fan on earth. His name is Rick Johnson and he was close friends with Mickey Monus, the disgraced former president of Phar-Mor who was convicted of embezzlement and fraud.

Rick, who I called "J.J.," claimed he could pick up any girl anywhere, just by using the line, "I may not be much. I'm only 5-foot-8 and 260 pounds—and eight grams." They fell for that one every time, he said, because they knew those eight grams meant a supply of cocaine.

J.J. was probably the most normal guy I ever knew in prison. He had a great attitude, loved to tell jokes, and loved sports.

One time, they stuck J.J. and me in the hole together for seventy days. Just he and I, talking shit to each other about Ohio State and Michigan for seventy days! We played gin everyday and counted out the grams on each Dorito. We rationed out seven for each of us every night. We also had a small, transistor radio which kept us alive, at least until the batteries gave out.

I have to admit that not all of my prison stops were miserable. In fact, one county jail in particular, the Henry County Jail in Indiana, was almost like Mayberry. I had my own cell and a TV with cable. Inmates could actually order pizza on the weekends. It's where I spent six or seven months in 2001 and saw the events of September 11 unfold.

But the Henry County Jail was the exception.

It was nothing like the federal penitentiaries in which I was incarcerated. They were every bit as tough as you could imagine. There was no privacy anywhere. You ate, slept, and crapped with other inmates next to you.

Most prisons had common areas with one television.

I had never watched a NASCAR race in my life until I went to prison. It seemed that every white inmate wanted to watch NASCAR and the black inmates wanted to watch basketball and boxing.

So whatever demographic of the prison population had control of the TV at that particular time, I knew what sport I would be watching. TV, radio, and whatever mail you received were the lifelines to the outside world.

My best time watching TV in prison had to be the night of January 3, 2003, the BCS national championship game. Picture about 50 black inmates rooting for the University of Miami. Then there was me, the lone white guy, *the* lone person rooting for the Buckeyes.

Miami had that renegade image that appealed to the inner-city guys while Ohio State has always been regarded as the straight-laced, buttoned down football program. Let's just say that my commissary bin was very full after that game.

There is no denying that my prison existence obviously was different from most prisoners. Most people knew who I was, and they had an opinion of me before getting to know me. They either liked me or hated me. Some guys wanted to hang around me to talk about sports. Others treated me like a piece of crap. I came across inmates who were Ohio State fans in just about every prison, and those are the guys who spread the word about who I was to the others who had no idea.

It seemed I never ran out of people who wanted to talk sports with me, almost to the point where it became annoying. Answering the most mundane questions about playing football seemed to be just another penalty for me to pay.

Many of the younger guys who had never heard of me questioned my past over the years.

"I've never heard of you," some of the younger guys would say. "You played quarterback in the NFL? Prove it."

It wasn't something I could prove or cared to prove, but other inmates would verify my identity to the doubters.

One time, a convicted murderer—he had killed some drug dealers and was sentenced to 180 years—came to me and asked, "Are you Art Schlichter?"

We got to talking and I thought he was a real nice guy—as nice as a multiple-murderer could be, I guess. He mentioned that he had snuck a cell phone into his cell.

"Could I ever use it?" I asked.

One night, I heard whispering.

"Art," the voice said. "Look outside."

I looked out of my cell to see that phone dangling by a bed sheet. He had tied it securely and lowered it from his cell, a floor above. I untied it, called Mom and my kids, tied it back to that sheet, and he pulled it back into his cell.

One day, the hacks came rushing into his cell for a surprise search. When he heard them coming, he smashed it into bits and flushed the pieces down the toilet. That was the end of my undercover phone calls.

At the federal prison in Cumberland, Maryland, I wasn't the only famous prisoner. Riddick Bowe, the former heavyweight champion, was serving eight or nine months for taking one of his kids and going on the lam. All of the inmates in Cumberland certainly knew who Riddick was. Everyone called him "Champ," and after some of them explained who I was, he got to calling me "Quarterback."

He was a very nice guy. We walked around the outdoor track one day and talked about everything, but I could tell that all those fights took a toll on him.

———————— ⬤ ————————

Prison, and the thought of facing time in prison, took its emotional toll on me. After they had sentenced me to five more years in April 2001, while I was imprisoned at the Marion County Jail, my stress level soared. I became extremely depressed and would not see the outside for more than a year. My weight ballooned to almost 300 pounds and I had high blood pressure.

One day, the right side of my face suddenly went numb. My right arm was numb. I couldn't feel my right hand. I blacked out for a while and they rushed me to the medical unit. After the doctors examined me, they told me I had a mild stroke.

A stroke! At the age of 42.

That scare forced me to start taking care of myself and I shed some weight. I wanted to see my kids once I became free again. I know I prayed to God to give me more time on the outside to see my daughters again.

Like many inmates, I, too, often turned to my faith in prison. I found prison to be so unbearable at times that I had to seek something to get me through it. I didn't go to church in prison, but I prayed daily, mostly for my family and my children. I always struggled with a tremendous amount of guilt for being in prison and for not being there to help raise them.

What turned me off about religion in prison is that it always seemed there were 400 convicted child-molesters in the prison church. I worked at a prison chapel once and it was hard for me to forgive a child molester.

I always believed people should seek that higher power and to forgive others because I wanted forgiveness for all the wrong things I had done to people. Maybe that's why I've always been so forgiving. Despite some of the things that The Q-Man or Red Ronnie did to me over the years, I always forgave them. I guess that's because I wanted people to forgive me.

That said, I had a problem forgiving the child molesters.

And I remained skeptical of the people who found religion once they got to prison, and a lot of times, I was proven I had a right to be.

But even I needed somebody in there with me. Often, it was God. I read the Bible and a book by the evangelist, Joyce Meyer, while inside. If you're a Christian, as I am, you believe there's another life ahead of you after this one.

That's the one I'm looking forward to.

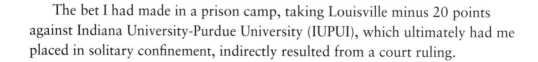

The bet I had made in a prison camp, taking Louisville minus 20 points against Indiana University-Purdue University (IUPUI), which ultimately had me placed in solitary confinement, indirectly resulted from a court ruling.

My release date had been set for December 4, 2004, but just before my pending release, the Department of Corrections reviewed my paperwork and announced that my sentences were to run consecutively, not concurrently.

All of a sudden, with one stroke of the pen, I faced prison until December, 2008.

I had been transported to Medaryville, Indiana, to a prison camp, working as a janitor at night, sweeping and buffing the floors. I became extremely depressed, realizing my freedom was much further off than I had originally counted on.

Again, when I celebrated the best times, when I faced my sorrow in the worst, I turned to my mistress.

I had placed a few bets over the telephone.

And this time I got caught because they had monitored the telephone conversations. One of the hacks came to me while I was lying on my bunk at the camp.

"Schlichter! You need to get up," he said. "Pack your stuff. You're leaving."

"Leaving to where?" I asked.

"You'll find out soon enough," he said.

"Can I tell my family?" I asked.

"When you get there."

They shackled and chained me and took me to Pendleton, Indiana, to the Indiana Reformatory and stuck me in the deadlocked cell, "The SHU."

It turned out that they had written me up for a transgression that would be on par with murder or rape in prison. Betting 20 bucks on a college basketball game shouldn't have been judged in the same manner, but they were trying to teach me a lesson.

It wasn't the smartest thing for me to do, but they were treating me like someone who had shanked another inmate.

They escorted my shackled body into the SHU at about three in the afternoon that day, January 13, 2005, and when I saw that steel toilet, no seat, those cement walls, an old thin mat for a mattress, a dirty blanket, no pillow and that dangling 20-watt light bulb, I realized I faced six months of pure hell—if I survived it.

It was about 100 days later when a hack came to me.

"Art, you'll be out of here sometime today," he said.

"Oh God, thank you," I said.

They let me out of the SHU approximately 80 days early, citing my good behavior. The SHU was for the unmanageable inmates, the worst of the worst of the prison. That wasn't me. But I laughed about the reason they gave me. I mean, how could I not be on good behavior in there? There was nothing to do, no trouble to get into because there was nobody to interact with.

They transported me to the medical block, where I stayed until July, 2005.

Eleven months later, when Marion County Judge Grant Hawkins granted a hearing on my case, I had hope. Dr. Valerie Lorenz, a leading expert in gambling addiction who had become a great friend of mine through treatment, testified in front of him.

"Your honor, gambling addiction is a disease," she testified. "He needs treatment. We have a place for him to get the treatment he needs. Being in jail does not serve his needs."

The judge listened and asked a few questions. At the conclusion of the hearing, he agreed with Dr. Lorenz and said he would sign the papers to grant my release.

"Okay, Mister Schlichter, I will give you a chance to turn your life around," Judge Hawkins said. "Don't make me regret it."

I understood what judges thought when they had sentenced me to prison through the years. Treatment would help the addicted help himself. Prison protects society from the addicted. They couldn't just stick a gambler in treatment if he had murdered a bookie over a debt, even if he was compulsive and addicted.

There is a line to be drawn. When you break the law, you go to prison —addicted or not—and I understood that clearly.

At the same time, I had paid my debt to society in the ten-plus years I was confined. I believed I was due another chance, and Dr. Lorenz believed it, too. Fortunately, so did Judge Hawkins.

When I walked out of the courtroom that day, however, I still wasn't sure his words would lead to my freedom. I figured there would be a last-minute glitch, or someone would overrule him, or he would change his mind. Until the second it happened, until the moment I walked out of the Marion County Jail the next afternoon and hugged my mother at the gate, I just never figured the day would come because the past six and a half years had been so draining on me, so downright horrible that I had almost given up emotionally.

It was Friday, June 16, 2006.

We checked into the Embassy Suites in downtown Indianapolis and the next morning I drove to Carmel to visit with my kids. Then on Monday, I reported to the probation office to make arrangements for my probation.

We returned to Mom's house in Washington Court House where I rested for a few days before flying to Baltimore for four months of intense treatment for my addiction.

I have tried my best to enjoy every moment of my freedom and do the right things ever since that Friday.

From that fateful day, November 10, 1994 in Las Vegas, when my wrists first felt handcuffs, until the day I walked out of the Marion County Jail, there were 4,233 sunrises and sunsets.

Four thousand, two hundred and thirty-three days.

I have figured that I spent all but 358 of those days behind bars.

My time incarcerated totals ten years, seven months and two weeks inside 44 various jails or prisons.

Those will forever be my dubious, disgraceful statistics.

More than a decade wasted, spent in "the system," as America's inmates call it.

I missed 11 Christmases, New Year's Eves, Thanksgivings, and Ohio State-Michigan games. I also spent 10 birthdays behind bars.

The thing I missed the most were my daughters growing up. When I first went in, they were four years old and six months old. When I was released for the final time, Taylor was 16 and Maddy was 12.

My regret isn't that I spent more than 10 years of my life in prison. It's that I spent more than 10 years of *their* lives there.

Chapter twenty

DISCOVERING MYSELF

After reading about the bad checks I passed out like candy on Halloween, all the stupid things I did, all the people I've hurt, the crimes I've committed in my lifetime… just as I once stated to my attorney in Las Vegas years ago, "*You must think I'm a piece of shit.*"

I felt that way about myself. I was ashamed for doing many of the things I did. I had a conscience and knew they were wrong.

At the same time, anyone who's gone through a severe addiction will understand what may have driven me to do what I did, why I did it, what I've gone through trying to fight it.

A reasonable person might say, "Art, you believe in God. You've been saved. You knew right from wrong. So how could you do all those bad things to innocent people?"

Let me say that being saved and believing Jesus died for our sins, as I do, isn't a cure-all for being a good person who always does the right thing. It's not always the crucial factor of whether you live your life the right way.

Many Christian people fall by the wayside. I'm one of those people.

For whatever reason, I had, and still have, an addiction. It's a severe, severe addiction. It's kind of like crack cocaine in that it takes away your soul and your character. It takes away your ability to always do the right thing. If you're addicted to crack, all you care about is the next fix. I was addicted to gambling and all I cared about was the chase. It wasn't about getting my fix, it was about chasing all the money I'd lost from an early age.

If you combine my addiction with my competitiveness, it's a recipe for disaster.

When I was seven or eight years old, I played the card game, Tonk Rummy, against my uncles and cousins for nickels and dimes and hated to lose. By the time I was a sophomore in college, it became $50 here and $100 there. I chased it, but never as intensely as I would later.

At 22, I signed a contract worth one million dollars and gambled away the money almost immediately. That affected me for the rest of my life. I started chasing that million dollars and the chase itself was worse than anything else. No matter what I had to do to get money to continue the chase —steal, lie, cheat—I did it. It was a never-ending journey, a battle that probably won't end until the day I die.

Subconsciously, I believe I was driven every day to somehow win back that first dollar I ever lost.

When I had my own money, I was driven to gamble it during the chase. When I didn't have any money, I was driven to do anything to get it. That led to me writing bad checks, forgery, and fraud. Here was my thought-process about passing these checks, and I passed hundreds of them:

Red Ronnie introduced me to this method a long, long time ago at a racetrack, when gambling establishments accepted personal checks. I would write a check to the casino or track, receive the cash, and then go gamble.

As I handed them a check, in *my* mind, I was sure that if I won, which I had planned to do, I would buy the check back.

Plus, I would have some profit in my pocket.

But I would almost always lose and wouldn't be able to cover the checks.

Therefore, a law was broken.

Red Ronnie told me one day in Las Vegas, probably in 1994 when I went on that severe binge, "Art, someday when they write your life story, the title should be, 'Insufficient Funds.'"

In my mind, I never, ever wrote a check that I didn't intend to cover soon afterward with my winnings. To me, they were all good checks at the beginning. As an addicted gambler, I always figured I would win money, and make that check good.

In the end, I lost so much that most all of the checks I ever passed resulted in insufficient funds.

Passing bad checks, stealing, lying, and conning people out of their hard-earned money just so you can gamble is a sleazy way to live, believe me. It's terrible. It's not the way I wanted to conduct my life, and I was not happy with myself when I did those things. I knew it was wrong. I just couldn't stop doing it.

Let me say it again, I COULD NOT STOP.

Today, people often ask me if treatment and counseling has cured me. I've been through countless hours of treatment and therapy in the best gambling and addiction treatment centers in America, but that doesn't mean I'm now a new person—a cured addict. Just look at alcoholics who go through treatment twenty or thirty times and still can't get it right. My desire to jump back into the chase, like their desire to drink again, is always there.

When I say that the chase is a never-ending battle, I mean it hasn't ended. It probably will never end for me. It never gets better. It only gets worse.

I've been in more treatment centers than the average addict. I was admitted for thirty days to the South Oaks Center in New York when the NFL announced my suspension in 1983. I spent time at the Taylor Manor, a psychiatric hospital in Maryland, in 1986. I was treated on an outpatient basis at the Charter Hospital in Las Vegas in 1989. I've been in what I considered the best—Harbour Center in Baltimore, in 1997. It later became Harbour Pointe, and I was treated there again in 2006, but the doctors who I believed were the best were gone by then.

The longer you're in treatment, the better the opportunity to discover who you really are and what drives you. Doctors told me at times that I was clinically depressed, had anxiety disorders, and Attention Deficit Disorder.

More important, I learned there were a lot of painful things in my life I never dealt with, mainly because I didn't want to deal with them.

Treatment led me to realize that I blamed myself for losing our son at birth. I beat myself up over that. I learned I was self-destructive and a self-beater-upper, if you will. I did things after that terrible day to punish myself. I believe that event triggered my behavior from 1992 through 1994 until they put me away.

A therapist once had me fill out a paper, listing the best times and worst times in my life.

"One thing stands out on the scale to me," the therapist said. "You wrote down the good times, you wrote down all the worst times, but you never mentioned that you lost a child."

That shows how much I tried to kill the pain, to bury that awful memory somewhere deep.

Another time, a counselor suggested that getting burned severely and almost dying at the age of 12, may have ignited my destructive behavior from that very day. I've always been a bit of a daredevil anyway, as anyone who's ever ridden with me when I drive, will tell you.

Red Ronnie loves to tell a story about the time we were headed to Scioto Downs, with me following in my car behind him, in his car. My cell phone, before they invented those handy cigarette lighter chargers, suddenly went dead. As we drove north on I-71 at about 80 miles per hour, I pulled up alongside his car in the emergency lane.

I reached out with my left hand and knocked on his passenger-door window. AT 80 MILES PER HOUR!

"Ron, I need your phone," I screamed through the glass. "I need to make a call."

He looked over at me. His eyes were as wide as the Ohio River.

During treatment in Baltimore, in 1997, counselors told me to invite anyone important in my life to join me, so one time I invited Dad to visit so he could participate in a session. That day, I said a lot of things to him that I needed to say for a long, long time. I was angry, because I felt he was overbearing to me in my early years and that he was trying to live my life for me. He made too many decisions for me and I know that now. He lived his life vicariously through me. Even later, he gave me advice on how to raise my kids.

As I rattled on, he started to cry. I cried.

"I was just a farmer, a simple man who tried to do the right thing by you, your mother, John, and Dawn," he told me. "I'm just a man and I have my faults."

He had no idea how much he had affected me in my adolescent years, but I had built him into an icon of a father whom I always wanted to please.

After he left Mom to marry another woman, we barely spoke for the next seven years. I never even called him when Madison was born. I was so angry with him, but I never really realized why.

Through treatment, I learned he wasn't an icon of a father. He never was.

He wasn't perfect. He was just a man who had his faults like every one of us—a man who tried to raise me, and my brother and sister, as only he knew how.

He may have manipulated me, lived through me, but I still don't think anything Dad did resulted in my problems. I don't blame him, or anyone else, for my addiction.

I have to say that session helped me immensely, as did many sessions there. I was making some serious progress and was doing better with every day until the feds stormed the place to take me back to prison.

Dr. Lorenz believed in me and cared for me at times when I felt nobody else did. She understood me more than anyone else because she understood the mind of an addicted gambler more than anyone I ever knew. Dr. Thomas Truss also was a brilliant doctor, a tremendous help to me to find answers into what motivated me to follow a destructive path.

Through all the therapy and counseling, I always wanted to know the answer to this question. What takes a person who likes to gamble and can walk away after an hour, or two hours, across the line to become a person, like me, who can never walk away—someone who gambles until their life is ruined?

I still don't know that answer, if one exists.

I've learned that a scientific aspect of it is the chemical dopamine, which affects how your brain works in regard to addiction and the pleasure system of the brain. Scientists believe it is what provides the feeling of enjoyment when it's released, by rewarding experiences such as eating, doing drugs, having sex, or drinking alcohol

I've believed for some time that dopamine rushes into my brain when I gamble.

There are drugs on the market that limit the flow of dopamine into the brain, but they do have some bad side effects, and I've never taken them consistently. That, along with being extremely competitive, may have been my undoing.

As a competitor, and I was more competitive than anyone, I often wondered, "How can I be this bad at gambling? I had a lot of success early in life in sports? Why can't I have success in this, too?"

If I was successful at gambling, and if I ever had re-captured that million dollars, would I have been happy?

Probably not, because I know I wouldn't have stopped. I would have gambled *that* million dollars until it was gone, too.

Instead, my gambling failures led me to do terrible things, put me in prison, and almost drove me to insanity, if not, at times, close to death.

Addicts who read this book will understand what I'm talking about. Other people, those people fortunate never to be addicted to any real vice like drugs, smoking, booze, sex, or gambling, may not.

How many times have you walked into a restaurant and seen an overweight person eating a pizza? That person knows the pizza will make them fatter, but they go ahead and eat it anyway.

How many times have you heard of a person who realizes that smoking causes cancer, or heard of a person who is dying from lung cancer, but they still smoke cigarettes every day?

I never drank and I never smoked, but I know what those people are going through. It doesn't matter how bad these vices are, the addiction to them overpowers the will *not* to smoke, drink, or gamble.

It's a war, a real war, inside the person's head and body.

People ask, " ... but you know first-hand how bad prison is, so doesn't the thought of going back stop you?"

Let me say, I have a *strong desire not to go back to prison*. I don't think I have one more *bit*—that's inmate slang for jail time—left in me.

But I'm not cured. This is a very tough addiction to treat. There isn't enough money to research it. People pour money into casinos by the billions. They're not worried about the addicted gamblers, the guys like me.

The addiction—that war inside me—is sometimes stronger than my will to stay free. Some days it's easier to deal with. Some days it's not.

Some people say to me today, "Don't worry, it's all behind you."

No, it isn't, because you can't just walk away from a disease like mine. It's always there, staring at me, just like my face when I look into the mirror while shaving each day.

Will I do bad things again that will send me back to prison? I admit the urge is always there.

Today, I know I'm still only one wrong step away from imprisonment, insanity, or death.

Chapter twenty-one

CRACK COCAINE OF THE 21ˢᵀ CENTURY

Every sports fan knows Pete Rose since he became a household name more than four decades ago. First, Charlie Hustle became a living legend, the all-time Hit King baseball fans loved for his hard-charging style. Then his image evolved into being a known gambler who was suspended from baseball, while a manager. He became an inmate, like me, having been sent to prison for not reporting income to the IRS.

And finally, after denying it for years, he succumbed to the overwhelming evidence and admitted that he had bet on baseball. I knew that fact a long, long time ago—years before he admitted it publicly.

He once came on my radio show in Cincinnati, because we had a mutual respect for each other. I had visited the Reds' clubhouse when I was in college and he was an Ohio State fan.

Point blank, I asked him on the air, "Pete, do you think you're a compulsive gambler?"

Not many people could get away with that question without him blowing up and storming out of the studio.

"Listen," I told him. "I know I'm a compulsive gambler, but are you?"

"No! I just got the money to do it, and I like it, so I do it," Pete answered.

Charles Barkley recently gave a similar response to a similar question when it became public that he owed a Las Vegas casino $400,000. Michael Jordan was another American icon who liked to lay down a wager or two.

Examining their lives from a distance, I really believe they are tip-toeing around a dangerous slope, one that could turn icy and slick if they don't have the self-control it takes to keep the gambling demons in check.

Pete and I never discussed if he ever bet on baseball, but I didn't have to ask him. I knew that he did. Everybody 'in the know' in the Cincinnati area knew it, too. Red Ronnie was in Cincinnati all those years and he was on the inside on all the big-time gambling and the bookie connections, and he knew how Pete was doing it. He had all the details and I was privy to that information.

There were times at River Downs in Cincinnati, during the '80s, when Pete and I would be doing our thing separately, hoping nobody noticed us.

I would wear disguises and sit downstairs and my buddy would joke, "Here you are downstairs hiding and Pete is upstairs hiding in the corner so nobody sees him. You two guys have got it bad!" That picture might have been funny if it wasn't so sad.

We had our own respective league commissioners to worry about— Pete Rozelle for me and Bowie Kuhn and then Bart Giamatti for him. Neither one of us was supposed to be at a racetrack, but we did it anyway, risking our futures for the thrill of the bet.

It was such a small track with a small handle (the total amount of money bet) that when Pete would be dropping $500 or $1,000 on a horse, the odds would be affected dramatically by his wager. We'd wait for Pete to walk up to the window and bet, and we'd watch the board to see how his bets had altered the odds. Then we'd bet on another horse that suddenly had much better odds.

Today, Pete's name and mine, are often regarded as a punch line to a gambling joke rather than as reflections of our athletic accomplishments.

I know now that gambling is no joke. It destroyed my life and certainly diminished his image, if not his life, as well. After all, his bust isn't in Cooperstown. And, like me, he's spent time in prison.

The bottom line is this: Pete Rose was a compulsive gambler. I know all of the signs and he owned them as sure as he owns the major-league hits record.

And another undisputable fact, whether Pete wants to admit it or not, is that he and I are likely the two most notable living, breathing poster boys of the three million compulsive gamblers who live in the United States.

Everybody knows our stories, but those other 2,999,998 stories are what concern me.

And sadly, there are more developing all the time.

Recently, I walked into a friend's living room and his 14-year-old boy and another friend were sitting on the floor, surrounded by poker chips, playing poker.

ESPN televises so much poker that they have this country thinking it's a sport. But we don't call blackjack a sport. Or craps. So why is poker televised on ESPN?

Because it's pure entertainment.

Kids of all ages are doing it now, thinking it's a perfectly acceptable sport, not realizing it could lead to destruction down the road. I sincerely believe we could be headed for an epidemic in the future.

Why do I feel that way? Let's start at the beginning.

Gambling is defined as a wagering of money or items of value on an uncertain event, dependent wholly or in part on pure chance. It appeals to our human desire for gain and the thrill of risk and has been practiced throughout human history in all places of the world.

I have another definition for it: Gambling is the "crack cocaine of the 21st century." It may not be quite as addictive as cocaine, but it's just as destructive and even more widespread and accessible, simply because it's legal.

The problem in the United States is undeniable:

* The National Council on Problem Gambling estimates that 86 percent of Americans have gambled during their lives and 60 percent gamble at least once in any given year.

The Council also claims that pathological and problem gamblers are much more likely to have problems with drinking, drugs, smoking, and are more susceptible to depression. Naturally, there's a strong link between pathological gambling and suicide.

* In addition to the estimated three million compulsive gamblers, another three million can be considered problem gamblers and even 15 million more adults are at risk for a severe gambling problem, while 148 million are low-risk gamblers, according to the American Psychiatric Association.

What's the difference between "pathological, problem, and compulsive"?

"Pathological" and "compulsive" gambling are virtually synonymous. It's a progressive addiction characterized by an increasing preoccupation with gambling, a need to bet more money more frequently, an irritability when attempting to stop "chasing" losses and a loss of control regardless of the consequences.

"Problem" gambling describes a gambling behavior that disrupts any important life function, but has not yet progressed to compulsive. The APA also claims that pathological and problem gamblers are much more likely to have been on welfare, declared bankruptcy, or to have been arrested and incarcerated.

* The Council on Compulsive Gambling found that the addicted gambler is typically a "competitive, bright, charismatic" male between the ages of 21 and 55. "But when you peel away the surface, these people suffer from loneliness and low self-esteem," said Edward Looney, the council's executive director.

That all sounds familiar.

As we were writing this book, I picked up the March 5, 2009, edition of *USA Today*, and noticed a story in the Life Section headlined, "Gamblers by 6th Grade?" The story detailed a study published in the *Archives of Pediatrics & Adolescent Medicine* that reported the more impulsive a child was at the age of 5, the more likely that child was to be gambling by the age of 11. Researchers had studied 163 kindergarten kids who were inattentive or hyperactive. By 11, many of those kids were betting on their video games and sports or playing poker. The research claimed that children's impulsive behaviors "snowball" as they grow older.

Anyone who knew me when I was 5, especially Mom, will tell you I was a hyperactive, ornery kid.

So this study, too, sounds very familiar to me.

A week after that story appeared, it was reported that Delaware Governor Jack Markell had proposed a bill in his state that would legalize sports betting. His plan was to institute a sports-betting lottery, offering parlay bets only (which was my downfall), to generate an estimated $50 million to $70 million annually. The Delaware governor came up with the idea after his state faced a $700 million budget shortfall for 2009.

In time, he may solve Delaware's budget crisis by paving an easy, legal path to debt and heartache for would-be sports gamblers. I'll tell you that legalizing sports parlays will unwittingly create hundreds of compulsive gamblers. Add this together and I believe the gambling problem is a runaway train in this country, especially if you examine the proliferation and increasing accessibility of venues.

In the 1950s, Las Vegas was a sleepy, little town in the middle of the Nevada desert and Atlantic City was known for its boardwalk and coney dogs. By the 1980s, they had grown into gambling meccas, but most people still had to catch a flight or drive there to get their fix.

Today, there are more than 500 casinos in seventeen states and Puerto Rico, producing gross revenues of more than $34 billion annually. More than seventy-three million people will step into a casino this year. There is *one* reason all of those beautiful, high-rise casinos along the Las Vegas strip offer free shows, food, and rooms to their best customers. They *make* money.

Furthermore, legal "gaming," another common term for gambling, accounts for an estimated $80 billion in revenue across the country when you throw in all the horse and dog tracks, card rooms, bingo halls, and state lotteries.

Think about that. That's $80 billion that could be used annually to pay mortgages, car loans, student loans, utility bills, and put food on the table.

Formal lotteries date back to the Roman Empire, but New Hampshire established the first during the modern era in this country in March, 1964. Today, 42 states offer official lotteries. What's interesting is that they seem to be recession-proof, too. The Associated Press recently reported that 25 states that offer lotteries reported sales had increased in 2008 and through the first few months of 2009, as the economy worsened.

That makes perfect sense. When people are struggling financially, they want to take that one long shot of a chance to reach financial security.

What may turn out to be the worst invention related to problem gambling is the Internet, of course. No longer do you need to leave your house or office to gamble. Now it's as easy as a click of your mouse. And there are hundreds of gambling websites, as well as off-shore gambling houses, offering toll-free telephone numbers so you can bet on any sport you desire without going through a shady bookie who may threaten to break your throwing arm if you don't pay in a timely manner.

Recognizing the symptoms and characteristics of a compulsive gambler is the first step toward getting help, according to Gamblers Anonymous:

1. An inability to accept reality. The compulsive gambler escapes into the dream world of gambling.

2. An emotional insecurity. A compulsive gambler discovers that he or she is emotionally comfortable when "in action." It's very common to hear a member of Gamblers Anonymous claim, "The only place I felt comfortable and secure in life was sitting at the poker table, or blackjack table, or in front of a video poker machine."

3. Immaturity. The gambler possesses a desire to have all the good things in life without putting in the effort to achieve them.

There are some positives. Today there are more places to turn for help, unlike when I fell into this dark hole.

There are several websites, including *gamblersanonymous.org*, *problemgambling.com* and *ncpgambling.org*, where you can research the problem, identify its symptoms and effects, and discover how to seek help and treatment.

Also, casinos around the country have posted toll-free numbers of help centers for patrons who believe they have a problem. Counselors, too, are better trained than ever before to identify a gambling problem and provide help. Treatment centers have a better understanding of how to effectively deal with the addiction than they did twenty or thirty years ago.

But there's still no consensus as to what creates a compulsive gambler. Some doctors have concluded through years of studies that many addicted gamblers have experienced severe traumas in their past. Others believe some of the cause is hereditary. And some believe it's the chemistry of the brain, related to dopamine.

I believe that treatment for this problem still is in its infancy compared to where it should be. The problem is that some treatment centers have failed financially. It's harder for them to operate long-term because there's little money. The gambler already has blown his or her finances, sucked their family dry, and has no ability to pay the center. Insurance does not cover treatment, unless it's linked to depression.

Another problem is that the severely addicted gambler's road, like mine, may lead to prison. Well, he can't receive the proper treatment if he sits in a six-by-eight cell for twenty-three hours a day. Still, judges want to protect society from the addicted gambler who has committed a series of crimes.

But once these people are released from prison, they do the same things that put them there in the first place, just like I did. They're still addicted because they never received the necessary treatment. It's a never-ending, destructive cycle.

When I was stuck "in the hole" in prison, at times I wanted to die. At other times, I wanted to figure out a different path for myself once I was released. So I started practicing what I'd say to people about my addiction, how I would describe the hell I've been through. I starting putting my thoughts together and forming the content of the speeches I would give.

When I was released from prison in June, 2006, people immediately started calling me to talk about gambling addiction, wanting to know all about it, or how to identify it and where to get help. That got me to thinking, so I contacted a friend from college, who helped me set up a website called *gamblingpreventionawareness.org*, a tool for me to reach out to help others.

I've also conducted several, what I call, "rescues." I use that name rather than interventions, because I like to think I am throwing the addicted person a lifeline.

It works this way. After a family member conducts an intervention that did not succeed, they contact me as a final resort. I meet with the family to get a picture of the loved one's story of addiction. Then I form a game plan to reach that person.

Let me say that I'm not Jesus and I don't have all the answers about this disease, but if I can get a few moments with that person, I'm confident I can connect with them. I don't think anybody is more qualified to tell gambling horror stories than I am and my name recognition also helps. Most of them know who I am or have read my story somewhere.

Some of them think, "Well if it means that much to him to come all this way to talk to me, then it means enough for me to let someone help me."

I start by telling them my story, what gambling did to me, and that there's help for them if they want it. I also educate their family members about the addiction.

Once the addicted is admitted into a facility, the treatment pulls them along until they can again stand on their own two feet and not gamble anymore. I know better than most that it's a long, difficult journey to reach that point. It took me approximately twenty-five years.

Most of these people's lives are unmanageable by the time I get to them. They don't know what to do or where to turn. They're in complete ruin, either in divorce or bankruptcy, and some have legal problems. At the same time, their friends and family are ready to give up on them. Almost all of their stories have the same theme.

During one rescue attempt, I traveled to Florida and met with an addicted man's family and I learned that he was hooked on slot machines, which illustrates the danger of their increased accessibility. Ten years ago, there were no casinos or slot machines in the state of Florida.

Anyway, as we all sat in the living room ready to confront him, he walked in the door. This man was in his late 40s, but he appeared to be in his late 60s to me. He looked like living hell, or like Sam Elliott's aging character in the movie *Road House*, as I told him later. The poor guy had been out all night gambling and had not slept.

His wife said, "Honey, this man is here to help you and talk to you about your addiction."

He didn't say a word. He turned around and walked out the door.

I sprinted from my seat and caught him outside.

"Look, my name is Art Schlichter and I just want to talk to you," I started.

He looked at me like I had just landed on Earth from Mars. There was a long pause and he didn't say anything.

"Do you know who I am?" I asked.

"Of course, I know who you are," he replied.

He sat down, lit a cigarette and said, "You know Art ... I'm just spent. I'm done ... I have no energy left."

So I began telling my story.

When I finished, I said, "I don't want what happened to me to happen to you. Now, I want you to come back inside and listen to your family."

Three or four hours later, he and I were flying to a treatment center to get him admitted.

That night, he told me, "You know, it's funny you came to me today."

"Why is that?" I asked.

"Tonight," he said, "I was going to *kill* myself."

Today, that man and I are good friends and he's doing very well in his recovery.

Naturally, when I experience something like that, I feel that maybe my life *does* have a little meaning. Maybe God placed me in this position, through all that heartache, pain, and misery I brought upon me and my family all those years, so I can be here today to save someone else.

Maybe I was meant to do this all along.

Maybe.

Chapter twenty-two

MY LEGACY,
MY PRESENT,
MY FUTURE

No matter what I do with the rest of my life, no matter how many people I educate about this disease, no matter how many successful interventions or rescues I conduct, I will never deny my path of destruction.

It was wide. It was long. And it was deep, carved out for more than twenty-five years. Those it touched, especially Mom, Dad, Dawn, John, Mitzi, Taylor, and Madison, were affected greatly. I hurt each of them in various ways.

How can I ever make it up them? How can I ever erase the pain or obliterate the emotional scars I inflicted? I can't, and nobody realizes that more than I do. All I can do now is live what's left of my life the right way, and tell those people I've hurt that "I'm sorry."

Apologies are so common and superficial these days, especially from professional athletes making millions of dollars who have shot themselves in the leg in a nightclub, used steroids, or gotten caught driving drunk.

Often, they're propped up in front of a microphone by a sports agent or team official, holding a statement written by someone else.

So my apology here may come off as self-serving, orchestrated, or superficial as well, but I hope that's not the case.

I feel regret, remorse, and a lasting sorrow deep inside my heart. I never set out to hurt anyone, most of all my family. I know I was out of control. I know that now. What I did was crazy. I really hope all the people I've hurt will someday forgive me.

I know I hurt my sister, because I spent ten years in prison and Dawn never

233

came to see me one time. Not once. I know I hurt my brother, because John visited me only once. Most of all, I know I hurt Mitzi and my daughters.

My dad came three or four times over the years, but he was battling his own problems at the end. My mom was always there for me, the one to drive hundreds of miles to cheer me up, to update me on the kids, or just to say a few words to give me hope.

There were others who visited me from time to time and offered their time and encouragement as well, such as Don Donoher, the retired Dayton basketball coach I always admired so much. I knew he was a great coach when I was a kid. Now I know he's an even greater man.

But don't get the idea that I ever judge people by whether they visited me in prison or not. I know prison isn't a pleasant experience, even for a visitor. Most of those who didn't come to see me had every right not to come … but for those who did make the extra effort, I will always hold a dear place in my heart for them.

There are several men in Ohio who have stuck by me through the years and have welcomed be back when I was released and I want to mention what special friends they are. Sonny Walters, Bill Beatty, David Ford, Bruce Kirk, Roland LeMaster, Jim Anderson, John Bryan, and Dick Holstein … all great, great people.

And Earle Bruce?

We've been through it all. It's true that I resented him at times during my playing days and by the end of my senior season, it's true that I couldn't wait to move on because of him. But he went to bat for me in Indiana when I was in prison. He visited me a few times in prison and for that I'm grateful.

These days, he and I work together on radio shows during football season and there are few people I respect more.

We may have had our differences a long, long time ago about what the offense was or wasn't, but I've grown to realize now that many of Dad's feelings for him may have rubbed off on me, fairly or unfairly. I really believe Dad may have poisoned my mind when it came to Earle. The farther along I get in life, I realize what a good man Earle Bruce really is. Thanks, Coach, for always being there for me.

Of all of my old teammates at Ohio State, there is no one I stay in touch with on a regular basis, other than Vlade Janakievski. None of them ever visited me in prison, although I am not blaming them for it. Once we left Ohio State, they went their way and I went mine. I always had the feeling they were scared to have any communication with me.

In the three-plus years I've been out, I've bumped into a few of them at the alumni functions and we exchange telephone numbers and they always say they'll call, but they never do. But I feel nothing but mutual respect when I see all of them. I'm looking forward to the 30-year reunion of the 1979 Big Ten championship team.

I saw Gary Williams recently and he's saddled with a bad back. He lives back in Wilmington and his son is a great high school basketball player who looks just like him and runs like him. It's like Gary has been reincarnated. He was a great receiver in his day, as was Doug Donley, who lives in Texas and is doing well in the golf supply business.

My mementoes from Ohio State—my two Big Ten championship rings and several bowl watches, including my prized Rose Bowl watch—are long gone. I've nothing left but a few pictures Mom kept. It's sad to think that I was so desperate for money at times that I sold those things.

What I have are my memories of all the special moments, the big plays, the big games, the laughs we all shared, and nobody will ever take those away from me.

As far as my legacy as a Buckeye, I know the people at Ohio State have not been eager to promote me during my post-career, nor do they have to, and I understand that's because of my past. I still hold most of the school's passing records, but you can barely find my name, let alone my picture, in the team's annual media guide.

I like to think I was a popular player when I was at Ohio State, and I hope that my off-the-field problems don't prevent me from being inducted into the school's Hall of Fame someday. If they do, I understand. I may not agree with it, but I do understand it.

My girls have never been to Ohio Stadium, but if that day ever comes, I'll bring them with me. That would mean the world to me.

When I think of Ohio State, I think of class. Ohio State stands for good things ... great things.

When I came back to Columbus for the first time after being released from prison a few years ago, I was bracing for the worst, but I discovered the best. People have been good to me, supported me, and have been very gracious. I can't thank them enough for that, especially the encouraging words I hear.

You know, I think the pride they have about being a Buckeye goes back to Woody Hayes and even earlier. When you play for Ohio State, you play for the people of Ohio. That's one thing he always preached to us, as players.

It's an Ohio thing.

Once you become a Buckeye, you remain one until the day you die, whether you've gone to prison or you've gone to the moon. The colors scarlet and gray seep into your blood, especially for a guy like me who grew up forty miles down the road from that campus.

And I will bleed those colors until they put me into the ground, just as Woody did until the day he died, March 12, 1987. I'll never forget his funeral, and sitting behind Bo Schembechler, and listening as President Nixon delivered the powerful eulogy.

He *was* Ohio State.

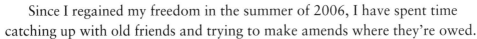

Since I regained my freedom in the summer of 2006, I have spent time catching up with old friends and trying to make amends where they're owed.

Sadly, Gary Vitto, the general manager of the Detroit franchise who introduced me to Arena Football and later became an executive with the Detroit Tigers, died of cancer in 2001. Sonny Walters, my middle-school basketball coach who re-introduced me to God, is still going strong and helping kids in Washington Court House. My old roommate Mark George owns several Wendy's stores in the Midwest. I'm very happy for him because he was one of the good guys.

I still talk to Chuck Grubbs, as well as Red Ronnie, and consider both lifelong friends. Ron is having serious health problems, and we may not always have agreed on everything, but I know he cared about me.

My high school basketball coach, Ron Hall, is retired and living in Marion, Ohio. Our basketball team recently had its 30-year reunion and it was as if three weeks had passed, not three decades. We picked right up where we left off, having a great time telling stories and reliving that memorable season.

My high school football coach, Fred Zechman, lives in Dayton, owns a successful insurance business, and I stay in touch with him often. George Chaump, Woody's offensive coordinator who recruited me to Ohio State, is back in Harrisburg, Pennsylvania, coaching high school football. I talk to him once in a while. I have to say that George is one of the finest men I ever knew.

My brother John has been married to his high school sweetheart, Debbie, since 1979, and has three grown children, Trey, Bethany, and Miles, who broke all of my passing records at Miami Trace High. One of my biggest regrets is that I never got to see him play. John and I talk maybe once a month and I wish we were closer than we are. He was a state representative for three terms and a well-respected man in our part of Ohio. However, his business dealings with Dad were used by his political opponents who wanted to bring him down when he ran for re-election. If people knew my brother as I do, they'd know that he's an honest, straight-forward man who cares about people. There's no question about his integrity.

Sadly, my sister Dawn lost her husband to a heart attack three months after Dad died in 2002. Today, she's a retired schoolteacher enjoying life more than ever. She has one son, Kristopher, who attends Morehead State University.

John and Dawn, I love you, I care about you, and I want you to have good lives. I know there were plenty of times I embarrassed you and embarrassed our family name, but I hope and pray that you understand that people can change. I hope you know that I have changed.

As for Dad, he ordered that his body be cremated. His ashes were spread into the Olentangy River in Columbus. He never told me why he wanted that. Not a day goes by that I don't think of him.

And Mila Schlichter? She's living in Washington Court House in what was once her parents' house. Her health isn't always good and her heart is still broken from the divorce in 1991. She still is the classiest, toughest lady I've ever known, but she's been through more tough times than she ever deserved. Mom, I love you with all my heart and my goal in life is to someday make you proud of me again.

Since our divorce, Mitzi spent a great deal of time in the 1990s testifying before various committees and councils that studied gambling and its effects in this country. I realize I put her through hell and I apologize to her for that. I know there probably is underlying anger left in her toward me, but who would blame her?

Over the years, there were times I cringed when she publicly told all the horror stories about my gambling and the things I did. That really bothered me. She worked for a few years in public relations for Trimeridian, a gambling abuse and addiction intervention and treatment center in Carmel, Indiana, giving many speeches around the country. Originally, an Indiana businessman started the company with me in 1996 when I was out of jail, and I brought Mitzi into company. When I went back to prison, he disowned me and made her the director of PR.

While I was in prison, raising the kids took 100 percent of her time and focus. I have no beefs with Mitzi today and we get along very well most of the time. She's a very good mom and I know she'd do anything for our kids.

Sometimes I wonder if we got married for all the wrong reasons, but when I think of the two beautiful daughters we have, I can't see beyond them. She keeps me updated on the kids, and I need to hear what they're doing because they're teen-agers now and teen-agers don't always have the time to pick up the phone and call their dad.

She's now re-married to a good man, a guy with whom I get along very well. They live in Indianapolis. When you see your ex-wife get re-married to another man, you'd think it would be uncomfortable, but it hasn't been. I have a lot of respect for her husband and he treats both of my daughters very, very well and I appreciate that. I'm grateful he's stepped in and was there for my family when they needed someone.

Having kids changed me, for sure, but didn't change me enough to prevent me from gambling, obviously. I didn't take the responsibility of being a father seriously enough, or I wouldn't have done things that led to me leave my kids to head to prison.

I always believed that if my kids were prosperous and were living a happy life with me gone, and I had to make that sacrifice by staying in prison and to not be around them, which may have made their lives worse, I would do that. What's that old saying? "You can get married 100 times, but your kids are your kids." You never divorce *them*. Now, they may divorce *you* …Today, Taylor is attending Indiana University-Purdue University at Indianapolis, majoring in English. Maddy is in high school. I'll never be able to adequately tell them how much I love them and how sorry I am for what I put them through by not being there.

Maddy, Taylor and me in 2007.

As for me, I'm older, fatter, and balder. Still, my life is better today than it was yesterday, but I hope not as good as it will be tomorrow. I may have suffered post-traumatic stress from prison and I've undergone psychiatric treatment. I also continue to receive treatment and after-care for my gambling addiction. Physically, I need to lose weight and I need to eat better. I used to love to work out, but now I'd probably drop over with a heart attack if I worked out strenuously.

I don't worry about material stuff. Heck, I never did. I don't care about making a million dollars anymore. I had my shot at that one time and it didn't work out for me. I just want to live a free, clean life, and enjoy my children and hopefully, my grandchildren.

I hope to continue to find joy. If you don't have any joy in your life, you have nothing. I know what that's like, because I was in prison. I know there's an abundance of joy out there if you work hard at it and let it happen.

I hope to be married again someday, to share the remainder of my life with someone.

I love my radio job and I've dabbled in coaching high school football on a volunteer basis. I'd love to get into it full-time someday, because I believe I have a lot to offer young kids, on the field and off of it. I give plenty of speeches to high school-age kids about the dangers of gambling, and by the time I walk out of those rooms, I never know if I am reaching them. You know, most teen-agers think they're Teflon-coated and that nothing bad will ever happen to them. I hope they're right, but I know life is full of twists and turns.

Most of them may not want to hear some guy they never met speak about his past troubles. But there just may be one kid in the corner of that class who listened. Maybe that kid will think twice about gambling away hard-earned money. Maybe he's the one who will hear my story and realize a dangerous addiction lies ahead if he doesn't stop.

That thought of that kid keeps me going.

Do I gamble anymore?

I bet every day in my head. Life is a gamble. Driving down the freeway is a gamble. Writing this book is a gamble, but I believe people need to hear my story.

Just this morning I answered the telephone and a man asked, "Are you Art Schlichter?"

"Yes I am, can I help you?" I said.

"I found your phone number on your website," he told me. "Art, I'm addicted to gambling and I'm suffering … I'm ready to kill himself. What can I do? Can you help me?"

I talked to him for a while and I'll find that man the help he needs, as well as any others who face this same addiction and want my help. He may be a stranger to me today, but we have a connection because I walked in his shoes yesterday. I don't want him stuck in some six-by-eight prison cell years from now, wondering why no one reached out to help him. I don't want him being forced to his knees to pray for his sanity as I did.

And I don't want him staring at that stinking light bulb day after day after day, wondering where it all went wrong.

If I'm not there for him, he just may be the one to unscrew it.

Index